S4 ✓

D0387020

17X/3-08
6-11

JUL 0 2 2001

Kindred Spirits

ALSO BY ALLEN M. SCHOEN, D.V.M., M.S.

Love, Miracles, and Animal Healing

How the Remarkable Bond

Kindred

Between Humans and Animals

Spirits

Can Change the Way We Live

Allen M. Schoen,
D.V.M., M.S.

BROADWAY BOOKS / NEW YORK

Broadway Books titles may be purchased for business or promotional use or for special sales. For information, please write to: Special Markets Department, Random House, Inc., 1540 Broadway, New York, NY 10036.

BROADWAY BOOKS and its logo, a letter B bisected on the diagonal, are trademarks of Broadway Books, a division of Random House, Inc.

Visit our website at www.broadwaybooks.com

LIBRARY OF CONGRESS CATALOGING-IN-PUBLICATION DATA

Schoen, Allen M.
Kindred spirits: how the remarkable bond between humans and animals can change the way we live / Allen M. Schoen.—1st ed.
p.   cm.
Includes bibliographical references.
1. Alternative veterinary medicine. 2. Veterinary acupuncture.
3. Pets—Social aspects—Anecdotes. 4. Pets—Therapeutic use—Anecdotes. 5. Human-animal relationships. 6. Schoen, Allen M.
I. Title.

SF745.5 .S338 2001
636.089'55—DC21   00-057891

FIRST EDITION

Designed by Richard Oriolo

ISBN 0-7679-0430-3

01 02 03 04 05 10 9 8 7 6 5 4 3 2

Contents

Introduction / 1

PART I / 11
Kindred Hearts:
What Animals Can Do for Humans

1 Do Animals Feel Pain?   13

2 From Heart to Soul: The Benefits of the Human-Animal Bond   49

   Healing the Heart   53

   Physical Healing: Recovery from Serious Illness   58

   A Touch of Youth: The Elderly   62

   A Touch of Love: Children   64

   A Touch of Hope: Working with AIDS   67

   Healing the Mind: Psychological Disorders   69

PART II / 79
Kindred Minds:
What Humans Can Do for Animals

1 The Love You Give   81

2 In Search of the Magic Bullet   96

   Acupuncture   99

   Traditional Chinese Herbs   108

   Western Herbal Medicine   111

   Preventive Nutrition   115

   Therapeutic Nutrition   118

   Homeopathy   121

   Chiropractic   125

Touch Therapy   128

Additional Options   132

P A R T   I I I   / 145
Kindred Souls:
The Wonders of Co-Species Connections

P A R T   I V   / 201
Becoming Kindred Spirits

1 Creating a Spiritual Bond: Seven Ways to Foster Kindred
  Connections   203

  Co-Species Meditation   206

  Kindred Relaxation   209

  Sharing Mindful Moments   212

  Think Like an Animal   220

  A Blessing Exercise   222

  Talking and Listening   223

  Practices for a Busy Day   226

2 The Journey Toward Kindred Healing   228

  A Natural Pet Scan   229

  How to Help Heal Your Ailing Animal   233

  Finding Kindred Veterinary Support   236

  The Natural Approach to Diet and Food Allergies   237

  Travel Tips for Dogs and Cats   241

  Preventing and Treating Cancer the Natural Way   244

  A Holistic First-Aid Kit   246

3 Bittersweet Farewells   250

4 The Single Best Way to Find Your Kindred Spirit   255

A Final Word (or Two) / 257
Resources / 258
Acknowledgments / 272
Index / 275

Introduction

Winter 1979. A cold, raw, blustery New England night, the winding country roads invisible beneath the white snow. Megan and I manage to arrive at Joe and Martha Starr's barn at the stroke of midnight, me all bundled up in thermal underwear, veterinary coveralls, a down vest, insulated boots, a wool fisherman's cap; Megan in her fluffy golden coat. I'm the veterinarian. Megan is my attending assistant, nurse, and helpmate.

The Starrs' eyes light up when they see me and my five-year-old golden retriever walk into the light from the dark cobweb-strewn corridor at the barn's entrance. They're both thoroughly exhausted from trying to help Jesse deliver her third calf.

Jesse is a doe-eyed brown Jersey cow, a favorite not only because she's a superior milk producer but also because she's exceptionally sweet and friendly. Jesse seems to enjoy the company of humans more than the other cows, perhaps because her mother died just after her birth and the Starrs bottle-fed her until she could manage on her own.

Also in the barn is Amy, the Starrs' eight-year-old daughter. Amy has always adored Jesse more than any other animal on the farm, and tonight, when she woke up to the sounds of her parents rushing to the barn, she begged to come along, too, in case she could help. Joe and Martha have let her stay. Amy's face is wet from tears and wrinkled with anxiety, and Megan runs over to her and starts licking her cheeks.

Jesse is clearly in trouble. Lying almost inert on the ground, her eyes are dull, her body exhausted.

"She seems to be giving up," Martha says. "She's not trying to push her calf out anymore. We've put more straw and shavings underneath her, but she's just lying there."

"Let me take a look," I say. After observing her from a distance, I take Jesse's temperature, do a comprehensive physical exam, and decide that she has mild milk fever, a calcium deficiency that can paralyze cows and prevent them from calving. I quickly insert a needle into the jugular vein on the side of her neck to give her fluids and calcium.

Moments later, Jesse's eyes brighten, and, emitting a mildly enthusiastic moo, she starts to push again. I tie her tail to her side and wash up her rear end. Next I put on my gloves, roll up my sleeves, and lie in the straw on the icy cold barn floor. Then I gently push my way up into Jesse's uterus to see how Jesse's calf is positioned. I'm two inches too short, so I must strip down more; I take off my vest, flannel shirt, and coveralls and try to extend my reach through the warm amniotic fluid.

Meanwhile, Megan is ambling back and forth from Amy to her

parents. She seems to understand her surroundings from having assisted me on so many late-night and early morning calving calls, and she knows that her job is to calm the nervous people by being present and loving, wagging her tail, licking everyone at the most appropriate times.

When she sees Jesse starting to strain once again, she approaches carefully, as though to make sure that the cow, who has met her many times before, recognizes her and accepts her presence. Once Megan feels she has a clear signal, she starts licking Jesse's face. The contact seems to have both a calming and a revitalizing effect on the struggling animal.

Martha Starr, who has not seen the two animals together before, is startled, but she is sure that Jesse appreciates Megan's presence. Rather than push her away, as she does to Martha's cocker spaniel, Jesse accepts Megan's comfort and licks, even pushing her head toward her mouth for more.

As I watch, I wonder what is going on in Megan's mind: Is this some form of interspecies maternal empathy? Are the two animals commiserating with each other? Does Megan, who's probably had a litter of pups, understand what Jesse is going through? Can she sense the cow's anxiety? From a scientist's point of view, I can't explain what was happening, outside of instinctual maternal behavior.

Meanwhile, with the help of Jesse's contractions, which are now regular, I'm finally able to place my hands around the calf's head and help ease it through the birth canal. Slowly the baby emerges into the wondrous world of a cold, dark New Hampshire night redolent with the warm smell of fresh hay and manure.

But our relief quickly turns to concern when we see that the calf, who's been stuck in Jesse's birth canal for so many hours, has stopped breathing and is turning cyanotic—or blue. I immediately direct Joe to hold the calf up by her hind legs as a way to clean mucous from her airway and begin performing cardiac massage, pumping on her chest and ribs. The baby does not respond.

I then give her an injection of epinephrine and begin my CPR once more; I also tell Joe to breathe into the calf's nose and mouth as if she were a drowning victim, to keep oxygen flowing. Still the calf remains lifeless.

Then I remember a trick my old mentor, Doc Tenney, had taught me. Whenever he had to treat an animal with severe respiratory problems, he would place his fingernail on a certain point of the nose and press down hard. He could never explain why this instantly stimulated breathing, but his experience taught him that it succeeded more often than not.

Remembering his placement, I dig my fingernail into the calf's nose. Seconds later, she screams wildly as a huge plug of mucus shoots out from her nostrils. She then turns to make her first moo to her mother. Jesse slowly lifts herself off the ground and begins to lick away the placenta that covers the baby's stomach and abdomen, massaging more life into her chest through the powerful licks of her large tongue.

I didn't know it at the time, but this was one of my first experiences with animal acupuncture. It turns out that Doc Tenney's little trick, which he picked up without knowing its ancient origins, succeeded because it put pressure on one of the most important acupuncture points, Governing Vessel 26, which stimulates the heart and respiratory rate.

As the newly named Dora gazes adoringly at her mother, she calmly allows Megan to help Jesse lick off the rest of the placenta. Perhaps, in her newborn innocence, Dora assumes that these golden animals assist at every calf's birth.

•

Megan's arrival in my life had been inauspicious. Diseased and abandoned, she was first spotted by a friend who felt sorry for the ragged creature struggling to survive by begging for food at a rural New Hampshire parking lot. After devouring anything offered, she would hack, cough, and collapse on the ground, writhing in pain, piteously staring up at her benefactors, pleading for help.

Once I heard my friend describe the symptoms, I immediately

guessed that the dog's problem was heartworm disease, a potentially life-threatening disorder caused by microfilaria, tiny worms transmitted from dog to dog through mosquitoes. At that time in New Hampshire, it was almost impossible for dogs to avoid the disease unless they took a daily heartworm preventative. But I agreed to do what I could, and I told my friend to bring her over.

I fell in love with Megan the moment she bounded into my small cabin. Despite her grave illness, the look of love in her eyes and the deep reservoir of soul lurking behind them were enough to make me not just want to save her but also to adopt her. Still, her gums were pale, and harsh, rasping sounds came from her lungs—both signs of serious infection. With my stethoscope I could detect a heart murmur as well.

Blood tests soon revealed that she seemed to have more microfilaria in her blood than blood cells. I'd never seen such an advanced infestation, and it was hard to believe this dog could still wag her tail and stare up lovingly at me. By all reckoning, she should have been dead weeks—or months—earlier.

I made a pact with her. If somehow she managed to survive, I agreed to adopt her as my companion.

Megan, who appeared to be about four years old, was weak and undernourished, but I had no choice but to go ahead with the intensive treatment. Twice a day for two days I injected an arsenic derivative into her bloodstream, hoping to destroy the worms before they destroyed her. Although tiny now, without treatment they could grow to almost a foot in length, clogging Megan's heart.

Megan seemed to understand that I was trying to help her. Unlike most animals, who flinch or run from a needle, she held up her paw as any cooperative patient would every time I went to administer the medication.

Once the worms had been killed off by the powerful medication, I had to make sure that they dissolved slowly. To do this, Megan had to be kept as quiet as possible because any physical exertion could cause the dead worms to form clots that could block her vital functions. So I brought Megan with me everywhere, watching over her, petting her quietly, letting her know through words and love that there was a reason for this strange behavior. At night, after I'd taken her from the cage, she'd lie in front of the warm wood stove in my cabin, somehow knowing that she shouldn't move.

I was sure Megan appreciated my efforts. Even though she wasn't allowed to walk, her eyes followed me around the room, and whenever I approached her, they lit up. Still, I feared the worst, and I often woke during the night, panicked that she had died.

But she didn't die. Her health slowly improved, and within a few months, she was a lively and happy addition to my household—and my practice. Indeed, not long afterward I learned that Megan had an unusual talent, which I realized when she met an injured baby lamb that had been attacked by wild dogs. The lamb was covered from head to tail with bite wounds; it was a miracle that she'd escaped death. I brought her home to recuperate, but it was Megan who took over her care: licking, cleaning, and nuzzling the lamb with her tongue, even cuddling up with her at night. By the next morning, the lamb was standing on her own, looking worn but alive and healthy.

My treatment for the lamb had been an intravenous electrolyte solution and medications to treat shock, but Megan's treatment of pure love may have been the key to her recovery.

Megan soon became my unofficial nurse and partner. She seemed to feel it was her job to offer tenderness to any wounded or needy animal. I let her accompany me on my nightly rounds and on emergency calls, where she'd always wait calmly outside the exam room door, wagging her tail and wanting to come in and see the patient as soon as possible. Invariably sensitive to the situation, she mastered the art of a cautious approach, so as not to frighten the animal. Once she was perceived as nonthreatening, Megan would shower her charge with soft, warm licks. Her maternal, loving nature permeated every room.

One rainy spring evening a Maine coon cat was rushed to the hospital after giving birth to a kitten at home; she was in great pain because another kitten was stuck inside her birth canal. I performed a cesarean section, and when I opened up the uterus, I found the tiny creature was already dead. But I also saw two more tiny babies who were alive; once delivered, they started crying for their mother, who was too anesthetized to attend to them.

Megan sprang into action, dashing over to the kittens, licking the amniotic fluid off their bodies, her huge tongue many times their size. But the kittens were happy, bathing in Megan's maternal love.

When the mother cat had recovered from the anesthesia and was ready to start nursing her offspring herself, she looked at Megan as if to say thanks and then immersed herself in her maternal chores. Megan simply stepped aside.

Over the ten years we spent together, Megan administered to a veritable Noah's ark of animals: dogs, cats, ferrets, horses, cows, lambs, and so on. She was truly an ecumenical aide. On one occasion she even saved the life of another golden retriever by giving her own blood. When she did so, she patiently extended her paw up to meet the needle, just as she had when I first saved her life.

•

It's now 2 A.M. on that same cold February morning in 1979. Megan and I are driving home down the snow-covered Temple Mountain Road after helping Jesse deliver her calf.

I thank Megan for becoming half of a solid team—the more intuitive half, the one who always seems to know to give animals exactly what they need to get better. I have a degree in veterinary medicine, and my understanding of the healing process comes through Western science. But Megan understands how to heal with love.

I talk aloud to her—as I always do when we're alone. "Is this due to your basic maternal instinct? Is it because you knew what it was like not to be loved? Or is there a deeper connection, a deeper communion?"

Megan doesn't answer—but that doesn't stop me from continuing. "Are you really a golden retriever?" I ask. "Or have you evolved to a higher level of functioning? Have you consciously evolved to be an angel in canine form, a four-legged teacher for us two-legged folk?

"How do you know how to do all this?" I ask her. She looks me right in the eye, and for one brief moment I flash on her thoughts: "I wish I could answer you, pal."

But, in a way, she did answer me. Throughout the rest of her life Megan taught me that a healing power exists outside of conventional Western medicine. My more scientifically minded peers might tell me that my companion was just a loving golden retriever exhibiting typical canine behavior patterns. I believe she was more than that. Megan was my teacher, a Florence Nightingale in canine clothing. She helped me realize that other species have a great deal to offer humankind. Megan taught me that there was more to healing than drugs and surgery. She guided me to open up my heart space after it had shut down during veterinary school, where animals' feelings and emotions were not acknowledged. Megan was my door back to my childhood and my memories of being a boy who loved spending time with animals more than anything else, who told the world at the age of six that his life's calling was to travel around the country aiding animals who could not be helped by routine approaches.

Megan and I drive back home on that blustery night—me trying to keep my tired eyes on the winding road, Megan occasionally nudging my body to make sure that I don't fall asleep. She had helped too many animals after too many accidents to allow the car to swerve over the edge of the road.

It is only moments after we arrive home that we both fall asleep in my barely insulated cabin, exhausted, trying to gain the strength to face tomorrow's patients.

•

Ten years later, Megan taught us all another lesson when she developed cancer. While my distraught wife and I fretted, we noticed that Megan was treating herself, regulating her own activities. Just as so many humans have sought out mud packs to heal inflammation, she was choosing to soak her tumor-ridden front leg in the mud by a natural spring behind our house.

Finally, when her time arrived and she could barely move, Megan lay on the floor of our living room, looking up at me as if she knew that we'd never see each other again on this earth. In her eyes I saw the enormous love and gratitude, and I hope she saw the same in mine.

When it was time to give her a final injection of euthanasia solution, Megan slowly—and without any prompting—lifted her paw to the needle, the same paw she had raised when I had saved her life and when she'd saved the life of that other retriever. She left this world with the calm grace of a wise soul.

For me, Megan was more than a companion (I prefer the terms "animal" and "human companion" to "owner" and "pet" because, as you will read in this book, I don't believe that the complex relationship between two species can be rendered accurately by such loaded words.) Megan was a profound teacher. And she continues to be.

The intensive education of veterinary school helped instill in me a dogmatic thought process focused on developing a diagnosis and a therapeutic plan based on medicine and surgery. Most of us graduate from school confident that this is all we need to treat an animal. But Megan was my guide on a journey to a deeper, clearer perception of all that is truly considered healing. Step by step, through example, metaphor, and insight, she reopened the doors to my heart and soul; she reawakened my sense of kindred connections to animals I had felt as a child.

These connections are what I would like to share with you in this book, as well as my belief that there is more to medicine than medications and scalpels, that there are many ways to treat and prevent disease: through nutrition, exercise, love, compassion, and above all, through forming meaningful bonds with the other species on this earth. And I will also walk you through the most recent research from the world of science surrounding these insights, combined with stories about my patients as well as other animal and human friends along the way. May these insights lead you to open further your own love and compassion to all sentient beings.

As Megan was dying, I lay beside her and promised that someday I would share the wisdom I had gained through her—and my other animal teachers—with as many people as possible. And that is why I dedicate this book to Megan and all the others who have taught me that our potential for connection to all the world's kindred spirits is deeper than I had ever imagined.

PART I

Kindred Hearts

What Animals Can

Do for Humans

One

Do Animals

Feel Pain?

There is little that separates humans from other
sentient beings—we all feel pain, we all feel joy,
we all deeply crave to be alive and live freely,
and we all share this planet together.

—Gandhi

everal years ago, Carol, a fifty-year-old single working
mother, entered my office with her fourteen-year-old son
Scott, and King, their German shepherd.

Carol was the only one of the trio in good physical shape. Tall and
handsome, Scott had difficulty walking; he didn't shake my hand but
limped over to a chair where he remained quiet and withdrawn throughout the visit.

Twelve-year-old King wasn't doing much better. Due to weakness in his hind legs, he had to drag himself into the office. It was hard to tell whose face looked more worried: Carol's or King's, with his heavy eyes and his tucked-back ears. Struggling to remain composed, Carol told me that King had been diagnosed with degenerative myelopathy (an atrophy of the spinal cord) and hip dysplasia (physical malformation of the hip joint).

Their veterinarian had treated the dog with conventional medicines, steroids, and nonsteroidal anti-inflammatories. Nothing had worked. The veterinarian now felt it was time to put King to sleep.

"Is there anything at all you can do?" Carol asked, despair permeating her voice. She told me about a friend whose ill cat had lived years longer than expected by taking a series of nutritional supplements that I had recommended.

Carol had brought along King's X-rays and medical records. Looking them over, I saw extensive arthritis in the back, a condition called spondylosis, as well as in the hips. After gently lifting King on the table to conduct a physical examination, I noted that the dog's eyes were still bright, with no evidence of cataracts or other signs of aging; that his teeth were solid, showing little dental tartar; and that his lymph nodes and abdominal organs were normal-sized. His heart and lungs auscultated—or sounded—normal, too. His coat was in good condition, though a bit dry.

But when I conducted my neurologic and musculoskeletal examinations, I found that the dog had significant pain in his hips and back, which correlated with the findings on the X-ray. The nerve reflexes in his hind legs were greatly diminished, and the muscles were significantly atrophied, probably from disuse. When King placed both hind feet on the ground, they knuckled under, indicating that he had little sensation in the top of his paws, suggestive of decreased feeling from the nerves in that area. Fortunately, the reflexes in his knees were still good.

The nerve damage in the hind legs could have resulted from either degenerative myelopathy (a progressive debilitating disease more prominent in German shepherds) or from the spondylosis in the back impinging on the nerves to the leg. It is not uncommon to see both of these conditions simultaneously in German shepherds, which makes differentiating between the two quite challenging.

As gently as possible, I shared with Carol and Scott my sense that King's situation was indeed serious and then went over the treatment options available via conventional Western medicine.

Next I reviewed the possible approaches with alternative medicine and how they might work, especially if the nerve damage stemmed from arthritis.

I explained how—if the damage was not due to degenerative myelopathy—acupuncture could help by increasing the circulation to both the muscles and the joints (thereby increasing the blood and oxygen supply to them) and by stimulating the nerves to the hind legs. Acupuncture might also relieve some of the pain of the arthritis by stimulating the release of endorphins, the body's own painkilling hormones. It could also relieve inflammation (without the side effects of synthetic cortisone) by stimulating the body's own cortisone release mechanism. I also suggested we try supplements of vitamins E, C, and a B-complex to improve nerve functioning, as well as King's overall health.

Moments after I finished talking, Carol broke down in tears.

"You've just got to help," she sobbed. "King means everything to Scott." She told me that her son had suffered from Lyme disease for more than two years but that he had only recently received the correct diagnosis and proper treatment. He was now taking intravenous antibiotics because he had responded poorly to the medication orally. Scott's father, Carol's ex-husband, had only a distant relationship with the boy, and it was King who was taking round-the-clock care of him, lying by Scott's bedside during the months when he was most ill. The few times when Scott was able to move about, King limped along beside him, guarding him against falling.

"My son lives for King," Carol said, "and King lives for him. If King dies, it'll destroy him." As Carol talked, Scott glanced away, but I could see tears running down his cheeks.

I listened, fully aware of just how closely the fates of the debilitated dog and his young companion were connected. To suggest that there was nothing I could do for King seemed tantamount to sealing Scott's fate.

After showing Carol and Scott some exercises they could do at home with King, I told Carol I'd do my best, but with no guarantees. I explained that we would have to work together as a team, combining our positive energy with the physical therapy, supplements, and acupuncture. When they left the office, mother and son seemed happier knowing that they would be doing their part to help King.

We started King on acupuncture treatments, as well as nutritional and herbal supplements, and over the next eight weeks his condition improved. He was stronger, happier, and walking more. Each time he and Scott entered my office I could see his progress.

We weren't out of the woods, though, and whenever the boy's health took a downturn, so did the dog's. The opposite was also true: If the dog's symptoms worsened, so did the boy's. Still, both showed enormous resilience and determination.

As King improved, Scott relaxed around me to the point where he started helping me hold King during his acupuncture sessions, reporting King's day-to-day movements, and letting me know the specific ways in which he was doing better.

Because Scott showed genuine interest in the acupuncture, I explained to him how it worked and why I was using certain acupuncture points, such as Gall Bladder 34, located just below the knee at the common peroneal nerve, one of the most important nerves to the hind leg, or Bladder 40, near the tibial nerve, right behind the knee joint, which is also essential in stimulating nerves to the hind legs.

Scott was fascinated to learn that acupuncture had a scientific basis, that it was more than, as he put it, "just that yin and yang stuff." He observed how I chose my acupuncture points and how I attached electrodes to the acupoints on the legs. He watched intently when King responded to the electric stimulation with various groans and mumbles, and he noted how King was able to use his hind legs a little more after each treatment.

King started wagging his tail and holding his head up high. He was now barking at other dogs in the clinic, clearly showing more interest in life around him than he had just a few months earlier. Scott was also showing more interest, talking to other people in the waiting room, walking with more confidence, acting happier.

Despite his improvement, King suffered a series of setbacks. He was weakened from an attack by another dog. And he too came down with Lyme disease, but we caught it early enough to treat it successfully with antibiotic therapy. He then developed a tumor on his shoulder, but we were able to keep that under control for an extended period, too. At one point Scott told me that King was beginning to remind him of a cat, because he seemed to have nine lives.

Meanwhile, Scott's own rally was dramatic. His overall health, as well as his leg strength, returned to normal. He was able to play his favorite sport—basketball—again, as well as concentrate on his studies. Over the next few months, his work was so excellent that he won a scholarship to a well-respected boarding school, and he and his mother decided he should accept it. While Scott was overjoyed at the opportunities the school offered, he felt sad leaving his dog behind.

Less than two weeks after Scott left home for school, King finally died.

I asked Scott about this the next time I saw him, and the boy surprised me with his insight. Scott said that his parting with King had been the toughest moment in his life.

"King knew I'd gotten better," he said, "so he felt his job was done. He was telling me that I was going to be okay but that he wasn't. He let go. I could see it in his eyes."

◆

Do animals feel pain?

Do animals have emotions?

Do animals know compassion?

Ask anyone who shares his or her life with an animal companion, and the answer to these questions will be an unambivalent yes. For example, Scott and Carol would tell you that not only do animals have feelings, these feelings can also create a wonderful life-affirming connection between the animals and the humans who love them.

But that's not the traditional view held by science.

In fact, if you care to believe many of the ethologists, animal behaviorists, and other members of the scientific world, animals are basically nonthinking, nonfeeling, nonexpressive creatures.

These scientists have a great deal of history behind their convictions. As far back in time as Plato and Aristotle, philosophers and scientists believed in a clear and precise distinction between humankind and all the other living creatures on earth. For instance, Plato felt that both humans and nonhumans had a mortal soul, which was located in the chest and belly, but that only humans had a second, immortal soul. Located in the head, it bestowed the unique ability to reason and served as the connection to the everlasting divine.

Aristotle separated humans from animals more severely. In his hierarchy of being, male humans occupied a place just next to the top, below angels but above female humans, slaves, and children. Animals, whose existence was solely predicated on the service of humans, could feel pleasure and pain, but lacked emotion and reason. They had little or no ability to make anything but instinctual choices or adapt their behavior to new situations.

Attitudes toward animals barely changed in the centuries that followed the classical era. Judeo-Christian tradition supported the prevailing view of humankind's fundamental superiority over other living beings through various biblical teachings. In Genesis, for instance, human beings are given dominion over the earth and all living things. (There is, however, some controversy over the translation of the word "dominion." Several modern scholars feel that the more accurate word is "custodian," which puts a refreshing slant on the relationship—and one worthy of new debate.) Church leaders developed this hierarchy further by describing biblical man as a unique animal created in the image of God.

During the Renaissance, science and philosophy began to establish themselves as disciplines independent of religion, but the gulf between man and nonhuman animals was not rethought. French philosopher René Descartes's famous dictum, "I think, therefore I am," proposed that only the thinking mind has the ability to confer conscious existence. Descartes felt that animals, mindless and nonthinking, were no better than machines, and he limited the possibility of consciousness solely to humans. An animal's range of action was restricted to species-specific behavior, its response to stimuli strictly physiological reflex, devoid of feeling, thought, or choice.

Followers of Descartes are said to have carried out torturous physical experiments on animals with the confident conviction that the animals' cries of agony were comparable to noises from machinery, no more, no less.

In their book on animal emotions, *When Elephants Weep*, Susan McCarthy and Jeffrey Moussaieff Masson quote a contemporary of Descartes: "The [Cartesian] scientists administered beatings to dogs with perfect indifference and made fun of those who pitied the creatures as if they felt pain. They said the animals were clocks, that the cries they emitted when struck were only the noise of a little spring that had been touched, but that the whole body was without feeling. They nailed the poor animals up on boards by their four paws to vivisect them to see the circulation of blood. . . ."

Descartes's belief dominated the scientific world for centuries, although some great thinkers, such as Voltaire, spoke out against cruelty to animals. He was, for the most part, ignored.

In my mind, the seminal work that signaled the beginning of the erosion of the classic distinction between human and nonhuman animals was Charles Darwin's *On the Origin of Species by Means of Natural Selection* (1859), which posited a developmental continuum of physical, mental, and emotional traits among all living beings, including humans.

In his 1872 book *The Expression of the Emotions in Man and Animals*, Darwin traced the continuity of emotions such as fear, grief, and loyalty across many species; he theorized that nonhuman animals did indeed possess the ability to reason, to use tools, to imitate behaviors, and to remember events.

Even as Darwin was still writing, England's antivivisection movement was organized to oppose the use of animals in biomedical research, eventually resulting in Britain's 1876 Cruelty to Animals Act, which imposed a system of licensing and inspection on Britain's medical scientists. On the whole, however, Darwin's hypothesis about animal thought processes was controversial and was hardly popular with those who wished to retain the age-old sense of difference between humans and lowly animals.

Darwin's writings were so powerful that they took not just many years but many decades to be understood and assimilated—and are still debated today. Even now a large number of Americans doubt Darwin's theories, as evidenced by the recent (1999) decision by the Kansas State Board of Education to equate evolution with creationism in school textbooks.

Nor has the concept of emotions in animals been resolved. When I was in graduate school, we read volumes of work by ethologists, psychologists, philosophers, and scientists, each offering different definitions and perspectives on the debate—but all basically sharing a bias against any discussion proposing that animals had feelings. The behaviorists, who dominated the scientific pecking order, felt that all animal behavior could be reduced to fixed behavior patterns based on genetic programming. Those who thought otherwise were unlikely to see their opinions published. As a result, most animal scientists studying animal behavior during that time completely avoided the subject of animal emotions.

All this perpetuated a vicious cycle: There was no interest in studying subjective behavior patterns such as emotions, because if they existed at all, they were private to the organism experiencing them and therefore inaccessible to scientific investigation. In other words, they were not relevant because there was no documentation, and there was no effort to find documentation because they were not relevant.

Of course, this syllogism conveniently allowed scientists not only to avoid the entire study of animals' subjective experiences but also to deny whatever pain they might have been inducing in the sentient beings on whom they were experimenting in laboratories. As a result, for most of the past century, the concept of animal pain was something of an orphan cousin to the debate over animal consciousness.

Just before I entered veterinary school, the greatest argument in the field was not about whether animals feel pain or emotion but whether behavior patterns were controlled by nature or nurture. In other words, was animal behavior due to hereditary, genetic predispositions, or was all behavior learned? The leaders in the field of animal behavior, including the renowned Konrad Lorenz, saw most behavior patterns as a form of imprinting, or innate responses based on genetic programming.

The one thing animal behavior wasn't: emotional, or even conscious.

There were some notable exceptions to the behaviorist view, including Donald Griffin, whose book *The Question of Animal Awareness*, published in 1976, posed questions that few other scientists were asking. Currently an associate at Harvard's Museum of Comparative Zoology, Griffin was one of the codiscoverers of echolocation in bats (the sensory system that allows bats to interpret the direction and distance of objects by using sound waves). Griffin, who has continued to make a career out of refuting the behaviorist position, was among the first scientists to posit the possibility that animals have consciousness and can feel pain. His theories, which have become increasingly popular, were widely rejected when first published.

•

When I was young, knowing nothing of these debates, I simply assumed that animals had feelings, no different from my own. The animals I knew demonstrated this to me every day. As I grew older, my goal became to help them feel as good as they could, all of the time.

As far back as my memory stretches, I can remember wanting to spend all my free time with animals. My grandfather always told me that the first words out of my mouth, after "Mommy" and "Daddy," were "animal doctor." My earliest reading material consisted of animal magazines. The pictures I tacked to my walls were of cats and dogs, and at the head of my bed, instead of a headboard, was an oversized poster of a mountain lion.

While some kids came home to their dogs, I ran home to my six turtles—my parents wouldn't let me have a dog or a cat until I was older. And while the bond between terrapin and boy doesn't pull on the heartstrings like the one between a boy and his dog, whenever I burst into the room, all my turtles would rise from their somnolence and move toward me. I would take each of them out and pet them, and our bond flourished.

My connection to animals had become my main focus by the time I went to camp. The other campers would awaken, see the sun shining, and look forward to a great day for baseball. I would think, What a great day to forage for wildlife—mostly small amphibians—to bring back to the cabins. The other boys were fascinated by these finds, but eventually I came to feel sorry for the little creatures and wondered aloud whether we were depriving them of their homes and families.

The counselors would sigh and say, "Give me a break, Allen."

One night all my pent-up frustration exploded. I snuck into the place where we kept all the creatures and set them free. The next day's scolding didn't lessen the joy I had felt at seeing them crawl, squirm, or hop to freedom.

As I grew older, my reputation as an animal lover quickly spread throughout the Queens, New York, neighborhood where I grew up, and the people on our block used to bring me injured animals to care for, because they knew I would. One of my first patients was a baby starling that couldn't fly. As I watched the tiny creature, fluttering his wings helplessly and pecking at the air, I felt terribly sad and believed he shared that emotion.

I placed him in a cage and taught him how to fly by letting him stand on one finger as I raised it up and down, up and down, so he could practice flapping his wings. One day he flapped mightily, took what I still believe to this day was a last, loving look at me, and flew away. My joy was indescribable.

Across the street from our home was a small bicycle path through one of the last remnants of woods in 1950s Queens. This path provided me with my earliest and happiest escape from the unnatural city with its concrete streets, lifeless views, and stale air. I didn't mind playing with other kids. But I preferred to play alone, in nature.

I particularly remember one dull eighth-grade Friday afternoon in early spring. I was feeling emotionally deadened after a long week in school, dealing with teachers who seemed bored with their subjects and students and coping with classmates who were fighting for top positions on the basketball team and in the local gangs.

Sitting in class, watching the trees outside swaying in a slight March wind, I suddenly felt as though they were pulling me out the window. The large branches were arms, the smaller branches fingers; they were pointing to me and whispering, "Come with me, Allen. Come into nature." The birds sitting on the branches were talking, too, and their songs tugged at my heart, because I couldn't respond. The teacher was droning on about math or history or French, but I only could hear robins.

When school ended, I ran off to my special path so I could stroll through the woods. After I had walked for a few minutes, a large ancient oak tree stood in front of me. When I saw its tiny new leaves opening up to embrace spring, a part of my soul opened up with it. As the sun beat down on me, I felt full of warmth and joy. For the first time in a week, my energies came alive. Reveling in my surroundings, I scanned the ground for signs of life, listened for any sounds of birds or mammals. My senses were awakened, my heart opened to absorb the beauty of nature and the unconditional love of God.

I spent the afternoon listening, watching, seeing, touching, and feeling nature. Are the turtles coming out from hibernation? I wondered. Are there spiders or worms under the leaves? What new life is emerging with spring? I lifted up a log to study what might lie underneath and a tiny red salamander squirmed away. Another stayed behind and stared back up at me. As I peered into his shiny black eyes, I wondered aloud, "What are you thinking when you stare at me? The other salamander ran off. But you're just looking right into my eyes." I was sure I saw no fear in the salamander as it pondered me, a creature a thousand times its size.

I wanted to befriend the salamander. I wanted to find in nature the kind of meaningful connections I longed for, the attachment to something larger, more wonderful than myself—a connection not to a single being but to an entire universe.

And I did find that, standing there, staring at this small creature. That moment had a spiritual quality; I felt we had forged a timeless connection, lasting beyond seconds or minutes, a communication beyond words.

I gently returned the log to its original position and continued my journey to see what else was alive, what else was hidden, what else was about to burst into life. Presently I reached a field with a grassy hillock and the sole remaining apple tree of a former orchard, and I climbed up into its twisted branches. Sitting in the V of the tree, which resembled a palm with fingers reaching upward toward the luminous sky, I felt as though I were one with it—its roots were my legs, its branches my arms, its new leaves were the new part of me opening up to spring and the sun.

I sat there for hours, absorbing the brilliant blue energy of the sky like a sponge, visualizing myself climbing up a rope ladder into one of the clouds, looking out over the earth. Here in the heart of this tree I looked up at the sky and prayed to God, asking what my purpose was. Surely it was more than to live in a concrete environment surrounded by people I couldn't understand. I prayed for the ability to accomplish what I was growing to believe would be my life's work: to take care of animals.

Whenever I was in nature, the blood that stagnated in my body during hours of sitting in classes or studying at home seemed to flow like a river, sending vibrating ripples through my arms and legs. Today

I might call that rippling force *chi,* as the Chinese do, or *prana,* as Hindus call it, or the life energy force that is within all life. Back then it was only a feeling, not a concept or a word.

For me, spirituality and the science of nature were one and the same, like a yin/yang symbol with two parts flowing graciously into one another. My heart and my mind were one in nature, not opponents battling each other for dominance. I did not realize until many years later that there could be a split between science and spirituality, between heart and mind.

•

My path to college was quite fortuitous. After my junior year at Francis Lewis High School in Queens, I applied for what I was told was a summer job in biology at the University of Bridgeport in Connecticut. My guidance counselor was mistaken, however, for the position turned out to be a summer scholarship for underprivileged kids sponsored by the National Science Foundation (my family had limited resources). I won it and loved every moment of that summer. It was like a biology boot camp, my wake-up call to life.

As the summer was winding down and the first days of my senior year drew closer, my professor approached me with good news. Knowing how much I hated high school and the city, the university was offering me a chance to start college right away, enabling me to skip my senior year. Seeing my long face upon hearing this news must have dampened his enthusiasm. As much as the prospect thrilled me, I couldn't accept—my parents weren't able to afford college.

Perhaps my unhappiness only made my professor more determined. A few days later, the head of the program announced that a full four-year scholarship had been secured for me. I was elated.

I immediately chose preveterinary medicine as my major, and my biology classes were everything I had hoped for. But the school's treatment of the laboratory animals was overwhelmingly depressing. In one small dark room with a single tiny window were wedged all the mice, rats, turtles, guinea pigs—level after level of rolling metal trays, all smelling of urine and feces.

Feeling sorry for the creatures, I'd try to find a time to wander in and clean the room, all the while whistling and talking to them. Whenever I looked into their eyes, I was overcome with sadness. I wondered why no one could make the effort to care for these animals in a more compassionate way.

One day, without thinking, I asked one of the school's most respected biology professors if there was anything we could do to improve the living conditions of these animals.

"Of course not," the man snorted. He looked at me as though I had suggested clothing them. "They're just lab animals. They're around to be studied." Period.

He scolded me as if I were a child, and I felt like one—confused and unhappy. But I still needed to help, so from then on, without telling a soul, I'd secretly bring the animals fresh fruits and vegetables and any other treats I could think of.

This incident raised some tough questions for me. Here was a man who was supposed to be the paradigm of the modern biologist, my ultimate role model. Instead, I found him intimidating, aloof, and utterly lacking in respect for the very animals he studied. Others in the department showed more empathy, but they were lower on the academic totem pole. All I could think about was whether or not it was possible to keep a compassionate heart and still become a successful scientist. Doubt weighed on me heavily, and I considered dropping out of college. But I also knew that if I truly wanted to work with animals, I had no alternative.

•

When I was nineteen, I spent a summer working at the Museum of Natural History in New York City on another grant from the National Science Foundation. The project's goal was to study the way the various parts of a cat's brain affect behavior patterns.

The job sounded perfect—until it started. Beginning with the first day—and every day thereafter—I thought I would burst into tears. The thirty cats that we were studying, mostly stray tabbies, had each been thrown into a small plastic cage with just a food bowl, a water bowl, and a small litter box. Apart from dissecting their brains, no one paid any attention to them.

I could feel them craving attention and love, and I began petting them every day. Soon, whenever I'd arrive, they'd jump to the front of their cages and start purring and crying. Some mornings I'd arrive long before anyone else, take a few cats out of their cages, and hold them, talking to them, reassuring them. No one knew.

Our first experiment that summer was to anesthetize a cat, open up its brain, and damage its olfactory bulb to see what effect this would have on its sexual behavior.

I became sick to my stomach during the procedure, and I asked our research team leader why we needed to be so callous.

"This is science!" the man erupted. "This is what studying animal behavior is about!"

He looked at me closely. "You better get used to it," he added and walked off.

But I never did. I had such a different vision, although, I was realizing, a naïve one. I had thought it would be possible to study animal behavior patterns by learning from the animals themselves, spending time at their level, watching how we interacted.

I mentioned this to another of the summer workers, who laughed. I never brought it up again. But I did make a private commitment that I myself would never perform any research that would intentionally hurt an animal.

•

In the 1970s, veterinary school was more difficult to get into than medical school, so I applied to both, as well as to a graduate program in animal behavior as a backup. I ended up being accepted into everything except the veterinary program, where I was wait-listed. In order to keep working with animals, I decided to study for a master's degree at the University of Illinois in applied animal behavior and neurophysiology, so I could take courses where I wouldn't have to hurt any animals.

The major part of my research focused on pigs. What would happen if they were given individual, caring attention? Would it increase their weight? Would it reduce their mortality rate? The answer to both questions was: No. But we did discover that pigs who were comforted and petted ended up higher in their dominance order than those who hadn't been given human attention. Petting, it seemed, was a form of EST (the popular personal growth seminar) for pigs, providing them with increased self-esteem.

However, given the prevailing zeitgeist and the fact that the pigs were thought of as data, we were not allowed to formulate such a conclusion. We could only say that we found no difference in the death rate or weight gain, but that we did document a shift in dominance order. I wasn't even allowed to say that the pigs seemed calmer when I held them in my arms. "How do you know that pigs feel calm?" people would ask—a rhetorical question if I ever heard one.

Occasionally, tired of hiding my feelings, I might make a comment such as "The pigs seem to like being petted." All hell would break loose. "No no no!" I was told. "There are no pig likes and dislikes!"

After graduate school, I was accepted at the Cornell University College of Veterinary Medicine, which had an outstanding reputation and curriculum, as well as state-of-the-art facilities. But again I felt like something of an outcast. Admitting any credence in animals' feelings only landed me in trouble, so I tried my best to stifle my beliefs. I didn't always succeed.

Once, during my senior year, I was on night duty in the animal intensive care unit. There a lonely yellow Labrador, recuperating from surgery for a fractured femur, lay whining and squirming around in his sterile stainless-steel cage, a pathetic ball of quivering fur and flesh, licking the crusted blood around his surgical site, whimpering as students and residents walked by, ignoring his calls for help.

I couldn't stand it. The moment the others left I started monitoring his intravenous fluids and antibiotics. Then I opened the cage door and lay down next to him on the floor, petting him, stroking him, talking to him.

Boom! The door opened and the resident on duty stormed in to angrily ask me what I was doing on the floor with this dog. "Petting him," I said. I asked if he had any painkillers.

The resident snorted. "How do you know the dog is in pain?" he asked. "You're anthropomorphizing."

"Isn't whimpering a sign of pain?" I asked.

"Absolutely not," the man retorted and strode away.

I wasn't the only one to feel alienated by the science and scientists we had once wanted to emulate. My good friend and colleague Michael Fox, currently the vice president of the Humane Society of the United States, once told one of his professors that humankind needed to develop more ethical ways of slaughtering animals, such as pigs, for food production.

"Why?" his professor asked.

"Because," Michael responded, "research has shown a pig's fear and anxiety increases tremendously when watching others screaming and squealing before being slaughtered."

The professor laughed. "Wrong! There are no double-blind, placebo-controlled studies to show that pigs feel that fear."

Like myself, Michael felt frustrated and alone. We both knew that there had to be some balance between science and emotion. We just didn't know how to find it.

Throughout my life I had been interested in nature—and therefore in natural healing. But there was no place for creative thinking or for expanding the boundaries of standard medical practice in veterinary school. Unlike human medical school, where students studied one species, at veterinary school we studied dogs, cats, cows, horses, sheep, goats, pigs, fish, lab animals, and wildlife. Everything was mechanical and all that mattered was memorizing the location and purpose of every muscle and bone, every nerve and neuron, every cell of every different species and the differences between them. And often we were learning techniques only to palliate and suppress disease, not to cure it or treat its underlying causes.

Though the majority of the professors tended to be cool and aloof, there were a few exceptions who did show some compassion for the animals under their care. I couldn't have explained it at the time, but I knew there was something special about them. One was a wonderful man in the large animal clinic named Dr. Delahanty, who had just returned from China, where he had developed an interest in equine acupuncture. I was lucky enough to land a summer job with him and hoped he would teach me how to use this technique to help animals stimulate their own innate healing abilities. Unfortunately, Dr. Delahanty passed away just before the summer started. No one took his place, and I was on my own again.

At this point in my training, I was also reading a steady diet of books and journals with spiritual overtones that gave me some sense of an alternative path. In particular, I was interested in the fact that so many things that were unexplainable in Western medicine were quite comprehensible in Eastern medicine. Eastern science was based on hundreds of years of astute observation of nature, and it focused not just on the disease but on all aspects of the being—mind, body, and spirit— and the interrelationships of different conditions. Long before Western medicine had any knowledge of neurotransmitters and neuroanatomy, traditional Chinese doctors were well aware of the body's ability to ease its own pain.

Although attracted to Eastern medicine, I was still too left-brain-oriented to give it its full due. I kept my interest to a background buzz while plowing ahead as a Western-trained veterinarian.

•

After graduating from veterinary school, my hope was to find a way to deal with animals in a manner that respected their rich emotional lives. It wasn't an easy goal.

My first job was in a highly esteemed large- and small-animal practice in southern New Hampshire. There I hoped to become the New
England version of James Herriot. And to a certain extent that happened. A typical day could mean delivering a calf in 10-degree Fahren-
heit weather out by a frosty stream in an isolated pasture, then driving
to the animal clinic to place a pin in an injured kitten's fractured leg,
and next dashing off to treat a goat suffering with severe mastitis. Each
day was filled with extraordinary experiences and I was grateful.

The practice was founded by Forrest Tenney, the first professional
I'd met who felt about animals as I did. A short, stout fellow with a
strong New Hampshire accent, he looked like the classic Hollywood
version of a New England veterinarian.

Lying across the top shelf of his exam room were bottles of old
remedies that he'd used prior to the advent of antibiotics. I couldn't
help but ask him about these bottles, which made him smile, because he
loved taking them down and telling me about each and every one of the
remedies: plants such as uva ursi, which he used for cystitis, or comfrey,
raspberry leaves, echinacea—many of which have recently come back
into vogue in the natural medicine field.

Whenever I came across a tough problem, he'd give me advice, and
it seldom came from the standard Western medical school of knowledge. His favorite remedy in an emergency was some whiskey for the animal and then the owner. To my surprise, this often worked.

Dr. Tenney was a great favorite among dog breeders in southern
New Hampshire. One of these women, an elderly prim and proper New
England Yankee named Mrs. Bibb, once came to the office to introduce
herself. Entering the examination room with three of her Irish
wolfhounds, she looked me up and down with obvious mixed feelings
about my beard and youthful appearance.

Still, she began chatting about her dogs and their performance at
the shows, and she gave Dr. Tenney's old-fashioned remedies much
credit. While she believed in modern medicine, she said, she hoped I
wasn't one of those arrogant young veterinarians who felt veterinary
school had taught them everything they needed to know.

I assured her that despite my faith in modern Western medicine, I had a strong interest in herbal medicine. Mrs. Bibb then went on to say that she knew many veterinarians disdained folk remedies such as garlic as a flea and insect repellent, but that she had great confidence in them, because ever since Dr. Tenney had suggested adding a clove of garlic to her dogs' food, their flea problems had lessened.

I was somewhat skeptical. But years later, while researching the pharmacological properties of various botanical medicines, I discovered over 1,000 scientific articles documenting the medicinal properties of garlic and its antiparasitic, antibacterial, and antifungal applications.

Still another dog breeder shared a similar story concerning the use of raspberry leaves for dystocias—or difficult labor. Many of her dogs had been having a hard time delivering; uterine contractions would leave them weakened and ready to give up, often requiring an injection of oxytocin and calcium to hasten the birth or—more drastic yet—a cesarean section.

Doc Tenney told her that raspberry leaves could strengthen the uterine muscles, so she began giving them to her dogs during their last trimester of pregnancy. Since then, she said, the puppies popped out one by one, without leaving the mother in severe distress or exhaustion.

•

One Sunday afternoon during a tough lambing season, I had already performed an above-average number of emergencies—running nonstop between horse cuts and colics, cows that were off feed, dogs covered with quills from porcupine attacks—when we received an emergency summons to attend to a sheep in a difficult labor.

Joe and Jackie, the couple who had called, raised prize-winning Suffolk sheep, and Dolly, one of their best, had been straining for at least an hour. But the little lamb didn't seem to want to come out.

After contacting me, Joe and Jackie put Dolly in the back of their pickup truck and rushed her to the yard behind the hospital attached to Dr. Tenney's house, hoping that the bumpy ride on back roads would stimulate Dolly to give birth. No such luck. She was still straining when she arrived—and looking very unhappy besides.

I quickly checked her temperature, pulse, and respiration. I scrubbed up her rear end and inserted as much of my hand and arm as possible inside her birth canal. The weakened lamb was completely stuck. There was no way Dolly could deliver normally. We'd have to perform a cesarean section—and perform it fast.

Because it was a Sunday, my technical help was not available. As I was pondering how to do everything—prepare the surgical instruments, clip up Dolly, scrub her up, and keep her still—in the most expeditious and sterile way, Doc Tenney emerged from his home to check out the commotion. He was always curious, especially when he wasn't on call. And he loved giving fatherly advice. After fifty years of excellent service, no one was going to deny him the option.

As usual, Doc arrived with his black bag containing his tricks of the trade. Sizing up the situation in a flash, he suggested that I get a wheelbarrow and spread some straw on it to make a cushion and to absorb fluids. Then he told us to place the sheep in it, belly up. The sides of the wheelbarrow would serve as a ready-made restraint.

The plan worked beautifully. Dolly lay as still as a sleeping baby, and I was able to clip the wool on her belly in an effort to create a sterile environment. I then administered a local anesthetic, scrubbed down her abdomen with disinfectant as she stared up at me with her huge brown eyes, all the while, I am sure, pondering what the hell I was doing. I calmly assured her that everything would be okay as I made my incision down her ventral midline. The uterus, filled with her baby lamb, popped right up into the opening in her abdomen.

Quickly, but with a steady hand, I made the incision into her uterus and delivered one little lamb drenched in amniotic fluid. The baby immediately bleated, and just as quickly Dolly replied. Meanwhile, I rushed to suture the uterus to keep it from getting contaminated and gently pushed it, the omentum (the soft tissue surrounding the intestines), and other organs back into the abdomen.

The procedure took barely thirty minutes—from the presurgical

scrub, through delivering the lamb, to suturing Dolly back up and helping her out of the wheelbarrow.

Dolly walked over to her newborn and began licking off the amniotic fluid. Once again a new being had entered the world with the help
of Dr. Tenney, who knew the best way to perform a C-section on a
stressed-out sheep.

·

Doc Tenney was a lucky aberration. Whenever I brought up the notion
that animals have feelings, the vast majority of veterinarians I encountered would respond with that smirk I'd grown to know so well in
school. I had hoped that after the dryness of academia, the actual experience of helping sick and wounded animals would have a warming effect on my peers. It didn't seem to.

Being forced to hurt animals was even more troublesome. I had
also hoped that becoming a veterinarian would mean the ability to provide pain-free care, something I had always assumed was possible—
since I believed animals could feel pain, the last thing I wanted to do
was cause them suffering. But again, I was mistaken.

One spring I was asked to dehorn some full-grown cows with an
instrument that was literally no more than a modified guillotine. The
farmer, a French-Canadian known locally as Frenchie, had never been
told that it was more humane to dehorn cows when they were calves.

So I brought out the guillotine, as well as my surgical bag, anes-
thetics, and nose clamp (a metal ring clamped between the nostrils to
restrain cows), and drove off to the farm.

Frenchie had always worked with my immediate predecessor in
Doc Tenney's practice, a man named Dr. Karl, who had been serving the
area for many decades but was now preparing to retire by gradually
handing over his clients to the younger vets.

Now Frenchie was watching some bearded newcomer do the job
quite differently from Doc Karl, and it was clearly confusing him.

I explained that before I dehorned the cows, I intended to block the nerves to the horn so the cows wouldn't feel any pain.

"Doc Karl never did it that way," Frenchie said.

I explained my rationale, and Frenchie listened carefully. But every now and then, speaking in a low but determined voice, he said, "Doc Karl never did it that way."

The procedure took several hours for all ten cows. It was a bloody mess, but as painless as possible.

When I finally returned to my office, I hadn't changed out of my blood-drenched overalls before Doc Karl charged into the room to ask where I'd been all afternoon.

"The nerve blocks took some time to take effect," I told him.

"Nerve blocks!" he screamed. "Why do you bother to do that? Just pull the cow's head over with the nose ring, hold it still, cut off the damn horns, pull the nerves and blood vessels, and they'll heal!" The man was livid that I had wasted time and money in order to prevent pain in these animals.

I had almost become used to being the target for people who believed that animal pain either didn't exist or, if it did, had no significance. But this time I was more astonished than usual. When I finally got up the nerve to ask him how he could perform such brutal surgery on a full-grown cow, he stormed out of the room, muttering angrily.

The next day one of the younger partners in the practice took me aside. Speaking as one would talk to a well-intentioned but wayward youth, he let me know that there was no need to change the established way of doing things. Anyway, he added, it wasn't financially worthwhile to spend all the time and money blocking a cow's nerves.

This time I spoke up, feeling that since the man was the youngest partner in the practice, we could at least have a reasonable discussion. "Such a painful procedure should not have to be done at all," I said. "The farmers should be educated to dehorn their cows with an electrical dehorner when they are still calves—that's the most painless approach."

"Maybe you're right, maybe you're not," my colleague said. "But you're not going to change the practice of generations. So forget it."

Sure enough, later that month, Frenchie requested that we dehorn two more of his cows, and before I could pack my stuff, Doc Karl appeared in my office, demanding I perform the operation his way. We had, he insisted, far too many other farm calls to waste the time.

As the low man on the practice totem pole, I had to do what I was told. But these incidents and others like them strengthened my conviction that something was grotesquely wrong. Veterinary school indoctrination was more powerful than I realized. I knew these were all good people. But hadn't they lost something along the way?

I remember that autumn day as cold and overcast. I got into my car feeling as bleak as the weather, but by the time I arrived at the farm, I decided I had to speak out. So when I met Frenchie at his pasture, I told him that I would go ahead and dehorn these two cows as Doc Karl ordered, but I didn't feel right about it. It would be much wiser if Frenchie dehorned his calves by electrical branding when they were young. Besides being more humane, it doesn't hurt as much, it's bloodless, and it would be more economical for him in the short and long run.

Frenchie surprised me. Speaking in a low, conspiratorial tone, as though he didn't want Doc Karl to overhear, he told me how much he'd thought about my last visit and how he respected my concern for his cows. He also acknowledged that in all these years he'd never thought about the pain they were experiencing.

Frenchie's was a poor, backyard family farm. Every penny counted toward survival. But the man loved his animals. He'd made up his mind that from now on we would dehorn the calves when they were young.

In the meantime, I did have to dehorn two cows the old way, and they bellowed and howled in pain. And with each bellow I cried inside, too, asking the cows and God for forgiveness. But I also saw that the farmer was feeling his cows' pain for the first time and acknowledging that this was not right.

We both came away with a new awareness. And I vowed that I

would never inflict that sort of unnecessary suffering on any animal again. My resistance to my Western veterinary school training was strengthened. I knew there had to be a better way.

Doc Karl was pleased that I completed all my farm calls that day in good time, but I could see his bewilderment when I told him that Frenchie had decided, in the future, to dehorn his cows when they were calves. Doc Karl was a kind man and an excellent veterinarian, but we were never able to agree on our basic approach to animal care.

From that day on, whenever I came over for an early morning calving or on a sick cow call at Frenchie's, he would offer me coffee and homemade apple pie and then ask me if there were any better ways to treat the cows.

◆

When I was in college in the late 1960s, we would discuss ethics and revolution as routinely as we did sports or grades, sitting carelessly on the carpets outside our dorm rooms until late in the evening, drinking wine and trying to imagine a new world. Although it has become unfashionable to say this, I am unapologetic for that decade. We brought up important issues that had long been overlooked. We altered the mores of the previous decades, and we had fun doing it.

One theoretical question that frequently arose: Should you try to change the world via revolution, or can you make a significant difference by changing one mind at a time?

My experience with Frenchie made me understand that the problem was not simply that other people didn't share my ideas about animal emotions. Perhaps they just weren't aware of those ideas—there was barely any literature on it. So from that moment on, I decided to change the world any way I could, even if that meant one person—or one cow—at a time.

I thought back to when I first entered veterinary school and felt so idealistic about animals' feelings; I remembered reciting the veterinarians' oath, specifically the part about "doing no harm." I recalled the scientists, animal behaviorists, veterinarians I'd met along the way. Most of them were genuinely decent people who had, due to daily life's incessant demands and challenges, shut down emotionally, unwilling or unable to find an opportunity for either introspection or retrospection about the original dream that brought them to the profession in the first place.

I shuddered. By closing off their reactions to their animal research subjects, weren't they closing a part of their own psyches? By denying that their animal patients felt emotions, weren't they limiting the amount of emotion that they too could feel? What impact did this mindset have on their own psychic lives, their relationships with the people they cared about, their interactions with people in general?

My concern wasn't simply for other veterinary doctors—I feared that, as treating animals became more of a daily routine, this same alienating process might take place within me, too.

After all, I was already changing. Whenever I became overwhelmed by my schedule, I would do whatever took the least time to resolve the immediate problem, forgetting to honor the animal as much as I would have liked. If I was already making such compromises, how could I expect more from others who had been working ten, twenty, fifty years longer than I had?

A friend once told me, "If you follow the same road map as everyone else, you end up in the same place." But this wasn't the destination I had in mind.

·

A few weeks after my experience with Frenchie, I was off on a mission to castrate a four-year-old brown Swiss bull. I had been given detailed instructions where to go over the phone: Turn right off the main road on the east side of Mount Pitcher, follow that road for two and a half miles past the third barn on the left, turn right down the dirt road past the fifth old oak tree. After half a mile, take the first left past the large old pine tree and, a quarter mile up on the right-hand side, pull over and look up the mountain. There I would find the lumberjack and his bull.

These instructions were more specific than many others that had sent me on wild goose chases (occasionally literal ones) into the middle of nowhere. And as oak trees flew past, I kept wondering, Is this one old enough to be considered one of the five? Was that last tree really an oak, or was it a hickory?

But whether I'd followed the instructions properly or not, I was now lost in the woods on a sunny autumn afternoon without a truck or person in sight. I looked up the mountain and could just imagine a figure in the distance that might be wearing a dark red-and-black wool jacket. I shouted hello.

"Come on up," the figure yelled back. "We're ready for ya."

Where is the barn? I wondered. Where am I supposed to perform this surgical procedure? Where is the water supply or an area to restrain a 1,000-pound bull? I climbed up the hill uncertainly, holding on to low-lying branches of second-growth New England forest.

Straight out of a childhood cartoon vision came an oversized, bearded lumberjack, followed by two brown Swiss bulls. "Thanks for coming. Looks like the directions worked for ya," the man said. His name, appropriately enough, was Jack.

Then he introduced his animals.

"I use these guys, Ben and Buck, to cut and carry timber out of these woods without having to clear-cut the whole mountainside," he said. "It preserves the trees and allows me to be with my buddies here. I'd rather work with them and enjoy the quiet of the forest than have the noise and pollution of diesel tractors."

He went on to tell me how he had trained them and how well they worked together. "The only problem," he added, "is that I had Ben castrated, but never got around to doing Buck. But he's getting a bit ornery and I guess I better do it now."

He was right—if Buck was going to keep working without hurting Jack or anyone else who got in his way, he needed to be castrated.

"Where can we restrain him?" I asked.

"I thought we'd just tie him with a nose ring around this tree and hold him," Jack said.

Are you crazy? I thought. You want me to cut off the testicles of a 1,000-pound bull who's just tied to a tree? He'll kill us both.

But I expressed my concerns more calmly: "Are you sure?"

"No problem," Jack responded. He could handle Buck.

I reluctantly decided to proceed.

I went back to my car to fetch my black surgical bag, a bucketful of water that I'd brought with me, sterile solutions, restraining ropes, and the emasculators, as they're noneuphemistically called. When I returned, Jack had carefully tied Buck's nose and head around one of the sturdier trees and was now quietly talking to him, telling him it would only hurt for a minute. He apologized for what had to be done but explained that it was for everyone's best interest.

The vision of this huge wild man soothing his bull with words impressed me enough to ask Jack if I could give Buck a mild sedative and a local nerve block to alleviate some of the pain.

"Pain?" Jack asked. As much as he loved his animals, he had never even considered that their pain could be lessened. No one had ever brought it up before. "Go ahead," he said.

And so, after Jack restrained Buck's head, calmly brushing his forehead and talking softly, I administered a mild sedative to make sure Buck would not collapse to the ground, and then a spinal block. Next I clamped the emasculators above his fully developed testicles. Buck did indeed bellow for a moment—as would anyone—but not nearly as much as if we hadn't used an anesthetic.

The whole time Ben watched us: suspicious, curious, but thankfully calm.

Afterward Jack helped me clean up my surgical instruments and carry my equipment to the car, and he thanked me for alleviating Buck's pain. He felt guilty that he'd never considered it before. Once again I realized that my judgments had been too harsh. It wasn't that people didn't care if their animals suffered. Most of them had simply never been offered another—painless—option.

•

Meanwhile, it wasn't just animal lovers who were rethinking the topic of emotions in animals. Science too was beginning to catch up, and over the last two decades, in a slew of books and assorted publications, a remarkable openness to the issue has become evident.

Today it often seems as though the more we study the differences between human and nonhuman animals, the more we see how similar we are. Only recently did we discover that human DNA is 98.4 percent equivalent to chimpanzee DNA, meaning that humans are genetically closer to chimps than chimps are to apes. Put another way, humans and chimpanzees share a closer genetic relationship than most species that humans consider identical, such as African elephants and Indian elephants.

In fact, humans are so genetically similar to both chimpanzees and bonobos (or pygmy chimpanzees) that some scientists suggest we may actually be considered a third species of chimpanzee, which is how physiologist and UCLA professor Jared Diamond came to the name of his book *The Third Chimpanzee*. In it, Diamond demonstrates that many of the qualities once deemed uniquely human are actually shared by our various primate brothers and sisters, as well as by other members of the animal kingdom.

For example, it was once thought that only humans could express themselves in artistic terms. But paintings created by captive elephants and monkeys are so outstanding that they can fool art experts. (When told that a series of drawings was done by an elephant rather than a human, the abstract expressionist painter Willem de Kooning was reported to have responded, "That's a damned talented elephant.") And the male of a species called the bowerbird in New Guinea creates highly decorated, visually arresting huts designed to impress the female of his mating ability. They are certainly as artistic, Diamond argues, as any architecture created by humankind.

Agriculture, considered to be one of the cornerstones of human civilization, is practiced by several different species of ants, which cultivate different kinds of yeast or fungi inside the nest, harvesting them just as humans harvest necessary food crops. Ants also practice a form of animal domestication. Says Diamond: "Ants obtain a concentrated sugary secretion termed honeydew from diverse insects, ranging from aphids, mealy bugs, and scale insects to caterpillars, treehoppers, and spittle insects. In return for the honeydew, the ants protect their 'cows' from predators and parasites. Some aphids have evolved into virtually the insect equivalent of domestic cattle. [They] excrete honeydew from their anuses, and have a specialized anal anatomy designed to hold the droplet in place while an ant drinks it. To milk their cows and stimulate honeydew flow, ants stroke the aphids with their antennae."

We are discovering that even communication skills are more developed among animals than science ever thought: Certain African monkeys, known as vervets, use a highly sophisticated form of verbal communication with almost a dozen different "words"—and it's possible there are many more that human observers haven't yet been able to interpret.

Even the use of seemingly self-destructive behaviors, which once seemed to be a unique human predilection, such as smoking or drinking, show up among other species of mammals as a means of displaying genetic prowess. (The underlying concept is that individual animals able to perform such dangerous acts without being killed must be unusually fit; therefore their genes make them highly valuable mates. In short, playing with death is actually a form of Darwinian natural selection.)

As bizarre, yet as hopeful as it may sound, even altruistic behavior, thought only to be present in a small number of benevolent humans, has been found in wide range of other animals. In his book *Cheating Monkeys and Citizen Bees*, Lee Gatkin describes numerous examples of self-sacrificing behavior in different species, not only illustrating that there must be evolutionary benefits to altruism but also offering us examples to extrapolate to our own lives.

The list of corresponding traits between human and animal keeps growing. In a new finding from Harvard University, another area of division between animal and human has been shattered. Standard biology textbooks state that the human internal clock operates differently from that of animals; theirs, regardless of environmental clues such as sunshine or nightfall, operate on a twenty-four-hour day. Experiments from earlier this century suggested that most humans had a longer cycle, perhaps twenty-five hours—and some had cycles that were even longer or, in some cases, shorter. But new research shows that the former studies did not rid the environment of possible cues, such as indoor light. When no cues are extant, humans' clocks turn out to be analogous to those of other animals.

Furthermore, thanks to the pioneering work of Jane Goodall, Roger Fouts, and other primatologists, we know that many chimpanzee behavior patterns are not dissimilar from ours—for example, the mother-child bond, which lasts for more than ten years in both human and chimpanzee families. In addition, chimpanzees have been shown to display what clearly looks to human observers like feelings and emotions—they grieve, they experience joy and anger, they medicate themselves, and, sadly enough, they seem to wage war.

Some of Jane Goodall's latest research, published last year in *Nature* magazine, presents considerable evidence that chimpanzees develop unique cultures within their specific communities. The study found at least thirty-nine customs related to chimps' tool use, grooming, and courtship—customs that vary widely from group to group, much as they do in humans. "What we see in wild chimps, on a lesser scale, is the sort of cultural diversity that we would see in traditional human societies," said primatologist Craig Stanford of the University of Southern California.

And certain apes, when given standard human intelligence tests, have scored surprisingly high. One twenty-four-month-old ape, tested on the Bayley Scale for Infant Development, was judged to have the approximate intelligence of a thirteen-and-a-half-month-old human infant; at five and a half, he tested at about the equivalent of a human two-and-a-half-year-old.

Given this body of research, some feel we should rethink the entire human connection to apes. In the book *The Great Ape Project*, edited by Paola Cavalieri and Peter Singer, the idea is posited that given our comparable genetic makeup, all the great apes, including humans, should be categorized within one family.

·

Some of the most compelling reasons to believe that animals have humanlike emotional systems come from Candace Pert, an AIDS researcher and a professor in the Department of Physiology and Biophysics at Georgetown University Medical Center in Washington, D.C. (Pert was one of the scientists featured on the PBS television series *Healing and the Mind*.)

Pert's extensive work has identified what she calls "opiate receptors" in the human body, which are the biochemical basis for all our feelings and emotions. These receptors are stationary molecules, located in the cellular membranes of our nerve cells, that function as binding sites for different neurotransmitters, or opiates, that travel throughout the body. Pert refers to these opiates as "information substances." Depending on the precise external or internal stimulus, different neurotransmitters—such as dopamine, seratonin, or endorphins—will be released. These opiates then move through the bloodstream and bind to their specific receptor molecules, much as a key fits into a specific keyhole. When this binding takes place, a particular neurological response, or emotion, occurs.

A typical nerve cell may have millions of receptors on its surface—and they function as sensing molecules, like scanners, constantly sensing the environment around us. Pert writes, "Just as our eyes, ears, nose, tongue, fingers, and skin act as sense organs, so, too, do the receptors, only on a cellular level."

Essentially, Pert has discovered the most minute biochemical basis for our changes in behavior and moods. She also discovered that these receptors are not just limited to the brain, but are located throughout the body on every nerve cell, making our entire body one large sensing and feeling organ.

Particularly fascinating to animal lovers is that these receptors are not limited to humans. They exist in all animals, from one-celled beings all the way up the evolutionary scale to humans. Even the tetrahymena, a primitive single-celled animal, manufactures many of the same biochemicals as humans.

I feel this is a stunning demonstration of the unity of all life. We humans share these emotion molecules with the most modest forms of microscopic life, even though evolution has caused us to develop into trillion-celled creatures of extraordinary magnificence. If emotions such as fear, love, joy, sadness, and sorrow are based on opiate receptors, how can we be so species-centric to think that only in humans can the results of these molecules be interpreted as emotions?

It seems that Darwin's earliest observations have proven basically correct. The evolutionary basis for emotions, feeling pain or pleasure, does seem to be present in all animals.

•

Between 1982 and 1991, I worked part-time at New York City's Animal Medical Center. Established as a not-for-profit facility by the American Humane Society, the center is a model for providing the highest quality, most advanced veterinary care.

Most of the veterinarians there accept traditional beliefs concerning animal feelings. My experiences there are still burned in my memory: When doctors would go on rounds, they would talk about the animals under their care as though they were used cars. Discussing a quivering, ill poodle physically restrained on a table, a doctor would say, "Here we have a 1986 model standard poodle with coxofemoral [hip joint] degenerative joint disease and an active hepatopathy [liver disease].…" Or a 1975 model cocker spaniel, a 1981 model Great Dane, and so on.

After seeing me wince upon hearing these descriptions, a senior veterinarian took me aside and calmed me down. "It's just our way of distancing ourselves from the animal," he said.

Then he confided that he felt as he knew I did, that animals deserved the kind of care and attention we give to humans. He also added that because there wasn't much support for that stand at the center, I couldn't expect him to back me up publicly—he just wanted to let me know that not everyone disagreed with my position, which by that time had become well known, due to my inability to keep my opinions to myself.

Not long ago, when I returned to the center to give a lecture, I saw the man again. He was fairly bursting with energy. "You remember all that stuff you used to tell us about animals' feelings," he asked, "and how the way we react with them could have an impact on their immune system? It's no longer out of fashion to believe that!"

Today, almost a decade since my work in Manhattan, more and more of my colleagues are not just open to the possibility that animals have emotions and feel pain, but are out-and-out converts. For example, not long ago I gave a lecture at the Cornell University College of Veterinary Medicine. There I ran into a former professor, one of the group that had always ribbed me for being overly empathetic with the horses we cared for. He was a good man, but one of the most hardnosed professors at the school. Now, however, when I spotted him in the stables, I saw him not only stroking a horse's neck lovingly, but talking aloud to her.

Even the *Cornell University Veterinary College Animal Health Newsletter* recently published an article called "Do Cats Grieve?" In it my friend, mentor, and colleague, behaviorist Katherine Houpt, says that a cat may well express grief by refusing to eat, meowing more often, or becoming less active. When I was in school, such a comment would have meant grief for me, given the hostility it would have aroused in my professors.

·

In one of my favorite movies, *Alice's Restaurant*, based on Arlo Guthrie's song of the same title (and filmed not far from the town where I now practice), the hero, Guthrie, has been forced to appear before his draft board. There they ask him if he's ever been arrested.

"Yes," he replies.

The authorities then shunt him into a side room to find out what transgression he had committed. In this room he is surrounded by hard-core criminals—arsonists, burglars, rapists, all sharing a macho camaraderie about their felonious past.

One of these men asks what Guthrie was arrested for.

"Littering," he says.

When the others hear that, they shuffle nervously to the other side of the room.

Not so long ago, when I would discuss emotions in animals at professional gatherings, the scientists around me would become very quiet or mumble softly to themselves as they too moved to the other side of the hall. These days, when I address a group of scientists and discuss animal feelings, I am no longer faced with polite skepticism or abject mockery. The benefits of this change in thinking are just beginning to manifest in the improvement of care for laboratory animals, as well as in the increased use of postoperative analgesics and painkillers for our companion animals.

But pain is merely one emotion. To me, it seems unreasonable to acknowledge one animal emotion and not others, even though animal behaviorists would still say all these indications of emotions are actually predetermined behavior patterns resembling the human responses that we label feelings, whereas still other scientists would differentiate between feelings and emotions. But that seems nothing more than a game of hide-and-seek, changing the pieces or definitions as evidence of one wipes out the belief system of another. If animals feel pain, don't they feel pleasure? If animals feel pleasure, can't they feel love? If they have the same neurochemicals that induce emotions in humans, perhaps they share the same capacity for all our emotions.

Meanwhile, more recent evidence of animal feelings has emerged—positron emission tomography, or PET scans as the technique is more widely known, documents the activity in different parts of the human brain associated with particular emotional states, such as anger or fear. The same activity has now been shown to take place in the brains of animals when they are experiencing similar states. As far as I am concerned, this proves that not only do animals have the same emotional responses as humans, but that they have a full range of feelings. To my mind, all that is left is semantics.

Two

From Heart to Soul:
The Benefits of the
Human-Animal Bond

A faithful friend is the medicine of life.
—Ecclesiasticus 6:16

It is unfortunate that science has yet to make a meticulous attempt to study the presence of feelings in animals. Science has, however, initiated a serious investigation of the effects that animals have on human feelings. In other words, we haven't yet made a commitment to prove that animals can feel, but we are willing to debate how important their presence is to our own emotional landscape. At some level I wonder if this isn't itself a blatant form of anthropocentrism.

In fact, interest in the human-animal bond is almost as old as science itself. Throughout history, from the Egyptians to the Greeks and Romans, and then into the Christian era, numerous claims for animal-induced cures have been made. Some of these included the Egyptian dog-headed god Anubis who, among his many roles, was physician to the gods. In ancient Greece, the cult of the healer Aesculapius liberally employed dogs who were believed capable of aiding sufferers with licks of their tongues. In medieval France, Saint Guinefort was a loyal greyhound who saved the life of his master's child, but was then wrongfully killed. His grave became the site of a healing cult that attracted thousands of supplicants pleading for relief from a myriad of ills, including fever, blindness, rickets, and lameness.

In the nineteenth century, prompted by the startling growth in popularity of domestic pets, a few scientific studies did begin to appear, notably those by the renowned American psychologist Granville Stanley Hall. Hall, who established an experimental psychology laboratory at Johns Hopkins University in 1882 and is considered the founder of child psychology, believed that ontogeny recapitulates phylogeny—in other words, the development of an individual organism from embryo to adult duplicates the evolutionary development of the species. Thus, as children mature, they replicate the development of our earliest forebears. To Hall, this meant that children should be surrounded by animals, just as humankind was in the hunter/gatherer stage of its evolutionary past.

Though provocative, Hall's theories did not spur much research. It wasn't until the 1960s, when psychologists observed changes in human behavior patterns due to animal companions, that serious study of the human-animal bond began. Especially notable was the work of child psychologist Boris Levenson, who studied the benefits animals could contribute as companions to adults and children.

Levenson's work stimulated research in other disciplines, such as social work, sociology, and veterinary medicine. In particular it spearheaded the efforts of Ohio State University's Sam and Elizabeth Corson, who examined what they called pet-facilitated psychotherapy (or assigning dogs to psychiatric patients), and who claimed to have witnessed improvement in these patients.

The field remained the domain of psychologists until the late 1970s, when a young graduate student named Erica Friedman published her research on the relationship between animal companions and stress.

Over the last two decades, the body of work in this area has grown enormously. Among other findings, studies suggest that animal companions can:

- Help lower blood pressure during stressful situations.
- Increase self-esteem in children and adolescents.
- Reduce blood pressure and stress level in healthy subjects, as well as produce changes in speech pattern and facial expression.
- Increase the survival rates for heart attack patients.
- Improve quality of life for seniors.
- Help the socialization of young adults with their peers.
- Aid in the development of nurturing behavior and humane attitudes in children.
- Provide a sense of emotional stability for foster children.
- Help establish appropriate social behavior in mentally impaired elderly people and prisoners.
- Help patients in psychiatric institutions work through anxiety and despair.
- Improve balance, coordination, mobility, muscular strength, posture, and language ability in developmentally challenged children.
- Reduce the demand for physicians' services for nonserious problems among Medicare enrollees.

- Reduce minor health problems in the general population.

- Reduce feelings of loneliness in preadolescents.

For the most part, much of this recent work has focused on specific physical disorders. Only a relatively small number of studies have
looked at the impact on overall health. One of these was undertaken by
James Serpell, currently an associate professor of Humane Ethics and
Animal Welfare at the University of Pennsylvania Veterinary Hospital
and formerly the director of the Companion Animal Research Group
attached to the Cambridge University Veterinary School.

In 1979 Serpell had finished his Ph.D. (in avian behavior) and was
looking around for a research topic. "I had been thinking about why
people own pets," he says. "Most domestic animals have clear beneficial
roles—they give us labor, or food. Pets don't. But there are millions of
them. This struck me as an anomaly, so I wondered what theories
people had put out to explain it."

When Serpell researched the literature, however, he found practically nothing outside a few esoteric articles: "Here is this huge phenomenon and yet few social scientists or psychologists apart from some
oddball characters had even thought about it."

Serpell designed a ten-month study to determine the impact of
animal companions on human health and well-being. He enlisted sev-
enty-one adults who had applied to a local animal shelter for animal
adoption. He also ran a control group of twenty-six subjects without
animal companions over the same period.

Serpell ultimately found that the group with animal companions
reported a highly significant reduction in minor health problems beginning in the first month after acquiring the animal. This group also
demonstrated significant improvements in psychological well-being.
The households with dogs also showed a massive increase in the
amount of time they devoted to exercise—an increase of 400 to 500
percent in their walking. In general, Serpell concluded that: "Pet ownership can have a positive impact on human health and behavior and in
some cases these effects are relatively long lasting."

Despite Serpell's findings, research on the human-animal bond continues to center on specific health issues, including heart disease, recovery from serious illness, AIDS, the elderly, children, and psychological issues.

Healing the Heart

*D*r. Greg Ogilvie is the head of medical oncology at Colorado State University and one of the top veterinary oncologists in the world. He is also a dear friend; we met in 1995 when he was giving a lecture at a medical conference I was attending.

Not long ago he was telling me about a man and a dog who had identical heart problems: Tom, fifty-five, and his Scottie, Taffy, both suffered from hypertropic cardiomyopathy, which means that the muscles of the heart are worn out, with little likelihood of recovery—essentially the heart turns into an enlarged bag of tissue that can't pump blood.

The first time Tom fell ill, he was placed in a cardiac intensive care unit, where the doctors felt his prognosis was poor. With death imminent, the man pleaded that he be able to see his Taffy, because the thought of passing away without a last word with his dog seemed unbearable.

Tom's wife, Helen, managed to smuggle Taffy, carefully hidden in a pile of blankets and sheets, into Tom's critical care room. There man and dog spent some joyful time together before the dog had to be smuggled out again.

But Tom wanted to see Taffy more often, so for the next ten days Helen managed to bring the dog into his room regularly.

Very soon thereafter Tom began a remarkable turnaround. The nurses, impressed by the therapeutic value of the bond between man and dog, decided that Taffy should spend more time with Tom. And he did, hospital rules notwithstanding. As a result, Tom's health continued to improve and he was discharged from the hospital a couple of weeks later.

Taffy, however, soon became seriously ill himself. Grief-stricken, Tom took him to see my friend Dr. Ogilvie, who, after a thorough examination, found that the dog's disorder was almost identical to the man's and placed him on similar medications.

The drug, which had worked wonders for Tom, was equally effective for Taffy; they would take their medication at the same time and then go outside for walks. The pair flourished.

But one winter several years later Tom developed a bad cold, which put his health in jeopardy. And because he wasn't feeling well enough to give the dog proper care, Taffy also became sick again, coughing, building up fluid in his lungs, showing signs of physical weakness. Tom brought the dog back to Dr. Ogilvie, who readmitted him to the hospital.

The next day Tom's cardiologist told Dr. Ogilvie, "You won't believe this, but Tom just came back into the hospital. He seems so upset about Taffy's hospitalization that he's significantly weakened himself."

This cycle repeated itself several times. If Tom was ill, Taffy became ill. If one recovered, the other did, too. They were only both healthy when they were in each other's company. Dr. Ogilvie says that both he and Tom's physician were absolutely certain that Tom and Taffy's health were linked.

The connection was certainly hard to ignore. Once, when Tom was hospitalized once more and Taffy started to falter, Helen and the nurses smuggled the dog into the critical care unit (at a major Chicago hospital). The improvement in man and dog was so dramatic that it touched the hearts of the rest of the medical staff. Indeed, Tom's supervising physician decided to break hospital rules and let Taffy sleep on Tom's bed because, he said, his first responsibility was to keep the man alive. The administration averted its official eyes as Taffy became, to the best of anyone's knowledge, the first canine, or any other nonhuman mammal, to spend the night in one of their rooms.

The heart is among the most researched areas in human/animal correlational health. One of the most comprehensive studies was carried out on 5,741 adult men and women, from a wide cross section of socioeconomic backgrounds, at Alfred Hospital's Baker Medical Research Institute in Melbourne, Australia, one of that country's major heart and vascular disease research institutions.

The study showed that people with animal companions had lower blood pressure, as well as lower triglyceride (fat) and cholesterol levels, than those who did not. The report stopped short of claiming that the presence of an animal companion could in and of itself lower the risk for heart disease. But it stated that a relationship between cardiovascular health and animal companionship clearly exists and that it should be studied more extensively.

Several other significant studies in cardiovascular disease have been conducted by Erica Friedman, chair of the department of health and nutrition sciences at New York's Brooklyn College. Friedman, a highly regarded biologist who holds a doctorate from the University of Pennsylvania, is credited as being among the first nonpsychologists to study the health benefits of animal companions.

Friedman's primary area of interest is how social and physiological conditions combine with factors such as social support, psychological status, and mobility as determinants of health. Animals weren't her intended area of study, but as she was conducting her preliminary research in the late 1970s, she and her co-researchers discovered that patients with animal companions were more likely to be alive one year after discharge from a coronary care unit than those without animal companions.

More recently, Friedman examined people who had suffered from arrhythmia—or irregular heartbeats—after their heart attacks, making them at risk for sudden cardiac death. These men and women, all participants in a national clinical trial on cardiac-arrhythmic suppression, had low ejection fractions—a measure of the amount of blood emptied from the ventricle during contraction. A low ejection fraction means the ventricle isn't doing a good job of pumping blood into the body.

Friedman found that patients with an animal companion were more likely to be alive after one year, and that patients who had a dog were 8.6 times more likely to survive the year than those without.

In another study, Friedman and her co-researchers examined the relationship between the presence of animals and their companion's cardiovascular reactivity, or stress responses—for example, a sudden rise in blood pressure, one of the primary mechanisms in the development of heart disease.

"We were looking to see if just having a pet in the same room influences a person's cardiovascular responses," Friedman says. "We did a number of different studies, but one stands out in particular—in it we examined children's blood pressure while they were reading aloud and resting. We did that in two different situations: with and without a dog in the room. Basically, we found that blood pressures were lower with the dog present."

Friedman's work has generally been very well received, but she has run into occasional pockets of resistance. She tells me: "One of my coauthors, James Lynch, gave a talk at a medical school about the effects of a new therapy on heart disease patients. The attending physicians were very interested and wanted to know all about this new drug. But when they found out that the actual therapy involved having an animal as a companion, they lost all interest."

•

Dr. Karen Allen, a research scientist at the school of medicine at the University of New York at Buffalo, knows the exact moment she became interested in the effect of animal companions on human cardiovascular health. She was watching *Night of the Living Dead*, director George Romero's classic horror movie, and became aware that, as the zombies were devouring everyone in sight, her heart started pounding faster and her pulse began racing. She was sure her blood pressure was climbing as well.

Then her Saint Bernard entered the room, and she started petting him. As she did so, she could feel her pulse drop. "My husband was also in the room at the time," she says, "He didn't have that effect on me. He just said, 'Turn that drivel off.' "

Allen, who has a doctorate in psychophysiology, has been studying human and animal interaction for two decades. Her original research centered on social psychology, or how the presence of other people influences the development and progression of any kind of disease, especially cardiovascular.

Until recently, studying humans who either did or did not have animal companions, Allen had come up with dramatic results, not unlike Dr. Friedman's. But critics suggested that pet owners might differ from the general population—perhaps only happy, well-adjusted people acquired animals, and perhaps these people were more inclined to good health than those without animals. If this were so, studies of those who had already made a decision about having—or not having—an animal companion would be inherently flawed.

So Allen and her team decided to study people who had not given animals much thought: forty-eight middle-aged stockbrokers, all highly stressed and highly paid, all suffering from hypertension that required medication. After a careful series of screening tests and a random assignment of animal companions to half the study's participants, Allen found that six months later "the people with pets showed a dramatic improvement" in their hypertension.

In another experiment, Allen discovered that, during a stressful moment, a person's blood pressure rises in the presence of a spouse. It rises somewhat less in the presence of a friend.

"But with a pet," she says, "there's hardly any difference in blood pressure at all. To me, that means that no matter how hard people try to be nonjudgmental with each other, we don't see them that way. We do, however, see pets that way."

Physical Healing:
Recovery from Serious Illness

*J*oe and Sally are a couple whose short-haired cat, Samantha, was basically their only child. Their world revolved around her, their lives
were incomplete without her.

Shortly before her fifteenth birthday, Samantha began vomiting
severely. When the couple took her to their local veterinarian, they were
told that the cat had developed cancer and that it was a terminal condition that would be accompanied by intense pain. He recommended
they put her down.

Upon hearing the news, Sally collapsed. She had suffered from
asthma for many years, but the prospect of life without Samantha
caused her condition, previously under control, to take a bad turn. It
was soon accompanied by acute depression.

Joe took Samantha to my friend Dr. Greg Ogilvie's hospital, assuming that the only choice was euthanasia. But Dr. Ogilvie's examination indicated a better prognosis than the other veterinarian's, and he
suggested several options. According to Dr. Ogilvie, few people realize
that cancer in animals is not always a hopeless diagnosis—as with humans, successful treatment is possible.

On hearing this, Joe immediately left the cat at the hospital so Dr.
Ogilvie could perform more diagnostic work, and drove to see Sally,
who had been hospitalized for respiratory difficulty due to severe lung
disease combined with depression. Her doctor's private suspicion was
that the depression made a complete recovery doubtful.

When Joe told Sally about Samantha's improved prognosis, her
mood immediately lifted. In the weeks that followed, the cat was successfully treated with surgery and chemo.

Sally was then referred to Dr. Ogilvie's Changes Program at the
Argus Center—named after the Greek mythological figure Argus, the
many-eyed giant who cared for animals. The program's staff, which includes psychologists, psychiatrists, and veterinarians, focuses on the

difficulties that can arise in the relationships between pets and people—such as profound grief due to the loss of a pet, difficult choices in treating animals with chronic illness, or anxiety resulting from a separation.

After working with a social worker, both Sally's physical and mental health changed dramatically, and she was discharged from the hospital with the proviso that she continue to work with the Changes Program counselors.

Four years later, Sally is doing well, and so is Samantha, who recently celebrated her nineteenth birthday.

◆

Many recent studies have demonstrated the prophylactic effects of animal companions on humans recovering from illness. For instance, in a 1994 study out of New York City's Memorial Sloan-Kettering Cancer Center, researchers found that animals can have a beneficial effect on a healthy person who is caring for a spouse with cancer. They can also help terminally ill adults deal with their illness.

Sick children were particularly receptive to an animal companion's presence—they felt loved at a very difficult time, they were able to confide their feelings to their animal companions more easily than to adults, and caring for the animal gave them structure at a time when their own lives were disrupted.

These and other studies have helped to create a new field called Animal Assisted Therapy (AAT), which is being used in various areas of medicine, especially in recovery from physical injuries. Washington's Delta Society, the best known and largest not-for-profit organization to fund and promote the study of the human-animal bond, defines AAT as "a goal-directed intervention in which an animal that meets specific criteria is an integral part of the treatment process. AAT is directed and/or delivered by a health/human service professional with specialized expertise, and within the scope of practice of his/her profession."

Primarily used to help improve motor skills, wheelchair skills, and standing balance, AAT also has psychological applications in areas such as increasing self-esteem, attention skills, and verbal activity.

Shari Bernard is the executive director and founder of Therapet, a not-for-profit organization based in East Texas whose aim is to promote the use of specially trained animals in therapy—any type of therapy, whether that means working with physically or sexually abused children, or with adults in acute care, or in a hospital rehabilitation program. Bernard has even brought her animals in to psychiatric hospitals within the Texas Department of Criminal Justice.

Bernard, an occupational therapist with considerable experience training and showing dogs, first took her canines into nursing homes with her local canine-obedience club and noticed that the patients reacted immediately and positively. She also saw that the staff—some of whom were initially wary—was often able to witness real and even dramatic improvement in the patients' condition, even for those who hadn't been responsive to traditional types of therapy.

Bernard decided to expand her work with dogs in hospital settings and began a formal program in 1984. At present, most of her work involves patients who are severely impaired or semicomatose. "There's so little you can do for such people in a traditional clinical setting," Bernard says, "but by providing the sensation of an animal's warmth and fur, we get spontaneous eye opening, or tracking, or the moving of heads and hands to see a dog. If the patients are able, we try to get them to start following one-step requests. We tell them to reach for the dog's ear, nose, or tail. Then, as the patients progress, we slowly add more complicated requests, such as asking them to pick up a ball and throw it."

One sixty-year-old woman whom Bernard encountered, Wilma, had been baby-sitting for her two grandchildren when she accidentally started a fire, causing her trailer to explode. Trying to rescue the kids caused her to be burned on over 84 percent of her body. Eventually she lost an ear, part of her nose, almost all her fingers, and both legs, one amputated above the knee, one below.

When Bernard first met her, Wilma had been in an acute care hospital for several years and, because she still had open wounds, she was in isolation. Bernard treated her for a month, but due to her pain, Wilma couldn't do much therapy.

One day Bernard was able to get Wilma into a wheelchair and sat her in the hallway. There, one of the therapy dogs, a fat little Pembroke Welsh corgi, walked by. Wilma, who had barely spoken a word since the accident, actually tried to turn her head. She said softly, "Can you bring that dog with the cute butt back over here so I can see her?"

She even smiled, a gesture which must have been quite painful because of the considerable burns on her face.

Bernard asked Wilma if she wanted to work with the AAT program, and Wilma agreed. Soon the animals were able to help Wilma to move in ways she hadn't been able to manage since the fire, such as straightening her elbow and her arms so she could touch and pat the dogs. Finally, she had found the motivation to get past her physical suffering.

At one point, she wanted to throw the ball for a dog to fetch. This was difficult, but Bernard and Wilma worked together to find a solution. That kind of problem-solving helped teach Wilma to be independent, and when she returned home, she was able to live independently with a prosthesis on each leg.

All of Therapet's animals are owned by volunteers and undergo a basic obedience class, a temperament test, and a three-hour on-site hospital training session. The animals must retrain each year to maintain their certification, and every two years they must be retested.

"When we started," Bernard says, "the medical community was deeply suspicious. They had a lot of concerns that many people still have, such as infection control, the animals' cleanliness, the possibility the animals might hurt the patients, or vice versa. But over the last decade so much has been written about AAT, and so much success has been documented, that today many hospitals boast about their AAT programs in their advertisements."

A Touch of Youth: The Elderly

Minna is a close friend of a close friend. Formerly a therapist in Boston, she and her husband Fred, a professor of mathematics, were renowned for their wonderful dinner parties, their warm relationships with their friends, and their love for each other. They never had children, but throughout their half-century marriage they looked upon their social network as family.

When Fred turned seventy, he retired from teaching, while Minna maintained her practice, taking off the month of August to join her husband at their island home off the coast of Maine. They looked forward to a long, happy retirement. But one night, while Minna was driving Fred to a lecture in Boston, his heart gave out. She rushed him to an emergency room, but it was too late, and he died shortly thereafter.

Minna was devastated. She decided to sell the house in Maine as well as her apartment in Boston and moved into a condo. Within just a few months her mind, which had always been so sharp, began to drift, and her once-excellent health faltered. She would feel her heart flutter, become extremely excitable, and call her doctor, who would then tell her to come in for an examination. After sending her to a colleague for a consultation, it was eventually decided Minna had developed a heart murmur, a diagnosis which frightened her considerably.

She also began to lose track of her life. She would make a lunch date with a friend and then fail to appear because she had lost her purse or the address of the restaurant, or because she simply forgot. Considering this was a woman whose mind was always compared to the proverbial steel trap, her friends began to wonder if she had developed Alzheimer's.

Teddy changed everything. One of Minna's patients had a part collie, part cocker spaniel who gave birth to four tiny beige puppies, and she gave one to Minna. At first Minna resisted. She'd never owned a dog and she was worried that she wouldn't be able to take care of him, that she didn't have the strength to walk him, that she'd forget to give him food.

But Teddy not only charmed Minna with his winning ways, he had a profound effect on her health. Although her doctor refused to make the obvious connection, he admits that from the time Teddy showed up Minna's mind sharpened, her memory returned to an almost normal state and, most important, her heart murmur improved. Her doctor calls all this coincidence, but Minna refers to it as "The Miracle of the Mutt."

•

It is no surprise to me that there is a strong connection between an older person's health and the presence of an animal companion. What could be better for someone who has lost a spouse, who is in poor health, who has little social support, than a warm, loving, cuddly friend?

Yet here, too, convincing research has been gathered only recently. Some of the most impressive findings come from Dr. Judith Siegel, a professor at UCLA's School of Health. Siegel, who has a Ph.D. in social psychology and a master's in epidemiology, with an emphasis on cardiovascular disease, began to study the relationship between animals and health as an outgrowth of a UCLA study on the use of physician services among the elderly. Although animal companions weren't her priority, she asked if she could do an additional smaller study to see if pet ownership might reduce the impact of stressful life events on use of physician services.

For one year, the study tracked approximately 1000 senior citizens who were enrolled in an HMO through Medicare (which meant they felt no financial disincentive in seeking medical help). The researchers talked to the seniors regularly, asking questions about everything from the nature of their visit to the doctor to whether or not there were any animals in their households.

At the end of the one-year period, the researchers found that the people who had animal companions sought out their doctor far less frequently than those who didn't. They also found that stressful events caused the seniors to seek medical help far more often if there was no animal in the household. In other words, having an animal served as a buffer to stressful events.

"I was rather surprised at the magnitude of the effect," Siegel says, "because in social science research, you seldom get a clear pattern of results."

(According to Siegel, dogs had the best stress-reducing effect. She guesses that dog owners tended to be more attached to dogs and that the stronger the bond, the greater the impact. However, Siegel told me that her best friend, a cat lover, sent her a note "signed" by her five cats informing Siegel that she had "missed the boat.")

Other studies on the relationship between older people and animal companions have produced similar results, from studies in Germany that show the beneficial effect of owning budgerigars, to studies in Milwaukee on the advantages of companion animals for Alzheimer's patients and, from Colorado, the positive influence of animals on social interactions among nursing home residents. Loneliness, often a severe cause of depression among the elderly, has been shown to decrease in the presence of an animal companion; feelings of nurturance and optimism are increased. (One interesting note: 75 percent of the men and 67 percent of the women in this last study reported that their dogs were their only friends.)

Finally, in another study conducted by Dr. Karen Allen of 100 women with few human contacts and friends, animal companions played a vital role in moderating age-related increases in blood pressure.

A Touch of Love: Children

One of the deans in the field of study on animal companions and human health is psychiatrist Aaron Katcher, professor emeritus at the University of Pennsylvania. His interest in animals began when he read Erica Friedman's study showing that the patients recovering from myocardial infarction (damage to the heart muscle) had a better chance of survival if they had an animal companion.

With a grant from the National Institutes of Health, he and his team looked into the relevance of veterinary medicine to human health and initiated a series of investigations to monitor the interactions that occur when essentially normal people interact with animals.

Much of Katcher's research has involved the child-animal bond, including a study examining the effect of animals on children with severe ADHD, or attention deficit with hyperactivity disorder, who exhibited violent and aggressive behavior.

Says Katcher: "We set up a controlled experiment where we examined the effect of letting these children learn for two to five hours a week at what we called a companionable zoo, a place stocked with a whole variety of small animals. Their lessons at the zoo were structured around the care of the animals and nature studies. Using the best measurement of symptoms, and observing their attendance and number of aggressive episodes, we found a significant decrease in the children's aggression and symptomatology. This persisted for as long as the kids were in contact with their animals."

In fact, in the nine years the zoo has been in existence, Katcher says there has never been a single aggressive episode, remarkable among children who routinely had to be restrained due to their inability to control their impulses.

Katcher feels that his study shows that school can provide a poor environment for kids with ADHD. "It forces them to sit still and pay attention to highly abstract materials, so it makes them even worse. But if you put the children with animals, they become less aggressive, they learn better, and they lose their symptoms."

Through the Devereux Foundation, which helps children and adults with behavioral, psychological, intellectual, or neurological impairments, Katcher has become involved in special-education classes in Philadelphia, where the boys and girls raise animals, as well as in intergenerational programs involving children, seniors, and animals.

"Here we only have anecdotal observations," Katcher says, "but kids who weren't previously participating in regular special-ed class were active, happy, and verbal, whenever their interaction was centered around animals."

The lessons are directly drawn from the animals themselves. For instance, Katcher recommends chinchillas, who can be gentle and appealing ("They look like a mouse as designed by Disney"). The children learn what order of animal a chinchilla is (a rodent) and its defining characteristics (such as the continual growth of teeth). They also learn why the animals have such heavy fur (because they come from the high Andean plain where it gets bitterly cold) and why they take dust baths instead of water ones (once the kids see wet fur, they understand why the animals dislike water).

"Because of the animals, the kids are a lot more interested in what they are doing, more willing to learn and participate, and much more verbal," says Katcher.

Other studies offer similar results: At Purdue University, a project designed to investigate the role of companion animals in early development showed that animals may improve the quality of a child's life by helping create a sense of trust, one of the building blocks of character formation. Companion animals also may facilitate play, exploration, and identity formation, cornerstones of healthy development.

Still another study, published in the Delta Society newsletter, relates how a crack-addicted woman's baby, who wouldn't talk or walk and showed little interest in the world, underwent a complete transformation during a therapy session on the beach, where he was exposed to seagulls for the first time. He was enchanted by them. With family approval, the boy was then given a cockatiel; he looked at it and said his first word: "Bird." Eventually he received a dog, who worked with him for many months as the boy finally began to walk. The final result: The boy successfully enrolled in a regular preschool program.

A Touch of Hope:
Working with AIDS

J first met Michael Safdiah in 1985 at the Animal Medical Center when he brought his giant schnauzer, who was suffering from hip dysplasia. The dog was weak in the hind end and stiff all over, and medications had failed to help. Michael's regular veterinarian thought it might be time to put him to sleep.

Michael came to me hoping for a miracle. And through acupuncture and herbal and nutritional supplements, we were able to help his dog live a much happier and longer life.

A very stylish New Yorker, Michael owned a restaurant in Greenwich Village. He was so delighted with the effects of the acupuncture that he invited me and my wife to have dinner with him a number of times, and so we stayed in touch. Here is how Michael tells the next part of his story:

> *My first giant schnauzer passed away at the age of seventeen. We both knew it was time, and she died in my arms at home, for which I am very grateful.*
>
> *I then wrote to the breeder, who was surprised, because giant schnauzers don't usually live that long. Soon afterward she told me she had another dog whose father was a champion at Westminster. So I went to meet her, and she was everything she should have been. Lulu was standing on a hill while the other dogs were clamoring around below, and she'd run down the hill, literally running circles around the other dogs, then come back up to the top of the hill. We fell in love on the spot.*
>
> *In 1990 I tested positive for AIDS. My doctor had warned me to expect it and so I was pretty well prepared. But I wasn't optimistic about my chances. In other words, I didn't go out and buy a lot of green bananas.*
>
> *In the summer of 1994, I began to get stupid, dopey, tired, followed by heavy dementia—HIV encephelopathy. My memory from that time is so poor that I can't remember much. People tell me I just hung out on my living room couch doing nothing and feeling terrible. When I stopped being able to walk at*

all, a friend carried me to the doctor's office, and from there I was sent to a hospital. I was so weak I couldn't walk and my brother later told me my doctor thought I was a goner.

But then there was Lulu. Giant schnauzers aren't like other dogs—they kind of take you over. Lulu would put her head on my body, stay at my feet, always managing to let some part of her body touch me, so I could always feel her presence. She'd never been that physically close to me before. But now she knew I was ill.

She turned into a great licker, too. My first giant schnauzer didn't do that; she gave me maybe four kisses in her whole life. All in all, Lulu just radiated some incredible form of healing energy. She was also my guardian—she made sure that people she didn't like couldn't get close to me. A lot of the people from the home care agency were wonderful, but some weren't. They'd pick up valuables or act strange, and since I had no strength, I was very vulnerable. But if these people came anywhere near me, Lulu would growl under her breath.

I wouldn't have pulled through if it weren't for Lulu. There's a feeling of confidence you get from knowing someone is saying, "I am there for you." I swear that is the difference between people who I have watched die and those who have lived.

As I began to walk again, Lulu walked alongside me like a companion. Everyone else was so somber, but Lulu was funny, she'd try to get me to play with her. She didn't judge, ridicule, or criticize.

Wherever I went, there she was. If I got up in the middle of the night, somehow she'd wake up and be next to me. It's as though there was a piece of software that ran inside her brain saying, "Where's Michael?" And it never stopped working. To this day I will swear on a stack of Bibles that the reason I lived was a combination of luck, God, and Lulu.

Although there is considerably more research in cardiovascular health than in AIDS, several researchers have noted the possibility that animal companions might be able to ameliorate the depression among people who have AIDS or are HIV positive.

In a study conducted in 1991, UCLA's Judith Siegel discovered that the chances of an AIDS sufferer becoming depressed are greatly magnified if that individual does not own a pet. "Pet ownership seems to buffer the impact of AIDS on depressive symptoms," she says.

In another study, animal companions were found to provide a high level of support, nurturance, and acceptance otherwise lacking in the lives of most AIDS patients. The patients felt that their animal companion helped them feel better about their disease and themselves and was often considered to be the "one who really listens."

Healing the Mind: Psychological Disorders

*A*bby, who lives in her native Illinois, is a thirty-five-year-old paralegal. A friend of one of my fellow veterinarian's clients, she has had a tough life. Abby's childhood was intensely unhappy—she was physically and sexually abused—and she found it almost impossible to attend school. Although smart, she would often fall into a haze while the teachers were talking; unable to understand her lessons, she avoided classes whenever she could, and she was eventually expelled.

As her parents were divorcing, Abby was packed off to live with relatives; they in turn sent her to see a psychologist, who decided Abby suffered from bipolar depression. By the time she was eighteen, Abby had been checked into a hospital and was being prescribed a large quantity of drugs. For the next eight years, she bounced in and out of hospital care.

When she wasn't institutionalized, Abby would try to find work, but she wasn't capable of concentrating on any task, and she would end up in the hospital again, which she hated. She soon decided she wasn't right for either world. Abby went through a period where she simply couldn't talk to anyone, so enormous was her anger and depression. Luckily, another psychologist rediagnosed her as suffering from a dissociative disorder, and her prognosis improved.

But according to Abby, what really changed her life was Tigger. "One day," she says, "a staff member at the halfway home where I was staying came in with a really sweet kitten. He was tannish with little bits of white and a striped tail. I named him Tigger, from *Winnie the Pooh*, because he looked like a little tiger."

Tigger fell in love with Abby on sight, and she returned the love. Before Tigger, Abby had no friends, but now she felt that she had a soul mate. Whenever she had a really bad time, somehow Tigger seemed to know, and he'd come find her, no matter where she was hiding, and comfort her. The cat's love always made Abby snap back to life. The two soon became inseparable. "Someone had come into my world who loved me," she says, "at a time when I thought no one could love me. I wasn't a monster after all. That was my fear—that I had become too estranged from people and the world."

Abby feels Tigger taught her how to be responsible, for him and for herself. When she arrived at the halfway home, she had known nothing but hospitals and misery and pain. Tigger taught her to laugh—and to love.

Tigger even gave her the confidence to leave the halfway house— and more than that, Abby says, "he helped me end that terrible cycle of going from hospital to hospital. He helped me find myself."

•

The father of psychiatry, Sigmund Freud, used to see his patients with his favorite chows in attendance, although it's highly doubtful he employed the dogs in his actual therapy. But I know several therapists who believe that the presence of an animal during a therapy session can aid a patient in various ways.

One psychologist client, Kay, brings Gracie, her small fluffy white ball of Bijon Frise, to her office. Kay says her clients feel more at ease in Gracie's company. Their eyes soften and their moods change just by seeing Gracie wagging her tail. Although they may have started their sessions feeling disquieted or depressed, Gracie's joyous presence makes them more willing to open up, which makes Kay's job easier.

While most medical professionals are still hesitant to go on record endorsing the physical benefits of animal companions, many are willing to give credence to the psychological ones. The measure of how much psychological benefit animal companions can provide, however, is in debate. Still, study after study corroborates the relationship between animal companions and human emotional makeup.

For instance, recent research at Australia's University of New England examined people who lived with cats and those who did not, aiming to explore the relationship between psychological well-being and animal companionship. The study delved into general psychological health patterns, along with such focuses as depression, sleep disturbances, and anxiety. The results: People with feline companions demonstrated lower levels of psychiatric imbalance and fewer psychiatric disturbances than those without cats, although there were no significant differences found in regard to depression, sleep disturbances, and anxiety.

Outside of recovery, mental health has become AAT's most common application. According to the Delta Society, AAT is currently being used in psychological treatments in various modalities: to increase verbal interactions, to increase attention skills, to develop leisure skills, to increase self-esteem, to reduce anxiety, and to reduce loneliness.

I first met Maureen Fredrickson at the Animal Medical Center, where she was a social work intern providing grief counseling as well as helping to develop new AAT programs. I later learned that, as a child, Maureen had suffered from a debilitating heart condition that prevented her from attending school. Because it gave her an odd cyanotic—or blue—complexion, it also alienated her from other children.

Maureen's father, who came from a farming background, believed that all children should grow up around animals. With no friends to play with, Maureen bonded with her horses instead, so much so that whenever she went into the hospital for surgery, she would take her pony's halter with her. If things went wrong, she figured, she could always dream that she was riding away on her pony.

Maureen's relationship to animals goes deeper than most—an animal gave its life to keep her alive. During one of her many operations, a pulmonary artery valve from a pig, whose tissue is nearly identical to that of humans, was used to replace her own faulty valve.

After obtaining a bachelor's degree in animal behavior from Cornell University and a master's in social work from Columbia, Maureen spent many years as vice president of external relationships at the Delta Society. She also runs her own company, Animal Systems, which provides workshops in advanced techniques of animal-assisted therapy.

•

We try to get people to understand that their relationships with animals mirror their relationships with other people. For instance, when we're working with adolescent boys who have issues with anger, we'll pair them with a young horse or a dog who is also emotionally out of control. As the boys work with the animal, teaching the animal to keep itself under control, they begin recognize similarities to their own behavior. If it goes well, the boys grasp that being able to control their own emotions is a more adaptive strategy to life than being constantly stirred up.

If you try to teach these lessons in, say, a school setting, the payback is often too slow. It's hard to learn through words alone. We want to provide quick rewards—you have to if you're trying to motivate learning. It's like slot machines—people play longer if they have quick wins.

Our animals vary, but these days we have two donkeys, a horse, a turkey, a duck, a chicken, dogs, and cats. The turkey is amazing. He's not that colorless Thanksgiving turkey people have totally bred the brains out of. He's smart. He's quick. He knows which cars are ours, he knows which dogs are ours, he knows who works on the farm and who doesn't. He also has specific territorial issues. I've seen him take out a 240-pound man. Yet if you present yourself as a powerful physical presence, he will come up to the line, but he won't cross it.

We often have him work with abused women who have developed a victim framework and who continue to get assaulted. We use the turkey to teach them how to change. You can't fake it with that guy. Either you learn to stand powerfully in front of him, or he'll just chase you right out of the barnyard.

For example, one woman couldn't understand why she had terrible relationships with men. So I sent her out to get to know the turkey. A moment later, I saw she was crouching down on the ground, staring beatifically at him.

I thought, Oh my God, she thinks she's sending him love signals. In fact, she had inadvertently taken on the stance of a challenge: close to the ground, staring right into his eyes. The bird started heading for her with blood in his eyes, and I realized she couldn't see what was happening.

I ordered her to get up. That's the one rule on our farm: Do what I tell you— immediately.

She stood, which startled the turkey into taking a step backward. Then he went for her again. At that point my husband ran over and got her out of the pen.

Her first words were "I do that with men, too, don't I? I'm not aware enough of the signals I give off. I thought the turkey knew I was trying to be friendly. But he thought I was trying to challenge him."

In those few minutes, she learned one of the most powerful lessons of her life.

•

It is only common sense to realize that almost anything that humans can use in a positive manner can also be used negatively. Living with an animal companion is not a guarantee of mental or physical health, either for human or animal. It's the quality of the interaction that counts.

For instance, several years ago a former colleague, a gastroenterologist from the Animal Medical Center, called me and announced, "Have I got a case for you." He then told me about Martha, a single, middle-aged woman whose eight-year-old male dachshund, Harvey, was experiencing periodic bouts of vomiting and diarrhea as well as pain in his lower back region.

Martha's regular veterinarians could not discover the cause of Harvey's troubles, and they referred him to the Animal Medical Center for a second opinion. Two residents, an internist and a specialist in gastrointestinal diseases, reviewed Harvey's long history, repeated blood tests, ordered extensive ultrasounds and barium series, but found nothing.

Harvey just kept wagging his tail and was happy to be around friends. Frustrated, Martha went to the University of Pennsylvania Veterinary School for another opinion. More tests were performed, but once again Harvey seemed healthy.

Martha insisted on exploratory surgery and was delighted when one of their top surgeons reluctantly agreed. But again, nothing was found.

Determined to get medical help for her dog, Martha searched around until she found my colleague. He examined Harvey but also found nothing. When he told this to Martha, she mentioned that she'd read that acupuncture might help her dog's back problems, as well as his vomiting and diarrhea. My colleague agreed to talk to me.

A few days later, Martha brought in Harvey, who pranced into my office, wagging his tail up in the air over his trim twelve-pound body. After conducting a comprehensive physical examination, all I could come up with was the possibility that Harvey's back pain was due to the upset in his gastrointestinal tract, which in turn might be the result of exposure to certain household toxins or allergens (this would explain why the painful episodes only occurred at home).

I decided to try acupuncture. But as Harvey lay quietly, enjoying his treatment, receiving a release of endorphins, Martha was a bundle of nerves, continuously asking if Harvey could have cancer and trying to draw me into a worst-case scenario about his future.

As the weeks went by, Harvey seemed to thrive. When I made this observation to Martha, she immediately retorted that at home he wasn't doing well at all, and she wanted more tests undertaken.

That night I was reading a medical journal when I came across an article on Munchausen syndrome by proxy, a mental disorder whereby mothers report a fictitious disease, injury, or condition in their child in order to get attention for themselves. This psychiatric disorder, which necessitated taking the child from doctor to doctor, has potentially serious consequences for the child, depending on what extremes the mothers will go to make the doctors believe them.

Ah! I thought. Martha had Munchausen syndrome by proxy or "dachsy," if you will. (Harvey was a dachshund, after all.)

When I next saw Martha, I gently made her aware of my suspicions. Momentarily dumbfounded, she still insisted Harvey was at death's door. Poor Harvey.

A few years later, my colleague told me that Martha had continued consulting one veterinarian after another. Harvey did eventually develop an acute cancerous tumor and died suddenly at a ripe old age. Martha called to admonish my colleague. "I told you Harvey had cancer!" she said triumphantly. "I was right all along!"

In James Serpell's fascinating book *In the Company of Animals*, he recounts several stories of humans whose attachment to animals was, at best, excessive. For instance, he tells the story of the French student who loved her pet rat too much: "She risked severe penalties by smuggling the animal into Britain concealed in her pullover...the trip proved disastrous. The unfortunate rat was mistaken for vermin and was stamped to death by the patrons of a London pub. The girl was so distressed by the murder of her friend that she took a drug overdose and, when she eventually recovered from this, she was promptly fined 400 pounds for violating quarantine restrictions."

Serpell also recalls the story of the Texas hairdresser whose rottweiler killed and ate her four-week-old-daughter. The woman wept uncontrollably when told the dog would have to be destroyed. "I can always have another baby," she said, "but I can't replace my dog."

There's some science to suggest a challenging side of animal-human relationships. One recent study found that people between the ages of twenty-one and thirty-four who were strongly attached to their animals tended to have poor social support systems. This same study also revealed that strong attachments to animals in people between the ages of thirty-five and forty-four were associated with emotional distress when these people had no humans in their lives to provide support.

Other studies have shown that in children, unusually intense relationships with animals can make it difficult to develop friendships with peers. Children can also experience extremely severe emotional reactions when an animal companion dies or is taken away.

And of course, not every animal is going to make a great friend. We've all heard stories of loving families who've adopted a dog, a cat, or a horse, only to find that the animal resisted their loving overtures.

An animal's genetic predisposition can overwhelm any positive environmental stimulus. For instance, border collies, who have been bred to herd sheep, adapt to whatever environment they inhabit. That means, in a human family, they may well herd children into a group by nipping at their heels. If one child wanders off, the collie can become upset and continuously bark and nip until the child returns to the fold. The dog is only doing his job, and although the scene may seem funny, it can be potentially distressing to collie and child.

I don't want to pick on pit bulls, but many of these dogs were bred by their owners to be ferocious, and I have run into many who were so aggressively nasty that no amount of love could ever change them.

On the other hand, some pit bulls can be absolutely wonderful, and many experts consider them among the most loyal of all breeds. If given the proper affection and care early in life, they can turn into companions worthy of the very deepest, the very strongest love. Consider animal control officer Diane Jessup, in Olympia, Washington, who has spent much of her life helping the breed. Back in the 1980s, when so many pit bulls were destined for short, brutal lives, Diane found a litter of pups born in a house used for drug dealing and other illicit activities. The pup's mother, father, and uncle had been taught to be fighters, and his brothers and sisters were being trained to do the same.

But Diane snatched away her favorite pup, whom she named Dread, which was a common name for the breed earlier in the century. Diane went on to show the dog, who won many ribbons for his behavior. More than that, Dread became a favorite at nursing homes and eventually crisscrossed North America, working with thousands of police officers and animal control professionals, assisting in workshops on handling canine aggression.

In addition, Dread helped save Diane's life when she was diagnosed with cancer. "He was my only motivation to get well," she says.

"Frankly, my life revolved around him, and when I was sick, I felt so bad—not for me, but for him. So I had to get better—for his sake."

•

We live in an era in which animals have become almost as much a part of the human household as humans—it is more common for a home to support two species than not. And the evidence that animal companions can affect and support human feelings is enormous. Yet despite the research mentioned in this chapter, large-scale, well-funded studies of the impact of animals on humans are still lacking.

According to the Delta Society, few grants to investigate human-animal interactions amount to more than $10,000. And even well-respected researchers in the field readily admit that the scientific quality of many of the investigations does not hold up to the highest standards of theory, methodology, and empirical work.

Better and more research is needed to convince skeptics that animals are a gift to the human race—a gift that humans rarely take full advantage of. Only now are we even beginning to understand what a marvelous blessing animals truly are.

PART II

Kindred Minds

What Humans Can

Do for Animals

One

The Love

You Give

Mankind's true moral test, its fundamental
test (which lies deeply buried from view),
consists of its attitude towards those
who are at its mercy: animals.

—Milan Kundera

It was one of those bitterly icy mornings that give New England Februarys their character. Diane and Dan Green looked nearly frozen as they led Princess, a fourteen-year-old, forty-pound pure-bred mutt, into my examining room.

Princess (part black Labrador retriever and part terrier) was stiff—the cause, the Greens guessed, was an arthritic condition that often acted up in this frigid weather. Princess was also behaving lethargically and appeared to have gained some weight.

I had first met the dog five years earlier. At the time, after undergoing an ovario-hysterectomy, she could not control her bladder and was leaking urine throughout the Greens' apartment, despite all the conventional medications her veterinarian had prescribed. The couple loved Princess deeply, but the smell had become overwhelming.

After four acupuncture treatments, Princess was able to control herself again, the odoriferous trails were no longer evident, and the five years had happily passed without any complications.

Acupuncture had worked so well with the bladder problems that the Greens now hoped it could help relieve her stiffness.

To begin, the couple filled me in on the details of their lives. They still lived in New York City, but their weekends were spent at their farm in rural Connecticut. The Greens' children had moved out of the house, and Princess was very much their empty-nest surrogate child.

We commiserated about how sad it was to watch a dog grow feeble so quickly and how Princess had given them so much love over the years. Trying to be reassuring, I told the Greens that winter's cold and damp made it the hardest time of year for both people and animals who suffered from arthritis.

As I started the exam, I noted that Princess had indeed aged. Her shiny black coat was shaded with tinges of gray, and although her heart and lungs sounded normal, her gums weren't as pink as they should have been. Princess also had some evidence of arthritis, with mild crackling in her hips and knees. When I carefully moved my hands over her body, reaching behind her ribs to palpate her abdomen, I felt a large mass almost filling her belly.

I described my findings to the concerned couple with as much gentleness as I could muster. "She does have some arthritis in her hind legs," I said, "but there's no evidence of any nerve damage, and her heart and lungs sound great. Her coat is a bit dull, but we can help all of that with natural nontoxic approaches."

I then told them about the mass in her belly. "This is probably what's causing most of her discomfort," I said, and could feel the sudden presence of anxiety and sorrow in the room. "It may be a tumor in the spleen, and I'm sorry to say, the prognosis isn't promising."

I recommended that we do an ultrasound of the abdomen to find out if the tumor had spread and then make a decision on how to proceed. Following what seemed like an endless pause, the Greens questioned me about their options. Neither of them wanted to put Princess through chemotherapy or radiation therapy, since both had relatives who had endured those procedures and their side effects, only to have them fail, making their relatives' last moments on earth unrelievedly painful. Diane and Dan were happy that their friend had lived so long and did not want to put her through anything overly invasive or harmful, and if they could find something that could make her feel better without doing any harm, they decided it was worth a try.

So we discussed other possibilities—from surgery to natural approaches to euthanasia—and I suggested a consultation with an oncologist.

A week later, the Greens returned, walking into the office despondently with Princess slowly lagging behind, her once-bouncy gait now no more than a weak, stiff hobble. Between their tears, the Greens explained that the oncologist had given them the worst prognosis possible: The tumor, a hemangiosarcoma of the spleen, had metastasized to the liver and was already about five inches in diameter, filling her whole belly. Furthermore, there were large lumps on the liver, almost a half inch in diameter. At best, Princess could survive another three weeks.

The oncologist felt there was no point in surgery or radiation, and she recommended that the Greens simply try to make Princess comfortable until it was time to put her to sleep. The couple appreciated the doctor's honesty and just wanted to see if I thought natural approaches would be useful. Since Princess's appetite was still good, I suggested putting her on some vitamin, mineral, and herbal supplements to improve her general functioning and perhaps even to slow down the growth of the tumor. Because, according to traditional Chinese medicine, tumors are often thought of as toxins in the blood, I chose herbs that are considered blood detoxifiers, while I prescribed the vitamins and minerals primarily as antioxidants.

Diane and Dan looked into Princess's sad, dusky eyes and she looked lovingly back at them; then they cried, telling her that they would do everything they could so she might enjoy the time she had left. It seemed a small gift in return for all the love Princess had given them over the years.

I suggested they take Princess home and give her plenty of positive energy and enjoy the moments together.

Before departing, the Greens asked how Princess would go. I told them that either her death would happen quickly—if the tumor ruptured and bled—or it would be a slow bleed, leaking into her abdomen, making her weaker and weaker. They appreciated the information and left arm in arm, hoping against hope that Princess would remain alive until spring and enjoy one last season at the Greens' country cabin.

Four weeks passed before I heard from them again. I assumed the worst, but Dan's voice sounded energized. Princess was actually improving; she was happy and playful—her old lively and loving self. The Greens were only calling to report the good news—and to order more of the supplements.

Another month passed before the Greens called. Once more, I was greeted with the news that Princess was playing outside at their country home and enjoying spring's sounds and smells.

The next message came as the smoldering heat and humidity of August crept into New England: Princess was still frolicking like a puppy, but she'd developed a skin infection on her back and the Greens wanted to bring her in. I was startled to see the dog bounce into the same exam room that she had dragged herself out of seven months before with a prognosis of no more than three weeks.

Diane and Dan were ecstatic. They realized there was no way to know how much longer Princess would live, but they chose to shower her with love each and every day. Dan had always said that Princess was happiest when playing outside, so they restructured their work lives to spend as much time as possible in the country.

I hugged Princess all over as I examined her, and she responded by wagging her tail. Her gums were not nearly so tacky as before, but when I touched her abdomen, I found the tumor hadn't shrunk. Surprisingly, it hadn't grown, nor was there any evidence of tumors elsewhere.

In addition, Princess's coat had improved and the forlorn expression in her eyes had been replaced with a look of energy. New life had filled this furry black body, and she seemed proud to share it with everyone.

Diane and Dan were delighted with Princess's new vigor, but acknowledged that it would be hard to expect much more. They knew they had to continue to enjoy each moment and not agonize over the future.

As I continued the exam, the couple talked about how much they were learning from this remarkable experience. After the initial shock of the diagnosis and prognosis, as well as the grieving process that followed, the Greens had decided to be as upbeat as possible. They related how challenging it had been in the beginning not to break down and cry in front of Princess, which they knew wouldn't be good for any of them. They didn't want to deny their true feelings, but they wanted to be as positive as reality allowed.

Upon completing my exam and blood tests, I clipped and cleaned up the local skin infection at the base of Princess's tail, treated it with some antiseptic and natural solutions, and sent the dog home again.

A few days later, when Princess's blood tests came back, the news was good: Some of the numbers that had once been outside a healthy range had returned to normal, confirming that Princess's condition now resembled that of a much younger, healthier dog.

Over the next few months, the Greens checked in with me regularly, and Princess continued to thrive through the glorious New England fall and into the cold, damp months of winter. The tumor continued to be present, neither growing nor shrinking. The threesome celebrated their holidays by rejoicing in their gift of time.

In a conversation that I found particularly moving, the Greens told me that their experience with Princess had helped them develop a more loving, nurturing relationship with each other, as well as with their children. They had grown to realize that as they had aged, they had shut down emotionally and turned inward. They had each stopped showing each other—and their loved ones—how much they cared and how grateful they were for one another's existence. Now, having been able to experience this kind of expressive love for their dog, they were becoming more emotionally available to each other as well as to all their family and friends.

Then came a cold, dank February evening—and the phone call I'd been dreading for a year. Through his tears, Dan told me that Princess had become a bit more stiff and quiet over the past few days. On this particular morning it was sleeting; when she walked outside, she had sniffed the freezing air, looked up at the sky, collapsed, and died. She had lived almost exactly one year since receiving her terminal three-weeks-to-live diagnosis—a joyful, inspiring year for her and the Greens.

Still upset by Princess's passing, Dan told me that he and Diane were happy that Princess had never suffered and that they had learned to enjoy each month, each day, each moment together. Dan now realized more than ever how important it was to live in the present. He felt he had finally learned the meaning of unconditional love. Most of all, he had discovered how a special friend had been able to bring together a couple that the years had slowly drawn apart.

Despite the semifrozen ground, Dan and Diane buried their dog at her favorite spot by their mountain cabin. They knew that the wonderful times they had shared together and the lessons they had learned from Princess, especially during that miraculous final year, would live on in their hearts forever.

•

How can Princess's life and death be explained? How did she live for a year, with a massive tumor occupying most of her belly, when she was only supposed to last three weeks?

There are no definitive answers to these questions, but I have learned over the course of my career that the kind of love the Greens showered on Princess can be as powerful as any modern medicine. After the initial shock of the prognosis and the subsequent grieving, the Greens decided to act upbeat rather than despondent, to give their dog plenty of love, to get her out to the country as much as possible, to feed her natural foods—to take care of her just as they would take care of themselves.

Throughout my career, I have heard story after story of a human whose loving and caring nature has turned around an animal's life. In fact, for every story of an animal that has helped a human, I would like to think that there is a comparable story of a human who has helped an animal. Animals can help us tremendously through sickness and loneliness, through physical and mental ailments. Shouldn't we reciprocate whenever we can?

Since the beginnings of civilization, we humans have considered ourselves the caretakers of all animals. But we are not simply farmers who take care of our livestock for our own food production or herders who tend to our horses for our own utilitarian purposes. Our role as caretaker goes much deeper. As we dare to accept that animals are more than the automatons of Descartes, that they are able to think, that they have emotions, we realize that we have another level of commitment and responsibility to them: to respect and care for them as living beings with internal lives, not just as creatures with physical bodies. It is absolutely imperative that we all share this luscious planet Earth with each of its inhabitants—two-legged, four-legged, finned, winged, scaled—in a respectful and thoughtful way.

We have already seen that when animals experience fear, or love, or stress, they release the same emotion molecules as people do. This emission has an impact on their physical, mental, and emotional well-being, as it does on ours.

Still, some skeptics argue that even if animals do have feelings, humans are the dominant species on the planet and animals are our subordinates—and that they should be treated as such.

This strikes me as a remarkably unjust attitude, both from a pragmatic and a spiritual perspective.

For one, animals provide humankind with a remarkable range of benefits. On one end of the spectrum, they are a primary food source for all nonvegetarians; on the other, they provide loving companionship and friendship. Should we not also provide love and respect to them as well? Do we truly want to think of ourselves as a species that only takes, but never gives?

And considering the fact that we all live on this one planet together in a delicate balance, taking care of the animals can be viewed as a means of taking care of ourselves. If we pollute the environment, if we hurt other species, we are the ones who will ultimately suffer. Destroying species that we may not consider directly relevant to our well-being may harm us in ways that we will discover only when it is too late, ways that could have potentially devastating effects on the survival of the planet, our only home.

Just as environmentalists consider the South American rain forest to be the lungs of the Earth, providing all living creatures with the oxygen necessary for respiration, I believe that, as we learn more about our connections to animals, we will consider them our heart. More than anything else on this earth, animals have the facility to make sure we remain connected to our deepest feelings. Can anyone argue that this is not a good thing, that it is not essential for our continued survival as individuals as well as a species?

Look around the world and we can see evidence of the burgeoning care for animals everywhere. Just the growth in the number of dogs and cats in this country is staggering. Recent estimates put the dog population at approximately 53 million and the cat population at around 61 million. (Identifying the number of cats is much harder than dogs, because there are an additional estimated 25–40 million feral cats roaming the country in addition to the domestic population. This means that there are more cats in America than there are people in France and Spain combined.)

Animals are ubiquitous. Every day in the media we see expressions of the importance of preserving parks and wilderness areas for wildlife, as well as oceans for marine mammals. The *Valdez* oil spill produced an outpouring of heartfelt emotions for the injured and dying wildlife; children in schools throughout the country collected funds to save Keiko the whale. An entire cable television channel is dedicated to animals: Animal Planet. Even advertisements for tacos sell their products by using dogs, as do video stores, investment firms, and jewelry outlets. Bulletin boards have sprung up all over the Internet where people can discuss the emotional lives of their animal companions.

But it isn't enough to watch, to be entertained, to be passive. I recommend taking action—any positive action. Once we acknowledge that animals are more than just machines, we have a duty to respect and care for their minds, bodies, and spirits. This means not just providing them with a good physical environment, where their needs for exercise and nutrition are well tended, but a supportive emotional environment to ensure their continuing good health.

Over the last few years, I have watched people all over the country—and the world—create remarkable new techniques to pay back animals for all they have done for us. Diane and Dan Green gave their dying friend unconditional love in her final days. As we shall see, there are many other ways to care for animals—as evidenced by the following stories, such as Andrea Eastman's. Andrea, who works at one of the country's largest talent agencies, lives in Manhattan and Pound Ridge. I first met her when she called me in to examine a horse. Petite in size, she is absolutely colossal in energy and in her love for animals, as she explains in her own words:

> *I had heard that all around the country were farms run by the drug company Wyeth-Ayerst where they impregnate mares, and then keep them stall-bound for eleven months while their urine is collected to make Premarin, an estrogen replacement therapy for menopausal women. Mare-produced estrogen was one of the first ever produced for women, but today there are others on the market, including several natural ones manufactured from soy products.*
>
> *Because all the drug manufacturers want from the horses is their urine,*

they simply get rid of the foals. About a month after they're born, the baby horses—about 70,000 a year—are trucked up to Canada, where they're slaughtered.

About five years ago, I found out that there was a way to help. Both PETA and ASPCA send representatives to markets where the foals are sold to slaughterhouses and buy the foals for anyone who can guarantee to give them a home. This last year I saved six, keeping one for myself.

The October evening my foals arrived was one of those classic dark and stormy nights. The poor little babies had already been trucked three times in their lives, and by the time they arrived at my place, they were beyond terrified. I have no words to describe the abject fear they must have felt, being ripped away from their mothers, rounded up with hundreds of other newborns, dragged around the country. We had to carry them to get them off the truck, since they were too scared to move on their own.

One of my foals was a tiny little spotted Appaloosa, and I've never seen such terror in any being's eyes. He was standing still in the stall, panic-struck, hyperventilating, gulping air, trembling all over. I wasn't sure what to do, so I just put my arms around him and held him tight. Luckily, he was too scared to resist. I stayed with the little horse over three hours until he became calmer and started breathing almost normally.

I named the creature Lucky Star, because when I finally walked out of the stall at midnight on that horribly stormy night, the clouds had suddenly parted and one bright star was shining in the sky. I thought, That's who he is, a lucky star.

I would go to visit him quite often in his stall, and he would always walk away from me. He was afraid—humans only meant pain and fear. But after a while, he would let me pet him, although he still wouldn't come to me.

When he was turned out in the paddock, we put a halter on him, and, standing quietly, he gradually allowed me to pet and kiss him. Then I started training him. I'd take him on a lead rope and he would walk a little with me. We did this for a few months.

And then one day, about three months ago, it happened. Although he was all the way at the other side of the paddock, when he saw me arrive, he actually ran over to me. This was the most extraordinary feeling, to have this wonderful lovely creature come running up to me with such a sense of purpose. Now he does it all the time. The moment he sees me he comes over, following me everywhere, stopping if I stop, running if I run. We've bonded. His eyes, which used to be so filled with fear, are now filled with love.

The need for love and compassion is not limited solely to animals that have been abandoned or abused. Kelly Bollen is the close friend of a veterinarian I met while teaching acupuncture at Cornell. One night the three of us went out to dinner, and when I started talking about my theories on human-animal connections, Kelly chimed in to tell me about the program in animal enrichment she helped start while she was a keeper at the Syracuse Zoo. I was deeply impressed with what she was trying to do for those zoo animals. Today she's in graduate school, studying primate behavior. Here she tells her story:

> *I liked being a keeper at Syracuse, but I had a terrible time coping with animal captivity—it was just so difficult to see all those wonderful wild animals confined, looking so unhappy. I wanted to make their lives better. After all, they sacrifice themselves for us by entertaining us, educating us. The least we could do is try to pay them back.*
>
> *You develop a strong bond with the animals in your charge because you have to know them well—partly because you like them so much, but also because you have to assess their health. Even more than domestic pets, wild animals hide their illnesses, especially if they're at the bottom of their dominance hierarchy. So a keeper must know that animal inside and out in order to monitor the subtle behavioral changes that could indicate something is wrong.*
>
> *Too many times we aren't aware that an animal is sick until the day he dies, so you have to know these animals personally—you end up feeling like they're your children. Basically, at the zoo, I had twenty-eight kids.*
>
> *Enrichment programs have been around for about a decade or so; they're a means of stimulating the animals' minds, giving them a richer life, relieving their boredom, increasing their activity levels, developing their motor skills, and giving them opportunities to perform species typical behaviors.*
>
> *The main activity for animals in the wild is foraging for food. But in a*

traditional zoo, one meal is plopped on the floor, which the animal then eats in five minutes, leaving him twenty-three hours and fifty-five minutes to do nothing—whereas in the wild, they could spend ten hours foraging.

So I came up with a plan to make the great apes work for their food. Optimally I would split their big meals into three or four little ones and spread them all over their environment, so they had to hunt and work in order to eat. This also expanded their feeding time, which was good.

And we gave them new foods, like fruits and vegetables, and weird things, like sugarcane and kiwis, which they hadn't seen before but which I knew they could and would eat. We'd also give them whole coconuts, and they had to figure out how to open them.

It's been shown in many studies that, given a choice of receiving a pile of food or having to work for a meal, animals prefer the work. They're bored. So we made devices out of Plexiglas or wood and put the food inside—and the animal had to shake, maneuver, or rattle to extract it. Or we'd mix in small food items with hay or put the food in a burlap bag and tie it, and they'd have to figure out how to get it out. Or we'd make nut boards by drilling holes in plywood and pounding nuts with shells in them. It'd take them all day to get those nuts out.

When it snowed, we'd throw food in the drifts, and they'd attempt to forage it out. It was very cold and they'd have to stop and rub their hands, yet they couldn't resist trying again and going back.

The result of these enrichment programs was that our animals seemed happier. Maybe saying an animal is happy isn't scientific, but I was pretty sure that's what they were. I'd walk down the hall and they'd run over to the window wondering, "What the hell is going to happen today?"

All in all we were very grateful the zoo management allowed us to do this, but we're convinced the animals were even more grateful.

Even people who don't have the built-in support that Kelly did can make a remarkable difference with limited resources and a little ingenuity. Patty Wahlers runs an organization called HORSE of Connecticut, the initials standing for Humane Organization Representing Suffering

Equines. It's one of the most outstanding organizations of its kind in the country, and Patty manages to run it on a shoestring budget—until 1990 she had to work full-time at the post office and United Parcel Service to keep HORSE alive.

The first time she called me to look at one of her horses (Country, whom you will soon read about), I was somewhat startled by the conditions: The barn looked as though it were falling down, the paddocks were muddy, and horses were tied up everywhere to every hitching post possible. Then, when I met Patty, I realized how much she was trying to accomplish all on her own, putting in a sixty-hour week with no benefits, no paid vacation, not even a salary—and what an amazing job she was doing to save these poor animals. More than that, she also helps educate the public on the proper care of horses.

Eventually, as word of her work has spread, Patty has been able to attract increased donations and volunteer support. Today the farm is still time-, staff-, and space-challenged, but any horse who is rehabilitated by Patty is a very lucky horse indeed.

I've been taking care of horses since I was seventeen years old. A man I knew called to say he had two horses who needed homes. I wasn't able to take them, but I offered to help. When I saw them, I was startled—they were two skeletons. I went right home and drew up papers saying that I'd bought them for a dollar. The man signed. I walked the animals home. That's how I began.

Basically, I rehabilitate horses who have been abused, hurt, starved. At the moment I have twenty horses, but that number has been as high as thirty-five. We also have some dogs and cats, because people just throw them out of their cars—they assume that since we're a farm, we can use them.

One of my favorite horses is Country, who's twenty-two. He'd been bred and raised to be a show horse and was once so handsome that he was used in an advertisement for fancy cars. But then he injured his foot, so he was given away to another owner, who kept him for a while, then tired of him and gave him away again.

Nine years ago, Country's owner left him out on his own in the back field and then decided to sell him to slaughter. His weight had fallen to 650 pounds, about half of what would be considered normal. The horse was still alive only because of a stream in the backyard.

When a neighbor saw the owner leading Country out to the truck to go to the meathouse, she called me and I flew over. The horse was so physically exhausted he couldn't walk. We got him into the trailer and he sat down, and frankly I didn't think he was going to get back up again, he was so thin and weak and unhappy. When a horse loses half his body weight, he usually doesn't make it. He also had what they call heaves, a breathing problem, since the little hay he'd been fed was really bad. Normally if you give horses moldy or dusty hay, they won't eat it, since they're picky. But if they have no other food, they'll eat it and suffer. The stuff attacks their lungs, like asthma, and they can die from it.

We had to keep Country outside, in an open-sided stall, so he could get as much air as possible, and we had to put him on medications immediately. But first we had to see if he'd live.

All he could do when we got him was lift his front leg, because the owner had taught him to beg—so he would lift one leg when he saw you coming and then the other. It made me want to cry.

Six months later, Country was back to thinking he was hot stuff again. Once a horse knows he's gorgeous, he really shines. Country is very friendly, he likes people, he likes to be spoiled. He seems to have recovered completely, but I know he remembers, because when it comes to food time, you'll see him perk up a little.

His feet are still bad, so he gets special shoes every four weeks, and we keep leg wraps on him when he has a bad day. And he has a girlfriend, Patches, who's thirty-one and my original mare. The two of them do everything together.

HORSE of Connecticut is run only by volunteers. We apply for grants, and we've started to get a little money. But winter is always a tough time, and the veterinarian and the farrier usually have to wait a month or two for their money. But you know? Somehow we manage to survive. And so do the animals.

Every year I meet more and more people like Andrea, Kelly, and Patty, who are finding new and unusual ways to help animals. But every one of us has to help in his or her own way. Of course it's wonderful if you can save five hundred animals, or design a new animal care program, or run a helping organization. It would be a far different world if each of us made sure that every animal, whether behind zoo bars, in a scientific experiment, or out in the wild, leads a better life.

But it would also be a different world if everyone saw to it that each domestic animal was given the best care possible. And by best care, I don't mean spending thousands of dollars a year on fancy clothing or expensive haircuts. I simply mean providing excellent health care—and the first step to that is understanding all the options.

Two

In Search of the

Magic Bullet

Hear our humble prayer, O God, for our friends, the animals, especially for animals who are suffering; for any that are hunted or lost, or deserted or frightened or hungry; for all that must be put to death. We entreat for them all thy mercy and pity and for those who deal with them we ask a heart of compassion and gentle hands and kindly words. Make us, ourselves, to be true friends to animals and so to share the blessings of the merciful.

—Albert Schweitzer

here's no question about it: Health care—for humans and for animals—isn't what it used to be. Up until the latter part of the last century, our approach to medicine was a passive one. Whenever we were ill, we consulted doctors, we assumed they were omniscient, and we did whatever they told us to do. And with the discovery of penicillin, we began to believe that modern medicine would cure every disease that plagued our race.

However, as the years passed, we realized that this was a dream rather than a reality. Yes, modern medicine has made tremendous strides in developing such impressive diagnostic devices as MRIs, CAT scans, angiograms, as well as remarkable drugs, including painkillers and antibiotics. But when it comes to chronic conditions such as arthritis, cancer, and other immune mediated diseases, cures are sorely missing.

Meanwhile, over the past decade, a small yet rapidly expanding part of the population has begun questioning the authority of modern Western medicine and empowering themselves to take responsibility for their own health by exploring alternative routes to wellness. This has meant a reawakening interest in the approaches of the indigenous Chinese, Ayurvedic (Indian), Tibetan, Native American, and South American traditions, all of which Western medicine had denigrated as superstitious and ignorant.

Interestingly, much of this interest in non-Western healing sprang from President Nixon's visit to China in the early 1970s. Along with the consequent exchange of culture, art, and philosophy came information about traditional Chinese medicine, including acupuncture and herbs. One of the most notable moments of this interchange occurred when *New York Times* columnist James Reston underwent an appendectomy in a Peking hospital while under acupuncture analgesia.

The Chinese wholeheartedly embraced the advances of Western medicine and rapidly integrated it side by side with acupuncture and herbal medicine. Soon hospitals in China were dedicating one floor to acupuncture, another to herbal medicine, and another to Western medicine.

But because they challenged the belief that Western medicine already knew all the answers, Chinese medicine and acupuncture did not root as quickly in America, even though they seemed able to address, treat, and sometimes cure many conditions—including migraines, arthritis, and numerous gastrointestinal, musculoskeletal, respiratory, and neurologic conditions—better than Western medicine.

In the last thirty years, however, many Westerners have realized that not only can Chinese medicine and the other recently "rediscovered" medical approaches cure existing problems but they may actually prevent many diseases through natural, organic nutrition, and proper exercise. This awareness has transformed much of the public from passive consumers to active participants in their own health. (Unfortunately, this has also resulted in a proliferation of many false promises, placebo supplements, and a new era of what can only be called quackery, making it difficult for those seeking answers to differentiate between the valid and the hyperbole.)

This same pattern of active participation has emerged in veterinary medicine and animal health care as well. Over the past decade—and notably in the last five years—informed, responsible consumers have begun taking responsibility for searching out new options for their animal companions. Beginning with the dog, cat, and horse breeders who, as a tightly knit group, are constantly discussing their animals' health concerns, the search for new options has exploded into a major movement that includes not only breeders but educated individuals who are no longer satisfied with the all-too-frequent answer: "There is nothing more you can do for your pet."

The frustration associated with this answer was the beginning of my own search for the magic bullet. Although I realized that the Western medicine and surgery I learned at Cornell were beneficial for many animals, I knew that they also left much to be desired. My quest for alternative methods and answers began with acupuncture and then led me to Eastern and Western herbal medicine, nutrition, homeopathy, chiropractic, and other healing modalities. I soon realized that there was not a single magic bullet, but many options that, when incorporated together, could help many more animals live longer, happier, painfree lives.

As a result, today I can call myself an "integrative holistic veterinarian" without being considered a charlatan, which might not have been the case two decades ago.

I realize that many people respond to that phrase by saying, "What the heck does that mean?"

The idea behind that fancy-sounding title is much simpler than its thirteen syllables would indicate. It means I take the best of natural, holistic approaches to animal health and combine them with the best of contemporary veterinary medicine. In other words, East meets West for animals.

I firmly believe that no one treatment approach has all the answers. Why should we limit ourselves to one kind of medicine when there are so many good ones to pick from? Why not do everything we can to help our companions, regardless of which school of thought our treatment comes from, or which continent, or whether it is ancient or modern? If an animal becomes ill, we should look at every possible approach to both diagnose and treat the problem. This may include offering conventional medical examinations, using X-rays, and practicing surgery, along with every other weapon in the Western arsenal. In addition, it may also mean investigating such factors as environmental allergens, nutritional deficiencies, adverse reactions to vaccines, and a host of other possible causes.

For instance, if your animal companion develops a bacterial infection, the conventional approach would be to administer an antibiotic. For many years, I saw nothing wrong with that and prescribed thousands of antibiotic pills and injections. But today, looking at the problem from an integrative point of view, I would also look into the remedies available outside the Western scope in order to support the animal's immune system.

Let's discuss some of these treatments on which I have come to rely.

Acupuncture

I can remember the exact moment when integrative medicine became a part of my life—with my unexpected introduction to acupuncture.

The initial impetus was an awkward situation that developed after I graduated from veterinary school in 1978 and started practicing: People were constantly bringing animals in great pain into my office, but all I had to relieve their suffering were antibiotics, traditional anti-inflammatories like cortisone, and various nonsteroidal anti-inflammatory agents such as butezolidine.

Although powerful, these medications, particularly the steroids, had significant potential side effects, such as urinary incontinence, gastrointestinal ulcers, and bleeding. Even when they resolved the presenting problem, the animal usually remained in some form of pain.

The job of a veterinarian is to deal with ailing animals, but I hadn't realized just how much ailing I would have to witness. My empathy for the animals grew to the point where I began to feel their hurt myself. And I also grew increasingly frustrated and despondent at my own limited options and helplessness.

In the autumn of 1982, while working at a practice in New York State's verdant Hudson Valley, an elementary school teacher named Hattie brought Topper into my office. A fourteen-year-old Irish setter, Topper was bright and alert but suffering from painful arthritis in his elbows, hips, and back.

As customary, we started Topper out on some buffered aspirin, which seemed to help, but it also upset his stomach—he began vomiting and his stool turned bloody. We next tried cortisone, which seemed to lessen the pain, but it made him drink more and urinate all over Hattie's house.

We then tried a stronger, nonsteroidal anti-inflammatory drug, but that too caused gastrointestinal bleeding. Basically Topper wasn't able to tolerate any of the standard drugs used to relieve arthritis pain. And surgery wasn't an option, because he was arthritic all over his body, rather than in a localized area.

Meanwhile, the poor dog had reached a point where he couldn't climb stairs, so he would whine and then cry as he struggled to raise himself step by step, only to fall back down. Hattie tried to carry him upstairs, but she was a small woman and Topper weighed sixty pounds. Hattie started sleeping on the living room couch to save Topper the effort.

Within a short time the dog's legs became so weak that while he was eating, they would simply collapse and Topper would have to finish his meals lying on the ground with his nose in the food bowl. And finally, although he tried to wait until Hattie let him out, he lost control of his bowels and defecated on the floor. Knowing this was forbidden activity, he would look up at Hattie, frightened, expecting to be punished.

But Topper was Hattie's closest friend. He had been with her before she met her husband and had outlasted the marriage. Hattie pleaded with me. Wasn't there anything else we could try? Anything at all?

I explained to her as gently as possible that I knew of nothing else. "I wish I could offer you another option," I said helplessly. "But all we have is drugs and surgery. Drugs haven't worked, and Topper is too old for surgery."

Hattie knew that the dog's quality of life was poor. Moreover, she admitted that taking care of him was affecting her sleep and her ability to work. Topper howled in pain throughout the night, but she stayed next to him because she couldn't bear to leave him alone.

Hattie started weeping. "It's not fair," she said. "He's so alert, and his mind is so strong." But she knew that there was no choice, and on her last visit she came prepared to accept Topper's fate.

I gave him an intravenous injection, which was essentially an overdose of anesthesia designed specifically for this purpose. Hattie, tears rolling from her eyes, stood over her friend, petting his head lightly. "I love you," she said. "And I am sorry, but this is the best thing for you. You're not enjoying your life anymore. I don't want to keep you around just for my sake."

Topper looked up at her lovingly and licked her hand. Then he took a deep sigh and drifted away.

"I'm going to miss you so much—you've been through the worst of everything with me," Hattie whispered.

I left the room so they could be alone for their final moments together.

I knew that we had done our best for Topper, but I still felt defeated. That night I went back to my cabin and stared out the window at the Shawangunk Mountains, pleading with God to let me know if there was something more I could do that could help these animals.

A few days later, I received a pamphlet in the mail informing me of a veterinary acupuncture course to be given in New York City in a few weeks.

I hadn't thought much about acupuncture since the death of Dr. Delahanty, the one Cornell professor who had been interested in Eastern medicine. But now, after my experience with Topper, I decided it might be worth investigating. I reminded the veterinarian whom I was working for at the time that I was due for some continuing education, and he gave me the weekend off.

At the time I knew little about acupuncture beyond its Latin roots: *acus*, meaning needle, and *punctura*, meaning to prick. All this meant to me was sticking a bunch of needles into a body. But less than an hour into the first lecture, Dr. Altman, our teacher—and a man of remarkable honesty and sincerity—started discussing the scientific basis of acupuncture, as well as its interaction with the nervous system. Visions of my college and graduate school studies in neuroanatomy and neurophysiology lectures flooded my mind.

And this was the moment when I became hooked: Dr. Altman showed us how, without using a drug or a surgical procedure, acupuncture causes profound physiological changes in the body. It works by stimulating what are called our sensory afferent nerves, the nerves that send impulses up to the spinal cord and then to different parts of the brain. When these nerves are stimulated, they release different biochemicals and neurotransmitters, such as endorphins, throughout the body.

At that time science was just realizing that endorphins are more than just the body's natural painkilling hormones. There are endorphins in the gastrointestinal tract that affect gastrointestinal function, endorphins in the heart that affect heart function, and so on.

Dr. Altman told us that a needle inserted into a muscle spasm would immediately dissipate the spasm. I began thinking how wonderful this could be for relieving the spasms around a cat's fractured pelvis, or a dog's hip dysplasia, or a horse's back problem. When he told us how acupuncture increases the local circulation to a specific part of the body, I began thinking how this could accelerate healing in a lick granuloma—or slow-healing wounds. This was my answer to pain relief, I was sure of it!

As I listened, furiously taking notes, one patient after another came to mind—Gertrude, the sweet-tempered pony with a nonhealing wound on her leg; Moussa, the black Lab who wasn't recovering quickly enough from a slipped disk; Ariadne, the calico cat with irritable bowel syndrome. And since acupuncture seemed to boost the immune system by stimulating the blood cell count: Tiger, the Maine coon with feline leukemia.

Traditional Chinese medicine refers to the life energy force as *chi*. Every medical philosophy has a name for this force—in homeopathy it is called "the vital force," in Indian Ayurvedic medicine, *prana*; in chiropractic, the "innate." The closest term for it in Western medicine is the "bioelectric current."

What is the life energy force? Whenever I teach acupuncture, I ask my students this question: In these days, when we think we know everything, can you tell me the difference between you and a cadaver? Think about it. We both have a brain, a liver, a heart.

The difference, I say, is this *chi*, this bioelectric current, this ineffable force that flows through all of us. Some consider *chi* the equivalent of circulation.

In traditional Chinese medicine (TCM), when the body is in a good state of health, the *chi* flows freely through the meridians (the twelve major energy pathways in the human body) and the body's opposing forces (for example, hot and cold, light and dark) are well balanced in a state of yin and yang.

Disease results from a blockage of that flow. Goes an old Chinese dictum: Where there is no flow, there is pain. Acupuncture brings the body back into balance; by stimulating our nerves and circulation, it gets the *chi* flowing.

Traditional Chinese medicine integrates and unifies symptoms that, according to Western medicine, aren't in any way connected. For instance, an older dog with arthritis will often have mild kidney failure and exhibit signs of deafness. In Western medicine, this is called coincidence. But in TCM, these conditions are related. Bone conditions such as arthritis are associated with the kidneys, and hearing is the sense that is related to kidneys—so if a problem exists in one of these places, it will probably affect all three. TCM would consider this pattern a kidney yin deficiency and treat it with acupuncture and herbal medicine to help not only the arthritis but also kidney function and the hearing.

Later in my practice, while treating a German shepherd with severe allergic dermatitis, I witnessed a perfect example of the way in which the various systems of the body are connected. In TCM, a skin inflammation is considered heat, and as I examined the dog, I could feel extreme heat emanating from his body. After evaluating the dog's diet, I discovered he was eating poor-quality commercial food filled with red meat. According to TCM, red meat creates too much heat; it was literally turning him into a hot dog. So we changed his diet and gave him what the Chinese would call cooling foods. That cleared up the heat and the inflammation in the skin much better than cortisone.

·

Because I wanted to take more training immediately, Dr. Altman referred me to the International Veterinary Acupuncture Society, formed by three veterinarians who had brought acupuncture over from China in 1974. I took the six-month training course in 1981, and as I had become friendly with a Downstate Medical School physician who was conducting research in human acupuncture, he invited me to take a course in scientific human acupuncture there, too.

As soon as possible, I adapted acupuncture to my practice. My first patient was Blackie, an eleven-year-old black Labrador retriever.

Smart and alert, like Topper, Blackie was suffering from crippling arthritis in his elbows, hips, and back. Not atypical for dogs who ran unleashed in the country, he also had some buckshot in his back.

Blackie had been my patient for a number of years. Every summer he was fine, but each winter he became stiffer and stiffer. Buffered aspirin and corticosteroids had helped, but they also had undesirable side effects, causing Blackie to drink and urinate too much and lose muscle mass.

Blackie's companion, Mark, a middle-aged shopkeeper, was torn between his desire to prolong his dog's life and his reluctance to cause him further pain.

"Isn't there something more we can do?" he asked each time he brought Blackie in. "He's trying to be so cheerful, yet every day it gets colder, and I can see the pain taking over his body." The dog was having an increasingly difficult time getting up, and due to the increased need to urinate, he had to be let out each night after midnight. He would end up falling down on the snow and lying still, howling and shivering, waiting for Mark to carry him back inside.

Implicit in Mark's lament was the question I had heard all too often: "I don't want to put him to sleep, but what else can I do?"

Before taking the acupuncture course, the only option I knew was euthanasia. Now we had something else to try.

"Let's wait until next week," I said to Mark just before I took my seminar. "We'll give him one more shot of cortisone and some vitamin supplements to help him get through this weekend."

On Monday morning I brought twenty acupuncture needles to my office, as well as several acupuncture maps and my anatomy book from veterinary school. I was practically shivering with excitement when Mark carried Blackie in from the car and placed him on the table.

Blackie lay still in the "I surrender" position that dogs adopt when they've given up.

Shortly after Mark left the room, I gazed blankly at my acupuncture maps and realized the challenge I had undertaken. During our practice weekend, I had stuck acupuncture needles into a navel orange, not a live dog. The maps, strange hieroglyphs dotted with uncertain points and wobbly arrows, were swimming before my eyes.

I slowly started feeling for the acupuncture points as Dr. Altman had taught me. Hmm, I thought, this seems to be one. Here's another . . . I wonder if this is another one?

I didn't have confidence yet. It took me a full thirty minutes just to identify the points I would work on.

Finally my technician said, "For goodness' sake, just stick a needle in!"

So I did.

Wow, I thought—I did it! I tried another, and another, and then I got carried away and did some for the hips, some for the elbows, some for the back, some for overall well-being, and some for old age. Blackie started to resemble a canine porcupine as he looked up at me with confused eyes.

When I began vibrating the needles, Blackie visibly began to relax. "Amazing!" I told my technician. "He really looks comfortable."

"Are you sure?" she asked.

The answer was obvious a few seconds later when Blackie started snoring lightly.

After twenty minutes, we removed all the needles, and when Mark reappeared to take Blackie home, Blackie had resumed the appearance of a normal dog.

When they came back the next day for another session, Mark told me that Blackie, who usually whined and woke up and circled his bed all night trying to make himself comfortable, slept deeply for the first time in months. And in the morning he was wagging his tail more.

We decided to continue the treatments. After five sessions, Blackie seemed happier, and he was sleeping better, but he was still bothered by the arthritis. I began to wonder if acupuncture was truly my miracle cure. But at our sixth session, Blackie walked into my office wagging his tail, jumping up and down, looking like a normal, happy, and pain-free dog. (To this day, when I teach acupuncture, I tell my students that the first time you succeed, try to hide your amazement—because I know at that moment my jaw dropped open.)

We had a few more sessions that month, then reduced the number to one a week, then once a month, and eventually a few times a year. Blackie continued to do well and started to gain weight. Happy as I was at the outcome, I remembered Topper, the Irish setter. I wish I had known about this a month before, I thought.

Today acupuncture is the mainstay of my practice. I am continually impressed with its efficacy and remind those who think this is something new that the first acupuncture textbook was actually published in 650 B.C., and the practice is thought to have been in existence for two thousand years before that. And although we tend to think of acupuncture as a recent phenomenon in the West, the earliest European work on the subject appeared in 1671.

Initial research in the 1970s demonstrated acupuncture's ability to ameliorate chronic pain and treat a variety of disorders, and further studies in the last two decades have backed these initial experiments. Recently the World Health Organization cited 104 different conditions that acupuncture can treat, from migraines to asthma to sciatica.

And I can promise you it works for many conditions—because I see evidence of it session after session in animal after animal. In fact, in 1986 I conducted my own study of sixty-five arthritic dogs who had been treated unsuccessfully with Western medicine and who had been recommended for euthanasia. I had performed acupuncture on all of them; 84 percent showed a marked improvement in mobility, energy level, and overall health, while over 50 percent improved dramatically. Many studies since then have borne out the efficacy of acupuncture as a treatment method.

In one particularly intriguing study conducted in China and reported in the *Journal of Diagnostic Imaging Asia Pacific*, such modern Western diagnostic methods as MRI (magnetic resonance imaging) were used to monitor changes in the brain as volunteers underwent acupuncture. When a needle was inserted in an acupuncture point, researchers found that blood flow and oxygen metabolism increased in a corresponding area of the brain.

Traditional Chinese Herbs

"ACCHOOOOO!!!"

I'd never heard a cat quite like Spot. Sometimes humans sneeze so loudly you wonder if they're erupting, but for the most part, cats do it with all the fury of a whisper.

Not Spot. This unusually large gray and black male tabby sneezed with such ferocity it sounded as if he were going to exhale his internal organs. Sometimes he achooed three times in a row, each more violently than the last. And when he finished, he always had that same surprised look in his shockingly blue eyes, as though he were saying, "Was that me who made that terrible noise?"

When his companion first brought him to me, Spot was suffering from a high fever, as well as what appeared to be an upper respiratory infection. His nose was running, his eyes were watering, he was barely eating. And so I tried the usual approach of prescribing a course of antibiotics to clear up any lurking bacterial infections.

Over a period of several weeks, we experimented with two or three different medications, but nothing seemed to work. If anything, the cat's sneezing seemed to grow louder as his once hefty weight began to drop as precipitously as his appetite. Seventeen pounds, fifteen pounds, thirteen pounds; the poor thing kept getting thinner and thinner, as though every sneeze knocked off a few ounces.

I tested Spot for numerous other diseases, from feline leukemia to feline AIDS to toxoplasmosis, all of which came back negative. Finally, his companions, a young professional couple, asked if we could try some herbal remedies, since they used herbs to improve their own health.

A few weeks earlier, a friend had told me about an ancient Chinese herbal preparation, Yin Chiao, which is supposedly able to relieve the symptoms of the common cold. Formulated by Chinese herbal specialists in the Ching Dynasty, it is based on ingredients such as lonicera japonica and forsythia.

I had already tried out the formula on myself, as I usually do before I give it to any other living creature, and found myself cured of my cold.

So we decided to try Spot on Yin Chiao. Less than two days later, the cat's temperature had returned to normal, as had his appetite. Within another week, all his symptoms had disappeared, including the extraordinary sneezing. Spot had never looked better.

It's fairly impossible to study traditional Chinese medicine without becoming interested in herbs. One of my first acupuncture teachers, Ihor Basko, would, after delivering his acupuncture lectures during the day, give lectures on Chinese herbs at night. What an amazing experience—to spend a day being taught one way to deal with ailments that I had thought were untreatable and then twelve hours later to learn of still another treatment. Ihor would rattle off one remedy after the next: ginseng and royal bee jelly for cats with feline leukemia, bupleurum for liver disease, rheumania for kidney problems—all of them conditions for which Western medicine didn't have satisfactory treatments.

Like acupuncture, Chinese herbal medicine has been practiced for millennia. Unlike Western herbal medicine (see page 111), it relies on a combination of medicinal plants and other natural products—such as roots, stems, and branches taken from various flowers, herbs, and trees—and is based on what is called the four "properties" and five "tastes." The properties refer to the cold, hot, warm, and cool nature of different drugs. If a disease is considered cold, a warm Chinese herbal medicine, such as ginger, is prescribed. A condition producing a hot response such as a fever would be treated with something cool, such as coptis root.

And each taste—bitter, sweet, salty, sour, and pungent—has a particular medicinal action. For instance, sweet herbs reduce pain; salty herbs nourish the kidney.

Not long after I started using Chinese herbal medicine, I began treating a charming tortoiseshell cat named Daisy, who was debilitated and suffering from a high fever. Hoping it was just a bacterial infection, I prescribed antibiotics, which brought down her fever. But the cat was still quite weak, so we tested her for feline leukemia, and the test returned positive.

Melissa, Daisy's human companion, was devastated; Daisy meant the world to her. A secretary at IBM, Melissa explained that every night when she returned from work, Daisy would be waiting by the door to play with her, and in the morning, she would jump on the windowsill and stare out the window to give her a last loving look as she drove away.

We were able to keep Daisy's fever down as long as she was taking the antibiotics combined with vitamins, but whenever we stopped them, the fever returned, accompanied by sneezing and chronic infections.

"Isn't there something we can do to build my friend up?" Melissa asked.

Then I remembered what Ihor had told us about using ginseng and royal bee jelly to stimulate the appetite and boost the immune system. So I went to the health food store and bought several vials. I told Melissa to feed Daisy six drops, two to three times a day.

Within a few weeks, Daisy's temperature was normal, her appetite had returned, and her energy flooded back. She stayed that way for many years.

A note or two of caution: Just because herbal remedies are natural doesn't mean that they are always safe. Like any medicine, they can be dangerous if used incorrectly. If you are interested in these herbs, it is essential you find a veterinarian who has extensive training in them. And make sure that you only work with herbal products from high-quality manufacturers, always checking the expiration dates to make sure that the preparations are fresh.

Western Herbal Medicine

A forty-year-old woman with a long mane of chestnut hair, Molly is a well-known interior decorator in New York City. A huge two-year-old with a black- and brown-spotted coat, Major is a Great Dane who possessed an uncanny ability to tear Molly's apartment apart.

Whenever he was home with Molly, Major was loving and obedient. But as soon as she left he would run amok, tearing the stylish place apart pillow by needlepoint pillow until all the down feathers were floating around the room, as though someone had detonated a duck. Major, it appeared, suffered from severe separation anxiety.

Molly's veterinarian had recommended that she give Major tranquilizers, which only seemed to make him sluggish rather than tranquil. He still went out of control if Molly was gone for more than a few hours—just more slowly than before. The doctor also prescribed some stronger human antianxiety drugs, but Molly found them to have unpleasant side effects.

Hoping that natural medicine could help Major where Western medicine had failed, Molly brought Major into my office for a consultation.

An examination revealed that the dog was healthy but highly excitable, which was hardly a surprise. Unfortunately, no specific cause for his behavior was evident. Still, New York City can be problematic for domestic animals, as it exposes them to a wide range of stimuli from street traffic and helicopters to unfriendly pedestrians and startling noises. I began to wonder if Major's hectic surroundings were the cause of his problem.

Because friends of mine had recommended it, I had recently tried kava, the root of a tropical shrub purported to have anxiety-relieving effects. I suggested we try it out on Major. Molly agreed, and it quickly did the trick, relieving him of anxiety without sedating him.

I then asked her to keep him on the kava and try to desensitize Major both to noise and to being alone. She did as instructed. Slowly,

Major reached the point where the apartment was in good shape when she returned home, and he was simply wagging his tail rather than panic-stricken.

Over a six-month period, Molly was able to reduce the dosage until she could stop using kava. At that point, Molly said, Major seemed as calm as a Fijian watching a blue lagoon at sunset.

(Unfortunately, as kava has grown more popular over the last decade, its quality has plummeted. The best way to test it is to place a pinch in your mouth and see if it numbs your tongue. If it does, it's the real thing.)

•

The difference between Chinese herbal and Western herbal medicine arises from the remedies used—and the way they are employed. After all, it's not as though only the Chinese were aware of herbal remedies. The Sumerians were using caraway and thyme 5,000 years ago; the Greeks wrote several medicinal guides to plants, as did the second-century A.D. Roman physician Galen, whose herbal guide *De Simplicibus* was widely read.

From the Middle Ages through the beginning of this century doctors routinely worked with herbs and folk medicines, but they fell into disfavor as modern Western medicine, along with the modern drug industry, began to monopolize the medical profession.

A recent revival of interest in healing has helped return Western herbs to favor. In fact, it has become difficult to ignore them, as certain ones, such as echinacea and St. John's wort, have become increasingly fashionable and receive a great deal of media attention.

Unlike the Chinese, who as a rule mix various herbs together, Western herbal medicine relies primarily on just one herb and its specific pharmacological properties.

One of the first of these I encountered was milk thistle, which was being touted for liver disease. According to an impressive article in an alternative medical journal, milk thistle can stimulate the regeneration of hepatocytes—or liver cells. Western medicine by contrast has no equivalent—an animal or human with liver disease has a poor prognosis. Steroids may relieve inflammation, but they can further damage the liver over the long term, and the animal is more likely than not to die.

Most of the work on Western herbs was coming out of Europe, particularly France, as herbal research in the United States was basically suppressed due to a lack of financial support from the pharmaceutical companies, which don't benefit from remedies that are widely available without prescription.

As coincidence would have it, at the very moment I was reading about milk thistle, a local lawyer named Fred brought in Jelly, a nine-year-old yellow Labrador retriever who was vomiting regularly and eating poorly, as well as shedding weight.

My physical examination revealed that not only was Jelly's fur a golden yellow color, so were his gums. And when I lowered his eyelid, the conjunctiva—or the mucous membranes that line the eyelid—were also tinged with yellow. All of this meant one thing: The dog was icteric—or jaundiced.

"Did this dog get into any toxins or poisons?" I asked.

Fred explained that Jelly had free rein to a large field behind his house, where he could have found and eaten anything from a deer carcass to toxic waste.

On palpating Jelly's abdomen, I discovered hepatomegaly—or an enlarged liver—and from palpating the borders of the liver beyond the rib cage, I could tell it was extremely sore.

I then palpated the diagnostic acupuncture pressure points in the back, specifically acupoint bladder 18, the association point for the liver, and found it to be extremely sensitive.

Jelly's blood tests revealed a normal blood cell count and no infection, but the liver enzymes, including alkaline phosphatase, were extremely elevated.

My diagnosis was hepatitis—either bacterial or viral, or from a poison probably deriving from some toxin that the dog had eaten in the field. We decided to hospitalize Jelly and administer IV fluids and antibiotics in case the condition was bacterial. Using conventional medicine, Jelly improved, but the liver enzymes remained high.

"We have some serious liver damage here," I told Fred. "Although he's passed through the acute crisis, Jelly's still not gaining weight—and he doesn't look well, either."

Since we had done what we could with Western medicine, I mentioned this herb I had been reading about.

Fred felt he had nothing to lose, so he went to the health food store and picked up the milk thistle—I had yet to learn which herbs to keep on hand in my office. We figured out a dosage based on the dog's weight of sixty pounds, or about half the human dose.

Jelly started on milk thistle on a Monday, and within a week he had begun to improve, looking less and less yellow. By two weeks, his appetite returned, and after three weeks we took more blood tests and found the liver enzymes were completely normal.

A skeptic might say that Jelly would have recovered on his own. But I always ask these nonbelievers: How many cases of spontaneous remission following natural remedies can you accept?

Not long after meeting Jelly, I was introduced to Whitney, a very nervous border collie. As soon as his human companion, Jeri, brought him in, she apologized for having to run back to her car.

"I have to go clean it up," she said. "Whitney threw up all over the front seat again." It turned out the dog suffered from car sickness. The situation had been getting worse and now even a small trip around the block caused Whitney to start salivating and vomiting.

Jeri and her family wanted to take a car tour of Maine, and they didn't want to leave Whitney behind. But who looked forward to a vacation in a foul-smelling vehicle with a constantly vomiting dog?

"We've heard that car sickness can be treated with tranquilizers," Jeri said, "but we don't want to drug the dear for the entire two weeks. Isn't there any natural remedy?"

I told Jeri that in my readings on Western herbal medicine I'd seen considerable research on ginger as an excellent antidote for motion sickness in people and in animals. I acknowledged that I had never used it, but thought it might be worth a try. So once again my patient went off to the health food store for medication.

"Experiment with it," I said. "Try giving him small doses before taking drives around the block and see how it goes."

A week later, Jeri called to express her happiness—as well as that of the rest of her family. "We have a new dog!" she said. "The ginger works great. He even seems to like the taste."

Since my success with Jelly and Whitney, I've discovered that many other Western herbs are useful in treating a variety of ailments. Today I use Western herbal medicine as routinely as Eastern. Just to give you an idea, gingko biloba can be beneficial for canine senility; garlic can be used to fight bacterial, fungal, and viral infections; St. John's wort can help calm the nerves and lift the animal's spirits.

Preventive Nutrition

You are what you eat, whether you're a dog, cat, lion, dolphin, wombat, or human being. But in veterinary school, as in medical school, comprehensive classes in nutrition are rare and often the information is provided to students by pet food companies.

In fact, as far as I can remember, whenever questions about nutrition would arise, most of our professors would say, "Just read the information the pet food companies give you. That's all you really need to know." But these labels only provided information on the calorie count and the percentages regarding the carbohydrates, proteins, and fats necessary for normal health.

No one ever talked about the benefits of fresh vegetables and meats versus processed foods or the advantages of organic versus regular food sources. Certainly, no one discussed the concept of *chi* in processed versus homemade foods.

The only warning from the pet food company literature: Avoid feeding animals table scraps, because the pet foods were perfectly balanced and the scraps weren't. (And to some extent this was good advice. For example, scraps of extremely rich foods, such as fatty pork, can cause an extremely painful, life-threatening inflammation of the pancreas. Certain surprising substances can be toxic to dogs and cats—far too many dogs have died from a "treat" from a well-intentioned chocoholic companion. And while a carrot stick or broccoli spear can be beneficial, more gaseous vegetables, such as cabbage, should be avoided.)

During our junior year, we were wined and dined by the major pet food companies, who hoped that once we were set up in our practices, we'd recommend their products to our patients. "We'll help you get going," they'd say. "That's how everyone does it."

At the time, few of us resisted these efforts or doubted whether these heavily processed products were the proper way to feed animals. In the early 1980s, however, as some of us began researching the natural approach to animal medicine, we also began questioning our indoctrination by the food companies. My first awakening took place at my acupuncture training, where the teachers told us that artificial foods don't possess the same kind of *chi* as natural food. They have no energy—no life force—in them. The more I read about the deleterious effects of pesticides, artificial flavors, and preservatives, the more I questioned what we had learned in veterinary school regarding diet.

They say that what you don't know, you don't see. It had never occurred to me to look for nutritional deficiencies. But at that time in my practice, as I saw more and more dogs and cats who had poor coats, flabby bodies, allergies, and ear infections, I began to wonder.

For instance, the normal treatment of choice for a poor coat due to allergies was cortisone, which was used to relieve the underlying inflammation. But I began to suspect that the real problem wasn't an allergy but a deficiency of an essential fatty acid. And if that were true, wouldn't flax or sunflower oil be a better remedy?

Around this time my veterinary journals were publishing articles linking nutritional deficiencies to poor-quality dog foods. I started doing my own case-by-case research as well. Whenever I would see dogs in poor health, I would ask about their diet. Sure enough, the ones eating the poorest-quality foods consistently had the poorest coats.

One client brought in an eight-year-old mutt with a history of itching. His bright red ears were filled with wax, his coat was dull and dry and covered with dandruff.

I did a skin scraping to check for mange, an ultraviolet light test for fungal diseases, and various other tests, but we couldn't find anything wrong.

Before doing biopsies or trying cortisone, I said, "Why don't we change his diet for a few weeks?" I recommended meals consisting of organic meats, fish, chicken or turkey, whole grains and sweet potatoes, and certain vegetables such as broccoli and green beans.

A month later, the dog came back in, transformed. His coat was beginning to shine, his itchiness had disappeared, the wax in the ears and the redness was gone. This was the first time I had suggested a dietary change alone as a means of correcting a symptom and, as with acupuncture, I was slightly startled that the treatment worked.

After I had made the connection, I began seeing nutritional therapies succeed over and over. One day Chakra, a trim, forty-pound fox-like mutt, bounced into my exam room, all sniffing and tail-wagging, with the joie de vivre of a puppy exploring everything in sight. I was amazed to discover, when his Birkenstock-clad human companion swayed gracefully into my exam room, that the dog was actually fourteen years old.

Chakra leaped up on my exam table and proudly looked me right in the eye, examining me as I examined him. His ears showed no signs of wax or purulent odors, just a nice clean ear canal with healthy tissue. His eyes were as clear as a two-year-old's, without any evidence of aging. His teeth were immaculately clean without excess tartar buildup. His coat was shiny and sparkling, and his skin showed no evidence of dryness, flakiness, scaliness, hyperpigmentation, or sores. His heart and lungs sounded clear and normal, and all his other organs palpated well within normal range.

Basically, Chakra was as healthy a dog as I had ever seen, and I told this to Vanessa, the woman who had brought him in. I also asked why Chakra was here (for a checkup, Vanessa said) and how she managed to keep Chakra in such good health.

"Homemade organic food," Vanessa said, explaining that Chakra had been a vegetarian dog since she had rescued him from the pound as a puppy.

Chakra certainly made me believe that it's possible for a dog to live a healthy life as a vegetarian. But while this type of diet can have tremendous benefits, I don't advocate it wholesale for all dogs; different breeds have different genetic requirements. And I do not in any way advocate feline vegetarianism. Cats are carnivores. Forcing them to eat a vegetarian diet can destroy their health over time.

Today in veterinary school, classes are addressing nutrition as it relates to specific disease processes, such as kidney and urinary-tract disorders, because, to some degree, the food companies are now developing supplements to address these conditions. For instance, one company has developed a food with fructooligosaccharides, which benefit dogs with inflammatory bowel disease, while another firm has developed a diet high in omega-3 and omega-6 fatty acids (in the proper ratio), which help slow down the progression of cancer.

To me, these products mean that pet food companies are finally taking nutrition seriously. Still, it's important to consult with your veterinarian about your animals' diets to guarantee that they are nutritionally complete.

Therapeutic Nutrition

Early on in my general practice, because I was willing to try alternative treatments which other veterinarians tended to resist, I amassed a reputation as someone to call when other veterinarians were stumped.

One day Zeke, an old-time dairy farmer with a herd of 100 dairy cows, called me up. "Doc," he said, "I'm losing one cow after another and no one can figure out why. I heard about ya and figured I'd give a call."

I thanked him and began my inquiry. How many deaths? Over what period of time? What were the cows' ages? What were the initial diagnoses? Was any blood work done on the sick and dying animals? Were autopsies performed, biopsies taken? Was there any change in the cows' environment—feed, water, sprays, insecticides? Were they exposed to any new animals? Were any of them sick?

Zeke answered everything, but his responses led nowhere. The cows had become sick for a variety of reasons—a bad foot, digestive upset, mastitis, pneumonia, diarrhea, stress after calving—then they would stop eating and die.

My training in epidemiology has taught me to think like a detective. And so, like a Sherlock Holmes of the cow pasture, I tried to cover all the angles, examining cows and calves of all ages, wandering around the farm and the meadows smelling and sniffing and collecting.

Back at my cabin, after reflecting on my findings all evening, I decided that, despite the fact that the cows had initially become sick with a variety of illnesses, their deaths had to be related. The only things I knew the animals all shared were their food and their natural environment. I woke up the next morning convinced that some nutritional deficit was leaving them susceptible to stress and illness.

Many deficiencies were possible, but I knew that the animals in this area tended toward a selenium deficiency. I called Zeke and suggested that I take blood samples on some of his indisposed cows. I then sent the blood to the diagnostic lab at Cornell, and, a week later, the results came back: Every single one of the ten cows sampled had one-tenth the normal amount of selenium.

I immediately began injections of vitamin E and selenium, because the two work synergistically, and then added oral selenium supplements to the feed. Thus ended Zeke's bovine distress.

•

"Let your food be your medicine," said Hippocrates, and more than 2,000 years later, people are beginning to listen.

Preventive nutrition helps avert the occurrence of disease by maintaining good health and well-being. Another form of nutritional care is therapeutic, in which we use a food's active ingredients to actually heal and control an already existing disease condition.

Much research, as well as clinical observation, has shown that such therapy—which uses vitamins, minerals, enzymes, antioxidants, and other various biochemical components of animal and plant tissues (such as proanthocyanidin complex from grape seeds, oils from flax seeds or primrose, chondroitin sulfates from cow tracheas, glycosaminoglycans from mussels, and many others)—may work more slowly than drugs. But in the long run, it enhances physiological functions and allows the body to return to a state of balance—or homeostasis.

After surgery or an accident, a proper diet can help speed recovery. A therapeutic diet can aid in regenerating cells, relieving inflammation, improving circulation, potentiating immune function, and improving the activity of enzymes. For example, therapeutic nutrition for allergic dermatitis might include dietary changes, primrose oil, digestive enzymes, antioxidants, such as vitamins C and E, along with minerals such as zinc. For arthritis, a regime might comprise glucosamine sulfate, chondroitin sulfate, perna mussels, vitamins C and E, and sulfated minerals such as magnesium and zinc. Therapeutic doses of coenzyme Q-10, vitamins C and E, acetyl-L-carnitine, taurine, selenium, and fish oils have been shown to be beneficial for heart problems.

Not long ago, Gary, a reporter for a local newspaper, walked into my exam room with his fifty-pound English setter, Ajax. The dog was taking high doses of steroids because he had rheumatoid arthritis in all four legs and was somewhat depressed, with a pot belly and a poor coat—flaky, dull, and dry, as they say on television shampoo commercials.

Gary was quite concerned. Although Ajax was walking well enough, he was drinking excessively, urinating all over the house, and acting unusually droopy and depressed.

I reviewed all the blood tests, X-rays, and joint fluid analysis and agreed with the diagnosis of rheumatoid arthritis.

Gary then wanted to know if there were any other options besides steroids or other drugs with known side effects. I told him that both acupuncture and therapeutic doses of nutritional supplements might be of benefit. Because Gary lived a considerable distance from my clinic, which made a lengthy series of acupuncture treatments difficult, we decided to develop a program using homemade food that avoided wheat, corn, red meat, or other potential allergens; along with evening primrose oil (which acts as a natural anti-inflammatory agent); antioxidant vitamins, such as vitamins C and E, and selenium; as well as a Chinese herbal formula for rheumatoid arthritis.

I suggested that we try this approach for one month, reduce the amount of steroids, and then reevaluate.

Four weeks later, Gary returned to the clinic. He reported that about ten days after beginning the program, Ajax had begun feeling better and looking healthier. A few days after that, Gary was able to decrease the dose of cortisone without getting a reoccurrence of the stiffness. That, in turn, decreased the dog's urinating and drinking problems.

After a two-month recheck, Ajax was doing so well—his coat was improving and he was becoming his old self again—that we reduced his cortisone to a minimal dose. He continued to get better and lived happily for years on a minimal dose of medications—without side effects.

Homeopathy

Of all the different therapies that I've used regularly, homeopathy may be the most controversial. But as I removed all the various blinders I'd learned to wear during school, I kept seeing homeopathy on the landscape. Some of my new teachers liked it, some patients swore by it, and some consideration and possibly incorporation seemed appropriate.

My initiation came in 1982 when I attended a workshop given by Dr. Richard Pitcairn, a pioneer in holistic veterinary health who had begun to focus solely on homeopathy. The workshop, in Santa Cruz, California, was one of the first gatherings of holistic veterinarians—only twenty of us showed up.

The word "homeopathy" itself helps explain the methodology: The Greek *homoios* means similar, and the word *pathos*, suffering. Homeopathic practitioners use minute dilutions of plants and minerals that when given at normal doses create the symptoms of a disease. The patient is then given the solution that matches his symptom, which then stimulates the body's immune system.

Unlike most medicines, the more the homeopathic remedy is diluted, the greater its potency. Although Western scientists find this highly suspicious, according to new research it isn't the actual formulation that cures as much as the electromagnetic signals it emits; these may match the specific electromagnetic frequency of the illness and prompt the body's ability to heal. Quantity, therefore, isn't necessary.

Homeopathy is quite incongruent with Western medical theories, to the point where most Western scientists see it in adversarial terms. But some of its elements made sense to me. After all, traditional doctors give patients vaccines that supply a small amount of the disease, in order to circumvent the actual disease process. And I like the idea that good homeopaths spend a great deal of time with their patients, taking a lengthy case history. Also impressive was homeopathy's goal: to cure, not just to treat. Many well-known healers, such as the late Dr. Robert Fulford, strongly respect homeopathy (for a brief, excellent summary of how homeopathy works, as well as information on many other alternative treatments, read his book *Dr. Fulford's Touch of Life*). And while many studies produced in this country claim to have disproved its efficacy, studies in England, France, and Germany, published in such reputable journals as *Lancet* and *The British Journal of Clinical Pharmacology*, have validated its effectiveness.

Not long after I returned to New York from the workshop, I developed a terrible bout of poison ivy. Every year since I was twelve I've had a bad case—when I was young, I didn't seem to be able to keep away from the stuff. As an adult, I seldom encounter it, but dogs are always running through it, and even when they are not affected, they're somehow able to pass the itching and inflammation along to me.

I was frustrated, for I knew that no matter what remedy I tried—and I've used everything from herbal preparations to cortisone—I was doomed to a couple of weeks of severe itching and inflammation.

But since Dr. Pitcairn had mentioned that homeopathy can cure poison ivy, I decided to try *rhus toxicodendron*, which is, essentially, poison ivy diluted to a homeopathy potency.

Fifteen minutes after taking the first pill, my itching had stopped. I thought, Let's see how long this lasts. Twelve hours later, the itching started again, so I tried another pill. After taking two pills a day for five days, the poison ivy went away.

Having been convinced that homeopathy can work in certain circumstances, I started using it on the animals. One of my first patients was Lester, a three-year-old springer spaniel who had been stung by bees—not surprising, given that Gus, his human companion, was an amateur apiarist. The dog's eyes and nose were terribly swollen, and he was in obvious pain.

Although Gus tried to keep Lester away from his hives, the dog had a way of breaking through fences and climbing over walls to join his beloved friend. In order to prevent the dog from going into shock after a bee encounter, Gus normally would take him in for injections of cortisone and adrenaline.

Gus, a natural-medicine advocate, asked if there were any other possible treatments.

I told him that Dr. Pitcairn had mentioned a remedy from crushed honeybees, or *apis mellifica*; I also explained that I was afraid to try something I barely knew. But Gus insisted.

I agreed to try the homeopathy only on the condition that Lester stay at my office, so that I could monitor him continuously. If he needed conventional acute care, we could immediately administer it. Gus consented.

I placed five granules of *apis mellifica* under Lester's tongue, closed his mouth, and put him in a nearby cage.

The dog quickly relaxed, which surprised Gus, who said he was usually quite anxious when he was so badly stung. Soon Lester was lying down peacefully in his cage, and the swelling started to diminish. A half an hour later, we gave him another dose, and the swelling continued to lessen.

Throughout the day, we watched the dog improve to the point where the cortisone was unnecessary.

We continued to desensitize Lester by giving him the homeopathic remedy periodically, and he hasn't had a serious reaction since.

Since that time, I've used homeopathy to treat a variety of ailments, from motion sickness to various phobias. It hasn't always been appropriate. For instance, some years ago, Rose, who had used homeopathy successfully for her own psoriasis, brought Tramp, a fifteen-year-old German shepherd, into the Animal Medical Center. Rose insisted that I use homeopathy to treat Tramp's severe arthritis and nerve damage. But after examining the dog, I told Rose that Tramp was in such bad shape that he needed a variety of treatments, including acupuncture, to build up his strength.

Rose, furious, shouted at me in front of the other patients. "My homeopath said I shouldn't do anything but homeopathy. If you won't do it, we'll go elsewhere."

I told her that I just wasn't convinced that homeopathy could work in this situation, whereupon she stormed away.

A few months later, she brought Tramp back in, this time on a stretcher.

"My dog is almost dead," she said. "Do something!"

But there wasn't anything we could do at that point, and we put him to sleep. I tried to be gentle and didn't blame her for insisting on homeopathy, because she honestly believed it was the correct treatment. But it simply wasn't appropriate in that case.

According to homeopathy, there's one exact remedy for every condition. That sounds like a wonderful formulation. And sometimes I've seen it work, but to be honest, I haven't witnessed the same kind of case-after-case success with homeopathy that I have with other holistic treatments.

Furthermore, unlike most other therapeutic approaches, homeopathy can't be combined with anything else (except nutritional supplements), because the combination will counteract its implementation. I find that overly limiting. As a result, I use classical homeopathy less frequently than the other treatments discussed here.

Chiropractic

J never gave chiropractic much thought until 1988, when the staff of the Animal Medical Center decided to invite veterinarian and human chiropractor Sharon Willoughby to give a talk on chiropractic on animals.

Sharon, who lives right on the Mississippi River in Port Byron, Illinois, is solidly built, with medium-length brown hair and truly remarkable eyes; whenever she examines a sick or needy animal, she reminds me of a loving angel of mercy.

Sharon's commitment to helping animals is so strong that long after she graduated from veterinary school, she began the study of chiropractic so she could help pioneer a new field of animal medicine, despite extreme animosity from both chiropractors and veterinarians. The former, sensitive to claims that their medicine was suspect, didn't want their techniques used on animals because they felt it degraded their work. Veterinarians, like other Western-trained physicians, thought chiropractic was quackery.

Knowing all this, Sharon nonetheless plowed ahead, obtained her degrees, and has become a leader in her field.

Chiropractic (odd as it sounds, that's the correct term. There's no such word as "chiropracty" or "chiropractice" or "chiropractical") comes from two Greek words, *cheir*, meaning hand, and *praxis*, or practice.

Founded in 1895 by Canadian-American Daniel David Palmer, a

student of anatomy and physiology, its underlying philosophy is that disease, human or animal, results from a disruption of nerve function. This in turn stems primarily from displaced vertebrae. Thus, chiropractors use their hands to massage and manipulate the spine in order to relieve pressure on the nerves.

The Animal Medical Center always asks its staff members to host visitors, and the moment I heard about Sharon, I was happy to volunteer—and to introduce her to my practice. Several animals weren't responding to acupuncture as well as I had hoped, and particularly troubling was Agamemnon, a six-year-old King Charles Cavalier Spaniel show dog with a mild limp in his left front leg. An orthopedist had diagnosed the problem as a pinched nerve in the neck, and though my acupuncture had helped, it hadn't cured the dog.

After examining Agamemnon, Sharon decided that his shoulders and one of his ribs were out of alignment. She performed an adjustment and it resolved the lameness.

Once again I was surprised that the treatment actually worked. Yet upon reflection everything made sense; while my acupuncture had relaxed the dog's muscles, relieving the pressure on the nerve, the vertebrae were still impinging on it. So whenever Agamemnon turned in a certain way, he experienced muscle spasms. By combining the two forms of treatment, a magical synergy relieved the muscle spasms and corrected the alignment.

The success of Sharon's treatment made me want to study chiropractic. I suggested that Sharon organize a comprehensive training program, which she did, and I enrolled in it.

I began using chiropractic on horses after acupuncture sessions and found that after just one or two treatments, the animals began improving. With acupuncture alone, I had found four treatments were necessary.

It wasn't long before horse owners were showing up at my practice asking specifically for chiropractic. The first was a woman named Sarah, whose seven-year-old thoroughbred cross gelding, Pride, had been in a trailer accident. Pride was unable to turn his head more than ten degrees in either direction and Sarah had tried painkillers, muscle relaxants, and anti-inflammatories, but nothing was helping.

I met Sarah at her barn. There, palpating Pride's neck and head, I found that the atlas—or the first vertebra—was displaced about half an inch forward and a quarter of an inch lower on the right side than the left.

When I tried to rotate the horse's neck to the side, he would just spasm and resist; I could feel muscle spasms all the way down the neck.

I inserted some acupuncture needles at Bladder 10, an acupuncture point just behind the skull, just over the first vertebra in the neck, and then at each intervertebral space down the neck. The horse immediately dropped his head and relaxed.

After leaving the needles in this very relaxed horse for twenty minutes, I then began my chiropractic adjustment, placing my hands over the wing of the atlas, my forefinger on the ventral side. Moving with my left hand on the right vertebra and holding the halter with my right hand, I did a quick thrust to mobilize the vertebra and allow it to return to its proper place.

The horse licked my face and then started turning his head all the way back and forward, to the right and to the left. He twisted around to look at his rear end, again and again, as though he hadn't seen it in so long he wanted to make sure it was still there. Sarah started to cry; seeing how happy Pride was only made her realize how much pain he must have been suffering.

In human chiropractic, we usually adjust someone several times a week. Here that was impossible, so I prescribed carrot stretches (or, if you can bear it, carrotpractic). You hold a carrot near the horse's hip (and make sure your carrot is long enough to save your fingers). Then have the horse turn his head around so he must stretch to reach it, the carrot providing the impetus to make him stretch further.

Although my chiropractic sessions with horses were generally successful, it never occurred to me to work on cats, because more than other animals, they do their own form of yoga and stretching exercises. But once I was working on my friend Michaela's horse when Michaela told me that Moose, her fourteen-year-old Siamese, could barely walk. The poor thing ambulated by moving her front legs and then dragging her hind legs behind.

Michaela's regular veterinarian had already ruled out infectious diseases, and there was little he could do except recommend cortisone, which can cause behavioral changes as well as frequent drinking and urination. Michaela feared that Moose was going to die.

When I looked at the cat, I could find nothing amiss—until on a long shot I did a chiropractic evaluation and felt decreased flexibility in the pelvis and the back. So I tried some very gentle manipulations, being especially careful because I'd never tried this on a cat. I told Michaela to let me know whether the adjustments helped and when I didn't hear anything, I assumed they hadn't worked.

Years later, I met Michaela at another barn. "You really helped my horse," she said, "but my cat! I never told you, but within twenty-four hours Moose was running, jumping, playing, and the best part is, she's been fine ever since!"

Touch Therapy

*D*affy, a nine-year-old schnauzer, had a history of chronic myositis, an immune disorder which causes the muscles in the head, skull, and jaw to atrophy. In Daffy's case, it had reached a point over the last eighteen months where his human companions, Bob and Betty, a doctor and an architect respectively, had to feed him with a straw.

While Betty was open to holistic medicine—she was clearly the instigating force in the visit to my office—Bob rolled his eyes and muttered, "I can't believe I'm here. I don't believe in this stuff."

Betty cut him off with a harsh look. "We've done everything," she said to me, her eyes moist. "Won't you please have a try?"

"Of course," I said, but I warned them that at this point the odds weren't good. Still, I would do my best—it wasn't Daffy's fault that Bob had resisted seeking alternative help.

I tried some acupuncture, and Daffy immediately began to relax and appeared to feel better. But because he was in such poor shape, I felt he required a daily rehabilitation approach, so with Betty's consent, I decided to perform some acupressure, too. Acupressure is a form of massage therapy where the hands and fingers are used to stimulate or sedate (depending on the condition) certain acupuncture points.

Poor Daffy's masseter muscles were so tight, and there was so much fibrous scar tissue that though the treatment was effective, the scar tissue still restricted some movement. I told Betty that she should try some cross-frictional massage at home—that is, she should put her fingers on each side of the muscle fibers, where they're really tight, and string them gently like a guitar. When used in conjunction with acupuncture, this often helps to release the tension and break up the scar tissue.

Every day Betty would massage the inside of Daffy's mouth. Although the dog's eyes registered surprise at this intrusion, the movement felt so good that he quickly learned to relax. In fact, he seemed to look forward to the moment when he saw Betty reaching over to coax open his mouth.

After four acupuncture treatments and regular acupressure, the dog started opening his mouth by himself more and was able to lick his food on his own. Soon he could even chew a little. By the sixth treatment, he was able to eat normally and even brought his favorite rubber ball in his mouth during a visit. By the eighth treatment, he was completely healed. I've since taught many clients to try acupressure massage on dogs and horses to help potentiate acupuncture between treatments.

◆

The notion of massage therapy slipped in my back door. I'd always been aware of the healing nature of touch, but I'd never given it much attention until I became interested in acupressure.

Acupressure isn't as powerful as acupuncture. Its effects don't last as long. But there are times when the momentary feeling of touch can have an enormous influence on an animal's recovery.

It's also valuable because clients can do it at home, allowing them to become a part of their companion's healing process. What could be more pleasant than hearing your friend sigh with gratitude as your fingers and hands work to make him happier and more comfortable?

Besides acupressure, I've experimented with several other types of massage therapy on myself, such as deep tissue and neuromuscular therapy. They all seemed to work on some of my old camping injuries, where I was getting stiff. Because they helped me, I started extrapolating their use to the animals.

Massage doesn't offer the same dramatic results some of these other therapies do, but it can still be quite therapeutic. By increasing circulation to a specific area or by releasing muscle spasms, it can relieve stress in the body.

The other benefit of massage is more elemental. Throughout all forms of animal behavior, we see many aspects of bonding taking place via touch, whether it's humans holding hands, monkeys grooming each other's backs, or mother cats licking their kittens. Touch offers a subliminal communication beyond the merely physiological. So many studies have shown that primates and human children deprived of touch at a young age may fail to thrive developmentally. Furthermore, as seen in Candace Pert's work on opiate receptors, touch stimulates neurochemicals.

In 1995, I first met Lori, a sweet-natured teenager who had been physically and sexually abused by both a relative and her boyfriend. Not surprisingly, Lori developed a deep fear of being touched, and she avoided contact with people whenever possible. But Lori loved animals.

I was called in to do some acupuncture on Lori's beloved horse, Ivory, and I showed Lori how to give her horse acupressure massage.

Although skeptical, Lori wanted to help her horse, so she began trying the technique before and after riding. Ivory would simply melt in appreciation each time, groaning softly, leaning into her. Eventually,

Ivory would turn around and, using her muzzle, massage Lori's neck, just as horses do to each other. Because Lori was still young and healthy enough to learn from this experience, Ivory's gentle, loving touch helped Lori lose her fear of human intimacy.

Though entirely unspectacular, touch can work subtle wonders. For many years, my sister Beverly has worked at her local humane society, where she deals with abused dogs, many of whom have become terrified of being touched. One little beagle broke Beverly's heart. Quivering and shaking, he would cower in the back of his cage, and when Beverly tried to clean the space, he would huddle in one corner as far away as possible, as though he were trying to disappear. If Beverly did touch him, he wouldn't bite but he would tremble, whine, and hide his head. Clearly this little dog had been severely and repeatedly beaten.

But Beverly didn't give up. Every day she would whisper sweet words into the dog's ear and stroke him gently, hoping to gradually desensitize him. Her persistence paid off. He stopped squeezing into the corner when she approached and actually started looking up at her. Finally, he reached a point where, when she stopped petting him, he would turn around with that wonderful look dogs have that says, "Why are you stopping?"

Once he had learned through touch that contact can be loving, because he was so cute, he was adopted by a family who fell in love with him on first sight.

Like acupressure, I've found that massage works particularly well in combination with acupuncture. For instance, Alfie, a six-year-old collie-Lab cross, ruptured his anterior cruciate ligament, which is often called "Joe Namath knee" after the New York Jets quarterback who suffered from it. It's a typical and painful injury that is not uncommon in dogs, because canine knees are as fragile as ours.

Alfie was hyperactive, and his favorite trick was to jump off the backyard deck into the flower garden like a champion diver arcing into a pool. One day, after an unusually dramatic leap, he howled, held up his leg, and keeled over in pain.

Alfie's regular veterinarian prescribed drugs containing steroids to relieve the inflammation. When that failed, he referred him to a board-certified surgeon, who operated.

But even after what appeared to be successful surgery, Alfie refused to put any weight on his leg. He was then referred to me for acupuncture.

The dog's knee felt good and stable, but I detected a couple of trigger points—or knots—in the muscles on the inside of the leg between the hip and the knee. I treated Alfie with acupuncture, which released the spasms, but the muscles were still very tight.

As a result, I instructed Alfie's human companions, Tom and Pat, how to massage those muscles to increase the circulation and prevent the knots from returning and also how to stretch Alfie's leg, using a combination of stretching and massage.

Every night Tom and Pat would sit in front of the television and massage the dog's muscles. Each morning Alfie would put more and more weight back on the leg. He grew to love the massage so much that he would jump around the television as though looking for a way to turn it on by himself, since he knew the massages didn't start until the television did.

It only took two weeks before Alfie was putting his complete weight on the leg. At that point, the acupuncture was discontinued.

Like every other treatment, massage has its advantages and its limitations. It shouldn't be used in place of another more helpful therapy, which unfortunately can happen when a naïve massage therapist insists that only massage is required. It works best in conjunction with other therapies, and its ideal application is to help increase circulation, most helpful for older animals or ones recovering from surgery.

Additional Options

Diva, a shaggy, gray-haired four-year-old mutt, came to me one day with her new friend, Lucia, who'd been kind enough to adopt her from the local humane society where Diva had been languishing for a year. Lucia absolutely loved Diva, but she was concerned because the dog would become stressed anytime she heard a loud noise or was approached by another animal. It appeared that there may have been a history of abuse somewhere in Diva's past.

Despite all the love and attention Lucia had given Diva over the past months, these nervous attacks hadn't stopped.

Because Lucia preferred holistic medicine for her own ailments, she was reluctant to put the dog on tranquilizers, which she knew would only relieve the symptoms. She came to my office with the hope of finding an effective natural treatment.

After giving Diva a thorough examination, I suggested Lucia try "rescue remedy," which is a *Bach flower treatment*; one drop on Diva's tongue two to three times per day until her nervousness abated.

Diva responded within an hour after the first drop, taking a deep sigh and significantly relaxing. The episodes of nervousness continued to decrease during the week until she no longer needed the treatment.

The more you become involved in one alternative therapy, the more you are exposed to all of them. Bach flowers was one of those remedies that I'd heard about for years, and I can't even remember exactly the moment I started trying it.

The remedies were discovered and promulgated in the early 1900s by Edward Bach, who was a highly respected pathologist, bacteriologist, and immunologist, and, eventually, an avid proponent of homeopathy. Bach felt that the treatment of one's personality and emotions played a vital role in the treatment of disease.

Basically, the remedies are essences of different flowers diluted in sunlight, and they are designed to manipulate the balance of energy. Bach's philosophy is based on the vitalist theory of life; humans are beings of energy as well as physical beings. Bach believed that the essences of the different flowers could help balance the vital energy force of his patients.

Through extensive research and practice, Bach found the remedies to be completely safe and requiring only the smallest dosage to be effective. He also discovered that they would not interfere with or be affected by other medicines.

Dr. Bach named the combination of essences I used on Diva "rescue remedy" because it had the effect of calming mental stress stemming from crisis situations.

Many veterinarians I know have found the other thirty-eight Bach flower remedies effective in animals. I often ask clients to give them to their dogs, cats, or horses prior to any stressful situation. Although not as effective as conventional tranquilizers in some cases, many clients swear by it and often take it for themselves as well.

I can't tell you exactly how Bach flower treatments work, as no one really knows, which I readily admit to my clients. There are no published studies on efficacy and little research. But as they say—and as I firmly believe—a lack of evidence doesn't mean a lack of efficacy.

But if I wanted to be a skeptic, I could point out that the Bach solutions contain 20 percent alcohol, which may account for the results I have witnessed.

•

In 1996, when I met Susan Wynn at an alternative therapies conference, she had graduated from veterinary school, completed an internship in small animal medicine, and was getting her master's degree in immunology. She introduced herself by saying that she wanted to write a book on the scientific basis and clinical applications of alternative medicines.

I told her that I'd just signed a contract to do exactly that and we decided to collaborate. After she read my outline, Susan asked if we could include a chapter on *aromatherapy*. I was dubious, because I thought we should be as well grounded as possible to help form a solid bridge between Western medicine and holistic remedies, rather than give any potential adversaries reason to ignore us.

But Susan insisted good research on aromatherapy was available, and I decided the studies she sent were indeed impressive enough to warrant a chapter in our book: *Complementary and Alternative Veterinary Medicine*, which was published in 1998.

According to the research, aromas travel through the nostrils to the olfactory nerve, stimulating different parts of the brain. This causes the release of different neurotransmitters and neurohormones. In its simplest form, we experience the power of aromatherapy every day; the smell of a freshly baked cake releases pleasurable feelings, the odor of vomit produces the opposite.

Aroma research suggests that certain odors can give rise to strong physiological and/or psychological responses; specific aromas help accelerate different healing effects on your emotions—for example, the smell of lavender has an antidepressant and tranquilizing effect; the smell of fir needles is beneficial for musculoskeletal disorders; the smell of ginger can be used as an antiemetic and anti-inflammatory.

Although I have tried aromatherapy myself with some success, I have seldom used it with animals. One time I did was when Peter and Eric, both artists from Woodstock, New York, brought in their Jack Russell terrier Chloe, who was suffering from severe pancreatitis. The couple wanted to try a more holistic approach than their veterinarian had recommended, so they came to see me.

Going through the dog's history and the results of their regular veterinarian's exam, I agreed with the diagnosis: Chloe had probably eaten some garbage which inflamed the pancreas, causing vomiting and diarrhea. We decided to try an integrative approach: IV fluids and other Western medications, since the dog was severely dehydrated, along with some acupuncture to help with the vomiting.

The couple asked if we could also try some aromatherapy while Chloe was in the hospital. I was immediately skeptical, but since I didn't see how it could hurt and guessed it might make her stay more pleasant, I consented.

Peter and Eric tied a small vial of lavender to the cage bars, providing a soothing aroma. And Chloe seemed much calmer than most dogs I've seen hospitalized for pancreatitis. But did the aromatherapy have a definitive effect? I don't know. Still, there was no downside—the dog seemed happier, and so did the hospital technicians, who appreciated a change from the naturally unpleasant clinical odors.

I haven't used aromatherapy routinely in a hospital since, but I do tell people that if their cat or dog has to stay in a kennel, bring along something that has their smell on it—a blanket, stuffed animals, or a pillow—so the animal can rejoice in your familiar scent while you're away. That's one aromatherapeutic application that everyone can understand.

•

Glandular therapy harkens back to the homeopathic concept of "like cures like." You eat a little bit of an organ to heal the diseased organ—if you have a bad heart, you should eat heart; if you have a bad liver, you should eat liver.

Mentioned in Egyptian and Ayurvedic writings and one of the oldest of all treatments, glandular therapy, also known as organotherapy, was very popular in America in the early part of this century and is still practiced today, but the therapy fell into disfavor because Western medicine was never able to determine how it worked. It is more common in Europe and some of the cancer clinics in Mexico, often in the form of *cell therapy*, where individual cells, rather than the organ itself, are employed.

Recently Dr. Harold Weiner at Harvard Medical School, who calls the process *oral tolerance*, was able to figure out the physiologic mechanism involved and is currently patenting specific remedies.

Weiner's work centers on the theory that a part of our immune system lies in the gastrointestinal tract. When you eat or absorb liver, it stimulates an immune reaction in your system which in turn stimulates the liver's restorative processes.

Because so many people I knew were talking about it, I tried oral tolerance myself, using a glandular supplement of different organs to boost my immune system. (Unfortunately, most of the organs come from cows or lambs who have been brutally slaughtered, which has greatly upset animal-rights activists. But I was able to find a company in New Zealand that uses more humane methods to harvest organs from organically raised lambs as a by-product of the lambing industry. This doesn't resolve all my issues with the therapy, but it helps.)

Glandular therapy has worked on some of my patients. For example, Rollo is a fourteen-year-old poodle with chronic bronchitis. Acupuncture was helping, but Rollo's companion wanted to be proactive and help at home. So I recommended pneumo complex, a combination of lung tissue with a few vitamins, and it worked wonderfully well. As long as Rollo was on it, his wheezing nearly disappeared. But if we took him off the complex, it returned.

•

Whether we save an alley cat stuck on the top of a city telephone pole or ten wild horses starving to death in a canyon or simply do our best to maintain our own loving companion's health, we help foster love between species.

Not every interchange between human and animal companions is a positive one, however. Just as animals can profit from our love and our caring, they can also suffer from our neuroses and sadism. All of us in the medical field have heard horrific stories of humans abusing animals. And a great many of these abusers graduate from animal abuse to human abuse, leading experts to warn those who see children hurting animals to be on the alert. Sadly, psychologists say that the overwhelming majority of those abusers were abuse victims themselves.

However, physical violence isn't the only way we harm animals. Many well-intentioned people do not understand either the remarkable bond that takes place between close companions or the power of our emotions. Hurt doesn't have to be physical—we can hurt the animals we love in the same way that we hurt the humans we love.

For instance, James Serpell tells the story of an Englishwoman who insisted that her dog sit at the table with her while she ate her meals, and she fed him his food off a fork. The dog apparently felt so much anxiety as a result that he developed an ulcerated colon. Serpell finds that many animals are chronically stressed by their companions, and many are also persistently overfed to the point of obesity. "The dog evolved as a scavenger," he says, "well adapted to eating small amounts of poor-quality food, and now we're stuffing them with these wonderful nutritious canned food products that cause them to gain too much weight."

I doubt any human has ever intentionally tried to hurt his or her dog by feeding them too much. People just don't always understand the consequences of their good intentions—or their emotions.

The first time I met Lucky I had only been practicing veterinary medicine for a half dozen years. An attractive woman named Lucy brought him in to see me. Lucky was a German shepherd–Labrador cross with a dark brown silky coat and white markings. He weighed about fifty pounds and was remarkably sweet-tempered, but he was also anxious. He would approach a human with confidence, but then would cower; his behavior alternated between sweetness and fear. And, as Lucy told me, he was constantly licking his left front paw, which was why she was concerned. She and her husband Craig had tried everything and had consulted numerous veterinarians. Nothing seemed to work.

It didn't take long to make a diagnosis: Lucky suffered from a lick granuloma, a common ailment in cats and dogs in which they persistently lick at a specific area of the body. A lick granuloma can be due to what is known as referred pain. For instance, an animal may have an arthritic hip and the pain radiates down to the foot; the animal thinks that by licking the foot, he will alleviate the pain.

Lick granuloma can also be a form of self-mutilation resulting from neurosis and anxiety. The question in Lucky's case: What was the cause? Since we didn't know the answer, we tried to treat the symptoms with a variety of treatments, including acupuncture.

After the sixth treatment, I was feeling very frustrated, because I expected to see more improvement. The condition would appear to get better but kept returning.

At that point, I began to wonder about the dog's environment, because I realized that one spouse or the other always brought the dog in—but never both at the same time. Perhaps something was going on at home that was affecting the animal adversely. I decided to try asking about the dog's environment at the next visit.

The following day Lucy and Lucky came in, and the moment I said the word "home," Lucy choked up and started hyperventilating. Finally composing herself, she described Lucky's domestic situation. It turned out that Lucy and Craig lived in a tiny apartment near the elevated subway trains in the Bronx. Every fifteen minutes the entire place rattled and shook, and the dog would become agitated. The more worried Lucy became over his anxiety, the more anxious he became.

Lucy didn't want to leave the dog alone, she explained, but she had to go out on job interviews because Craig was divorcing her. All Lucky ever seemed to hear at home, she continued, was the train rattling and the arguments swelling. Lucky would jump up to try to stop the couple from fighting—throwing his body between theirs—to no avail.

I told Lucy that Lucky needed a more peaceful home environment if he was to get better. She and Craig conferred and decided that Lucky would live with Lucy, who would find an apartment more suitable for a city dog.

Of course, in some situations, the dynamics are less clear-cut, and it can be hard just to tell who does what to whom. That was the case with another set of clients: Donna and Gretchen.

Looking rather sheepish, Donna walked into my exam room one day unaccompanied by an animal companion. Although curious about her coming in solo (but pretending not to notice because I wanted her to feel at ease), I welcomed her.

Donna immediately volunteered in a jokingly nervous manner that she thought an office visit might put too much stress on Gretchen, her two-year-old Great Dane.

It seemed that ever since Donna had moved from the country into Manhattan, Gretchen's behavior had deteriorated to the point that whenever she was left alone, she would whine or bark incessantly. But when Donna took Gretchen for a walk, she would tremble the moment she heard noise. Anything from a shout to the rumble of a garbage truck would send her tearing back to the apartment as fast as possible, dragging Donna behind her.

Donna's veterinarian had made a diagnosis of separation anxiety, as well as fear of noise, and prescribed the latest psychopharmacological drug.

This was certainly a reasonable approach according to Western medicine, but after reading about the drug's potential side effects, Donna was reluctant to use it unless she had no choice. So, having heard that homeopathy could have a positive behavioral effect, she tried a homeopathic veterinarian. But this too came up short. She next contacted an animal behaviorist, who took Gretchen through a modification program. This consisted of Donna's leaving the dog alone for extremely short periods of time and using positive reinforcement techniques.

Unfortunately, Gretchen seemed beyond behavior modification. She would shake, tremble, and put on her natural emergency brake whenever Donna tried to take her out. But she couldn't stand being left alone in the apartment, either.

Both Donna and Gretchen were wrecks, both on the verge of nervous breakdowns. So, as a last resort, Donna had come to me, hoping there was an option other than psychoactive drug therapy.

I listened patiently to everything she said and then explained that it would help me get a better grasp of the situation if I could see Gretchen. Donna seemed reluctant and finally said that first she needed to tell me more about the situation.

I slowly realized, as Donna continued talking about her dog, that she was talking about herself, too. She appeared just as anxious as she said Gretchen was and described her life in Manhattan with mixed feelings, loving the excitement but hating the noise, the small apartment, the pollution, and so on. She even looked like a brindle-colored Great Dane—perfectly thin, perfectly fit, with perfectly flowing long streaked blonde hair.

After taking down a comprehensive behavioral history and asking about behavior problems in other dogs in the litter or the breeding line, I began to wonder. Were Gretchen's actions speaking to Donna's subconscious about Gretchen's desires, or Donna's desires, or both? Who was picking up on whose feelings and behaviors? Where was the dividing line between Gretchen and Donna? Was there a dividing line?

Perhaps Gretchen was acting as Donna's surrogate messenger, telling her that New York wasn't working for either of them. I even suggested this possibility to Donna, and she listened with a perplexed expression that slowly eased into genuine openness. But then she refocused on resolving the situation with some magic bullet remedy.

Realizing Donna probably wasn't ready for more than a gentle hint, I made further medical and herbal recommendations for Gretchen and asked Donna to come back in four weeks.

A month later, Donna reappeared in my waiting room, smiling jubilantly, with Gretchen in tow. Donna shared that she had indeed concluded that urban stress was making her nervous and uncomfortable. She had spent a week in the country with Gretchen while attending a meditation retreat. The dog had been as calm and relaxed as a vacationer on a Caribbean beach, and Donna had realized that she too was more content. She understood that Gretchen had been expressing unhappiness for both of them, and Donna was now looking for a rural home.

Which came first, the chicken or the egg? Did Gretchen pick up from the subtle and perhaps not-so-subtle body language that reflected her mistress's unhappiness in the city? Or did Gretchen develop these patterns on her own? Did Donna's unhappiness stem from seeing Gretchen so unhappy? I don't know, but fortunately, the end result was that Donna was able to face the truth and make substantive changes that were healthier for all involved.

•

When animals come into intimate contact with people, they communicate in many different ways (just as they do with their own and other species): through sounds, touch, smell, looks, and so on. And they respond to their perceptions of our actions based on their genetic predisposition, their past experiences in this life, and a myriad of other factors which, frankly, science doesn't yet understand.

As they become sensitized to our every action and reaction, these responses allow them to form a bond with us. When that bond is at its best, animals and humans can perform veritable miracles for each other: We provide each other with love, we improve each other's health, we can save each other's lives.

There are limits, of course. We can't treat our companions exactly as we do ourselves. Psychotherapy is not an option for an animal; you cannot ask a cat to confront his pain at being abandoned by his mother as a kitten or his feelings of rivalry with his litter mates.

Nor do all human drugs and medications work for animals. The herb ephedra, for example, which in carefully limited doses appears to have some beneficial effects on humans, can be toxic to cats. I doubt hydrotherapy is a good idea for cats, either. Then there are issues that no one can answer. Are bilateral kidney transplants on a dog sensible? Is cloning an animal too much?

Texas A&M University recently obtained a million-dollar grant to research cloning dogs. I was discussing this with a colleague the other day, envisioning the animal hospital of the future, complete with its own laboratory so that veterinarians could tell clients whose beloved dog had died that an exact copy could be brought to life in just a few months. But would you truly want to clone your dog? Perhaps it would be better to go to the pound and save the life of some wonderful puppy who otherwise would never find a home.

My sense is that all of us must make our own decisions as to how much we are willing to do for our animals. As science develops, there will be endless interesting options and ethical situations that will make today's challenges pale by comparison. All that I am confident of is this: If you give your animal companion a nurturing environment, you are in all likelihood doing the very best.

Always remember: Do unto all animals as you would do unto yourself. When you do, you give them the opportunity to grow, to love, and, as science is just learning, to *heal*.

According to my dictionary, the definition of heal is: "To restore to health or soundness; make healthy again, cure; to remedy or repair; to cleanse of sin, grief, or worry; i.e., to heal the spirit."

Benjamin Shield and Richard Carlson say in *Healers on Healing*: "Love is the one common denominator that underlies and connects all successful healing. For healing means not only a body without disease or injury, but a sense of forgiveness, belonging, and caring as well."

From the author of *Spontaneous Healing*, Dr. Andrew Weil, comes this definition of healing: "Making whole—that is, restoring integrity and balance."

And says Brooke Medicine Eagle: "True healing is coming into resonance with the creator's one law: You shall be in good relationship with each other and with all things in the great circle of life."

For me too, healing is a return to wholeness. It is a state of harmony with all of life, inside and out. The root of the word heal is the Anglo-Saxon word *haelen*, which means to be or to become whole. Wholeness is the essence of healing.

Healing cannot be limited to the improved healing of one person or animal. How can one living being, human or animal, be whole in a sick environment, surrounded by a polluted environment of air and water, eating polluted food?

The more experiences I accumulate as a veterinarian, the more I realize that healing isn't only about an animal or a human. It is about the relationship between living beings. Likewise, I realize that healing isn't synonymous with prescribing drugs or performing surgery—too much of what I have seen during the healing process cannot be explained according to the laws of Western medicine.

But it does follow its own kind of logic. By means of a process that I call "co-species healing," animals and humans work together in harmony to create healing where it might not otherwise exist.

Science can't explain it. But I know it exists. My proof consists of all the anecdotal evidence I have amassed over my two decades as a veterinarian, and it has been corroborated by other like-minded women and men in the field.

I am certainly not disallowing Western medicine and surgery. All of us, both animals and humans, can benefit tremendously from these endeavors. I am simply saying that a wonderful kind of healing occurs between animals and people when they are able to bond in a healthy, appropriate way. That bond occurs at physical, mental, and emotional levels, and most likely in some other planes for which we don't yet have names. We can skirt around it, using terms like "superconscious," or "spiritual," or "metaphysical," but the lack of words does not deny its powerful, wonderful, life-enriching reality.

Co-species healing exists. We must now decide whether to ignore it or take advantage of it, for the good of all Earth's children.

PART III

Kindred Souls

The Wonders of Co-Species

Connections

We are at the beginning of that path that can lead humankind to humanity.

—Sviatoslav Zbelin, Russian environmentalist

The amazing, adaptable, admirable animal: Indeed, animals perform wonderful acts for humans—they help us take care of ourselves, they improve our physical and mental health.

But let's not forget the hospitable, helpful human. As we have seen, we can do extraordinary things for animals, too—we give them food and home, we nurture them with love and tenderness. Together, human and animal are able to help each other heal, and although science is just beginning to understand the ramifications of this phenomenon, animal lovers have been enjoying its restorative effects for millennia.

But is the human-animal bond only about physical and mental health? As important as health is, isn't there more to the connection between human and animal?

This was what I began to suspect as my practice grew, and as I realized that my clients, both human and animal, were telling me more, if only I were listening.

The day that April and Jay O'Neil fell in love with Molly, she was only six weeks old, but the puppy was already dominating her Akita siblings like a mother rather than a sister. She'd try to lie on them to keep them from wandering, she'd bark when they strayed, and if one did go too far, she'd nip it with her tiny teeth. But it was Molly's eyes that clinched it for the O'Neils, for in them April was sure she saw a glimpse of a wise old soul.

Molly's bossiness didn't stop when she came to live with the O'Neils—she was soon overseeing the household, ruling all the humans and the other O'Neil animals like some benevolent dictator. For instance, when she wasn't fed her favorite dinner, she'd bark furiously and lead April to the cupboard, where she'd point with her nose to the food she wanted. Once at mealtime, when April fell asleep in the hammock, Molly woke her by nuzzling on her ear, then pulled at her sleeve until April tipped to the ground. She next led April indoors, all the while looking at her as if to say, "How in the world can you sleep at a time like this?"

Life wasn't easy when Molly first arrived at the O'Neils'. April was suffering from peripheral neuropathy, an incurable diabetic condition that causes the nerves in the extremities to become overstimulated by aberrant blood sugar levels and results in extreme pain. April and Jay had traveled around the country to consult with various doctors, both traditional and alternative, but no one had come up with a way to alleviate her pain. Only Molly's love seemed to help. Whenever April felt overwhelmed by pain, Molly would appear at her side, gazing up at April with caring eyes that provided comfort and relief.

Eventually, Molly came to know pain herself. Both April and Jay noticed that as she grew older, her gait became labored. When they brought her to their veterinarian, his diagnosis was hip dysplasia—or a malformation of the hip joint.

April and Jay were determined to do everything possible to help their dog, and just as they'd once done for April, they consulted one expert after another, exploring every cure, trying every conventional approach, experimenting with herbal supplements. Nothing worked. Molly's symptoms worsened, and soon she was able to walk barely more than half a mile at a time. If she strayed too far from home, Jay had to heave her into his arms and carry her back. Sometimes, as they trudged along, Molly would turn to stare into Jay's eyes—to thank him, he thought, for the ride.

I first met the O'Neils when they decided to seek help at Brook Farm Veterinary Center, my former clinic in Patterson, New York, where we performed animal acupuncture. Molly responded well to her treatments, and soon she was able to walk several miles without difficulty.

As Molly's health improved, so did April's, and for a few years both fared well. Then another tragedy struck: April's mother became terminally ill. April couldn't remember the last pleasant thought she'd had about the woman, who'd always seemed ambivalent about being a mother, becoming angry over her children's normal demands for love and attention. When, as a child, April would fall sick, her mother, rather than soothing her, would blame her for taking up her time.

April, who was seeing a therapist in order to deal with her unhappy childhood memories, was now forced to become her mother's guardian, creating great strain on her psyche. As she tended to her mother's increasingly selfish demands, she found herself breaking out in sobs during daily chores, often falling asleep at night on tear-drenched pillows. Despite her own struggles, Molly was attentive to April's pain, following her from room to room, comforting her, licking her hand, nuzzling her to show how much she cared.

Eventually, Molly began slowing down. Jay and April thought that her hip dysplasia was worsening, but when I examined her, I noticed her gums were pale and her abdomen seemed enlarged. Additional tests revealed that a tumor on her spleen had ruptured and spread to her liver. The three of us discussed options and decided, owing to Molly's age and the severity of her condition, not to operate. Instead, we gave her a transfusion and administered some Chinese herbs to stop the bleeding. Molly began to recover somewhat.

A few weeks later, on a cold winter night, Molly's spleen ruptured. Her breathing became labored, and she let out a low-pitched groan that April says she'll remember forever.

Then Molly looked up into April's eyes, and April felt as though what she later called a "thought-ball" had exploded inside her head, allowing her to understand the feelings directly: "Take my pain." April gathered Molly in her arms and held her tight, giving back some of the heart-melting comfort that Molly had provided April during her own painful days and nights.

She told Molly how much she loved her and appreciated what she'd done for them. Molly let out a final whimper. The spark in her eyes disappeared, her body became limp, and she passed away in April's arms.

April soon found out that Molly had given her even more than she knew. A few days later, she was lying in bed, feeling bereft. Closing her eyes, she had a momentary vision of Molly sitting in another world—still watching April, still comforting her. April even felt the luxuriant warmth of Molly's coat on her skin. April finally grasped Molly's other gift.

The next day she drove to Manhattan to see her therapist and said, "I can leave now." April had realized that Molly, who had given her the nonjudgmental love every child needs, was really her second mother. "It took me so long to figure this out," April told me, "because I didn't know you could get what you needed from a different species. This was Molly's sacred gift to me."

•

Yes, something else was going on, right under my own eyes—eyes that had been considerably blinded by all my veterinary and surgical training, all of which seemed to have consumed every available neuron in my head in the absorption of every medical fact about every part of every dog, cat, cow, goat, llama, sheep, horse, iguana, and parrot. I felt like the student in the old Gary Larson *Far Side* cartoon who raises his hand and asks permission to leave the class because his brain is full. I had learned so much in school that somehow I had missed the most important lesson.

Even as I began to understand that there was something in the wonderful bond between human and animal that could lead to increased well-being, I saw levels of connection between humans and animals that were greater than health—they reached into areas that could only be referred to as mystical, magical, or metaphysical.

I had already spent much of my life wondering what lay beyond the tangible world of Western medicine and traditional values. My parents were Jewish and they encouraged my attendance at temple, but I avoided it whenever possible. Organized religion felt unduly social, and spirituality seemed more real and accessible when I was in quiet solitude. I sought God in nature, and whenever I ventured into the woods, part of me always relaxed back into that awe-inspiring state of heightened feeling that nature provides, the peace and joy that flows from knowing that you are one with the universe.

But as poet William Wordsworth pointed out, growing older means losing touch with the child's innate connection to spirituality. Furthermore, I was raised to believe that the best course through life is the customary one, so I did the expected. I attended the right schools, earned my degrees, fell in love, bought a house, set up a good life. It was a very predictable process and one that has served me well, as I have been blessed in both my career and my domestic life.

The inclination toward the more spiritual side never disappeared, however. But it wasn't until Megan stepped into my life that it truly reemerged—because Megan helped me to recapture that numinous connection to animals I had felt so deeply as a child. It was also Megan who showed me that species could connect in more remarkable ways than I had ever suspected.

One hot summer weekend in 1978, I was on emergency call on a busy day at the office when Billy, a sweet, learning-impaired teenager who lived in a neighboring town, ran bellowing into my office, followed by his mother. I had met Billy before—he was well known locally as a marvelous goat handler, a boy who could have easily fallen through society's cracks if he hadn't been lucky enough to discover a connection to his favorite animals. He seemed to understand goats. More strikingly, they seemed to understand him.

Today, however, Billy was just short of berserk. "Doctor, doctor," he kept crying, his large head bobbing and weaving uncontrollably over his slight shoulders. "My goat. My poor goat. My little baby."

Indeed his goat, whom he was cradling in his arms, was in terrible shape. Only one week old, she had been attacked by a pack of dogs and had scarcely survived. Billy could barely tolerate his animal's pain and his screams were drowning out the animal's low, barely audible bleats.

Billy's mother had driven him to the clinic, and if she hadn't been there now to comfort him, I'm not sure he would have pulled through, so convulsive was his agony.

"We'll do everything we can to save her," I said. We then rushed the tiny semiconscious kid into the treatment room, where I lay her carefully on the surgery table with blankets underneath her quivering body.

First I conducted a physical examination, checking her gums for circulation—and then listening with my stethoscope to her heart, which, remarkably, hadn't given up.

I quickly inserted a needle into her jugular vein and began administering IV fluids and medications for shock. The goat had multiple bite wounds and lacerations, but, apart from disinfecting them, we didn't have time to do more when there was so much else to tend to.

Billy kept demanding to know if his goat would live. I tried to explain that, despite our best efforts, there was no guarantee. This only caused his bawling to intensify. Meanwhile, I had two other emergencies to care for, including a kitten who had been hit by a motorcycle. So I asked Billy to hold and comfort his goat while I checked on my other patients.

Not knowing what else to do, I abruptly announced that Megan, my golden retriever, would help. Billy had met Megan before, so he seemed able to accept her presence, even though he must have been reluctant to trust anything canine at that moment.

Megan had already proven herself a superb healer from that first time I had seen her help nurse a wounded lamb back to health. Since then she had helped me with a number of the other cats, dogs, and miscellaneous creatures who had walked, limped, or been rushed into the clinic. Still, I had never paid close attention to how she worked.

Megan quietly approached the goat, who was now on a blanket on the floor. The moment she could, Megan started licking the injured creature, lying by her side, breathing heavily against her chest.

I took off to attend to the other emergencies, figuring I would check back in as soon as possible. When I did, the goat had revived somewhat and was looking around the room, while Megan was wagging her tail, lying right by her side—almost on top of her—providing her warmth and a heartbeat. The helpless week-old goat must have welcomed the familiar lost sound of the womb.

I had to make a snap decision. Do I stay here and tend to the gravely wounded kid, or do I return to the kitten, who would only pull through with major and immediate medical intervention? Normally, I wouldn't have considered leaving a baby goat attached to IV fluids unattended. But Megan looked straight into my eyes, as if to say, "Don't you worry. I have this one under control. You go back and do your triage."

I studied her. Somehow I knew she was right. So after checking the IV fluid level, I said to Megan, "I trust you. Be my assistant. Take care of this baby."

At that moment I lapsed into clarity. Megan had connected to me in some ineffable way. She and I had become so closely attuned that we had become a team, working together for the same goal. This was not a goal of physical survival, a human and animal connection which I had heard about before, but one of a shared vocation. Megan had intuited and understood my role in life, and now she had adopted that responsibility for herself. She was becoming a healer—just as much as I was. Although I had been very close to many animals before, this connection moved beyond any I had ever made. In a moment's time, my sense of the human-animal bond had changed forever.

When I came back a half an hour later, the situation was under control. The little goat was sitting up, looking around, bleating quietly, and Megan was providing her comfort that the goat readily accepted.

Megan's gift to me that day was twofold. First, she showed me that healing a living being wasn't a purely mechanical function, that an important part of healing invokes using the love, warmth, and inner strengths that we often undervalue, ignore, or suppress.

I now understood that my left-brained scientific veterinary education had shut down much of my heart. I had been trying so hard to be professional, scientific, and methodical: This is the temperature, this is the pulse, here are my thoughts, here is my prognosis. I had been the very model of a modern Western veterinarian.

Although practical at many levels, I now saw that this approach had definite limitations. How humbling it was to realize that, despite our extensive training in Western medicine, we veterinarians were not the only healers. There are many other levels of healing that have nothing to do with anything we learn in school. One of these involves reaching into that magical connection between species I was only starting to learn about, with my dog as teacher. And this introduction was Megan's second gift.

Despite my best efforts to go beyond my Western medical training, I still couldn't help but ponder the situation analytically: In the middle of the nineteenth century, Charles Darwin proposed that maternal behavior is so ingrained in mammals that it can manifest itself vis-à-vis other species, from a female dog to him, for example, or from a duck to a goose.

Was Megan acting purely instinctually? Was she simply extrapolating from her own maternal behaviors to treat the baby goat or Joe and Martha Starrs' calf as her own? Was her internal nursing instinct developed to such an extreme that she had become, to some degree, everyone's mother?

No, I decided. Megan had transcended her basic maternal instincts to a level of awareness that I had never seen in an animal. She seemed to be acting in a conscious way. She had watched me take care of animals day in and day out, and she had identified with that role. It was as if she said, "I see what you do, and I am going to do as you do."

If she had been motivated only by her maternal instinct, she would have mothered any and all animals around her. But Megan was discriminating. I felt I could observe in her eyes her thought process as she took the time to survey her environment, somehow extrapolating her past experiences on to present conditions, and choosing the animal who needed her the most from moment to moment.

In the case of Jesse the cow, as related earlier, most dogs would have chosen to remain with Amy, the Starrs' daughter. In the case above, Megan decided to devote all her attention to the goat, not the boy or any of the dozen other animals in the clinic who might have profited from her help at that moment. She realized that only the baby goat was in such a precarious condition that her life depended on Megan's assistance. Megan chose accordingly. And she made that same thoughtful evaluation over and over throughout her life: "This is the animal who needs me now, this animal may need me later, this animal doesn't need me at all."

I'd like to think my own gift to Megan was as profound as the one she gave me. When I first met her and nursed her back to health with medication and love, I believe that I gave her something else, too.

Spending time with me enabled her to become something more than the average dog: She evolved into a healer. Accompanying me on rounds and watching my day-to-day triumphs and failures guided her to a new level of purpose in life.

The more I considered interspecies connections like the one between Megan and me, the more I realized they transcended what Western science knows about biology or chemistry or anatomy. They make no medical sense, they can't be quantified, there are no rational explanations.

Something inexplicable must be taking place at an exceptionally deep level—something other than subliminal communication, something beyond an animal tuning into human body language and verbal cues, something past the recent discoveries about the biochemical reactions a human voice may stimulate in an animal's opiate receptors.

I don't believe that the connection between humans and animals can be boiled down to simple neurophysiology or neuroanatomy. And I hear story after story that only reinforce my beliefs. Some of these stories have been famous for centuries. One of the best known, from Scotland, concerns a little Skye terrier named Bobby, whose friend Auld Jock died in Edinburgh in 1858. Bobby refused to leave Jock's grave and became known throughout the city as the loyal dog who wouldn't allow death to come between him and his master. For fourteen years, he spent each night by the tombstone. When Bobby himself died, the townspeople erected a fountain with a statue in his honor.

Similarly, there's the story of Charles Gough, who died in a desolate part of the English countryside and whose remains were found by a shepherd only because Gough's starving, grief-stricken dog refused to leave his side for weeks. The scene was depicted by many artists and poets, including Wordsworth in his poem "Fidelity."

As my ears opened, the remarkable number of incidents I collected, combined with my own experiences, led me to believe in what I call "co-species connections"—that there are many extraordinary levels to the connections between people and animals, and at their best, these connections surpass any currently acknowledged scientific explanation. More importantly, *they can lead to a bond that transcends everyday reality and takes both human and animal to new levels—even to a new degree of evolvement.*

At base, those connective elements between human and animal include the five sensory stimuli, such as touch, taste, hearing, sight, and smell (so important to all mammals except humans), as well as innate behaviors, including maternalism, where both animals and people assume mothering attitudes toward other species—the childless couple who turns a cat into a surrogate son or daughter; the female dog who seems to adopt a human baby; or the famous story of Koko, the zoo-caged gorilla who fell in love with a little kitten and chose to spend her days cuddling her tiny companion.

Other connections include the familial, whereby animals act as if they are part of a group or herd. As Caroline Knapp wrote in her book *Pack of Two*, it's easy to grasp how certain domestic animals and humans see each other as "family." And most of us who have both a dog and a cat have seen (when the two species get along, that is) the two act related as they groom and care for each other and often sleep side by side.

I began to realize that these varying connections were among the primary reasons I became a veterinarian. Walking into an old barn is like walking through a sensory curtain that masks the hustle and bustle of life in the twenty-first century. Moving backward in time to a place where pungent smells of freshly cut hay permeate the air and ruminative sounds of animals munching their feed evoke a peaceful mantra, you are setting foot in a world of peace and quietude. How wonderful it is to be greeted with affectionate whinnies as the horses smell my beard, my jacket, my clothing, and recognize me as a friend; they rub their head against me, I scratch them by their withers (the area between the shoulder blades near the mane), and they lift their noses up in the air, wiggling them in sheer bliss. We bond by touch and mutual delight.

As I examine their bodies, the horses bend into me, loving the feel of my fingers. When I place my left hand on the horse's atlas, she lowers her neck at just the right angle to make it easier. As I do my work, she releases a mammoth sigh of relief and drops her head into my arms and nuzzles me again.

Her relief is so great it seems all her four-legged and winged neighbors heave an empathetic sigh as well. The animals seem to share experiences through their own unique individual sensory inputs. While I'm working on one animal, her compatriots in the barn quiet down and stare inquisitively. There's always a barn dog, lying down by the horse's side, ears forward and upright, listening intently, eyes wide open, wagging his tail across the ground, sweeping the hay from side to side. An orange tabby tomcat jumps up on one of the stall doors, rubbing against the neck of another horse waiting his turn for acupuncture. The cat then settles down into a sphinxlike position by the horse's side, also watching curiously as I work. The swallows, sweeping up into the eaves to feed their screeching children, stop their bickering. Somehow, all the kindred souls in the barn focus on the horse and me, basking in a field of positive energy. A healing resonance abounds, a sympathetic endorphin release throughout, a sense of relatedness that spreads through all the creatures.

◆

But true co-species connections are even more remarkable, they hold even more potential for the miraculous than the familial and the sensory bonds described above. And that was what I was beginning to learn as I opened myself to the lessons learned in the barns of New England, from my clients—and from my dog Megan.

I've always found that when you remain unaware of something, you don't even notice it when it's in your face. The moment you become aware, however, you see it everywhere. For example, you may never have heard of a certain breed of dog, and then, once you see one, you seem to see them everywhere. The same has been true for me and the growing number of co-species connections I began to learn about.

For instance, listen to the story of Southern California surfer and teacher Joe Wolfson:

I've pretty much spent my childhood on beaches in California. There the dolphins ride the surf with us, showing off underwater, swimming with the waves as they start to break, exploding through the surface, jumping out into the air and spinning like a helicopter blade.

The more we surfed, the more dolphins we met, until it became commonplace to have them around us in the water, bumping us, riding the waves.

Years later, after I'd been diagnosed with cancer and tried everything and grown tired of all the oncology wards and doctors, I decided it was time for me to say goodbye. No doctor in this country could help me, and I wanted out.

First I read the Hemlock Society's Final Exit *for advice. The organization discouraged drowning because there's a strong chance you might be found before you die. But I figured if I did it at 2 A.M., I'd be safe, so off I went. Only the dolphins were around, so I rode waves with them for an hour to tire myself out, and then took thirty pills and tied myself twice around a line of buoys about 200 yards from shore and put the rope around my wrist, because I didn't want to drift off and be eaten by sharks.*

Then I lay down on my board and curled up like a child in a crib, cheek to one side on my right palm. I set it up so that I would slide face down into the water and drown. It was physically impossible to do anything else—I should have died.

I didn't. I was still tied to the buoy when they found me. And the reason they found me was because of the dolphins. Their jumping and splashing caught people's attention.

I wore a wetsuit, but the water was so cold that my temperature was eighty-two. The doctors couldn't put a tracheotomy tube down my throat because my jaw was clamped shut. But I had no brain damage, no tissue damage.

I'd gone into the water facedown, and the dolphins must have said: "No." And they must have flipped me over because I was on my back when they found me. There's no question that the dolphins saved my life, by staying with me all night, by making sure my face never went into the water, by keeping my body moving so I didn't die of hypothermia.

Maybe they wanted me to ride waves with them. No one spends more time in the ocean than me, I feel like I'm part of their family. Perhaps they didn't want to lose a family member.

The first day out of the hospital I went back to the water to thank them. The moment I appeared they surrounded me and we rode waves together.

My old friend Seva Khalsa shares a similar experience:

A few Christmases ago, I went out for a walk near Espanola, New Mexico, starting about a mile from home. At one point, I took a shortcut, but the path led me down into some rough country and I lost my way. By late afternoon, I had reached the edge of a cliff and was looking over a ledge. I couldn't tell how far a drop it was. My choice was either to spend the night where I was, because I couldn't get back up the crumbly, rocky soil, or try to make my way further down.

I still had another hour and a half of sunlight, and I was afraid if I stayed at the edge of that crumbly ledge, I wouldn't be able to hang on all night. So I decided to try to climb down.

But going down the cliff, I fell and broke my back—I shattered three vertebrae and had two compression fractures—and broke all the bones in my left foot and my right ankle as well. It was unbelievably painful.

When I regained my senses after the fall, I looked around and saw a house off in the distance. I started calling for help, but no one heard me. I didn't know what to do: Who was going to find me here, hidden from view, four miles from where I started?

That afternoon had been warm, but I knew it was going to be cold soon and all I had was my down jacket and sandals. I figured that if I stayed put, I wouldn't make it, so I decided I had to get to that house. Because my upper body was okay, I started pulling myself along the ground with my arms. I didn't make it far by the time it was dark, so I tried to find some shelter next to a rock overhanging the side of the mountain. It was getting cold.

As soon as I settled in, a dog came running up, almost as if he'd been looking for me, and started licking me all over. He became my protector, staying with me, never leaving my side except when he heard coyotes or other animals. Then he'd run off and chase them away. He was only about fifty pounds, but he was tough.

He slept close to me to keep me warm—it went down to eight degrees. Be-

cause I couldn't bend my legs and cover them with my jacket, they froze solid; they felt like two rocks.

In the morning, the dog got up when I did and started running back and forth between me and that house, as if showing me which way to go. It turned out he belonged to the two families that lived there.

I started crawling toward the house again and despite the pain, I finally made it. I was terrified no one was home, but when I banged on the door, a man appeared. He didn't know what to make of me until he realized how hurt I was and carried me to a couch.

Soon I was in the hospital; it turned out I had extreme frostbite in both legs, which became gangrenous—I ended up losing one third of one foot and all the toes of the other foot.

Still, it was as though God had sent me a protector: That dog gave me the hope that I could survive, as well as warmth and companionship. I don't know what other kinds of animals were out there—coyotes, maybe mountain lions. But he kept them all away. He saved my life. Somehow I knew he wasn't going to leave me. I knew he felt it was his job to take care of me. I don't know why. He was a wonderful soul. Or maybe it's because I've had a relationship with dogs my whole life, and this was as though the dog spirit was thanking me for my help.

Naturalist and skipper Tom Averna has been running a whale-watching company in the San Juan Islands off Seattle, Washington, for over a dozen years. For all that time he and his cohorts, as well as the scientists and whale lovers, have been watching the various pods that live and play in the area.

When Ralph, a forty-two-year-old orca whale officially known as J-6, died over the winter of 1999, a small group, including Ralph Monroe, Washington's secretary of state (after whom the whale was named), gathered to commemorate his passing. Says Tom:

I knew Ralph well over the years—he was very identifiable by his markings and his dorsal fins: Actually, all the whales are, since the same ones live here year round, and once you know them, you can identify them easily.

After Ralph died, we didn't see any whales for about three days, but there was a lot of nice energy in the air because we truly cared about these whales and felt sad.

While Ralph Monroe was giving his speech, with his back to the water, someone asked: "What's that out there?" And there we all saw, coming toward the lighthouse, a V-section of the local orcas, lined up like Canadian geese. It wasn't just a few of them. It turned out to be every single one of the southern residents whales, all eighty-four of them.

Now this does happen maybe six times a season, but here they were exactly as if on cue. It might have been just a coincidence, but then we noticed that the first whale who came past was J-8, Ralph's sister. Then we noticed that the J pod was leading, and the K pod and the L pod were following, as if they were in some sort of processional order.

On top of that, they put on the most extraordinary display of breaching, which means jumping clear out of the water. Each whale in the J pod jumped two or three times, including Everett, a twenty-two-year-old whale who jumped for us right next to the shore, almost on top of us.

It's very rare to see a display like that. But to do it in order, led by Ralph's sister, just as Ralph Monroe was giving his speech, was amazing.

Once they were done, the J pod started moving north, and once again the K and L pods, who had not breached, followed, as though they were cars in a procession.

We all looked at each other, energized and spellbound. It was like being at a church revival. I truly believe that the whales knew what was happening. How else could you explain it? I think they have a sensory perception beyond anything we know, something that humans can only hope to emulate.

Constant exposure to stories like these has not only made me see how much communication exists between species, but how much of it takes place beyond the sensory levels—beyond the part which science can explain. Not, however, that scientists haven't tried. A score of men and women from extremely different educational backgrounds have weighed in in an effort to elucidate parts, if not all, of these kinds of connections.

One of the most eminent to venture into the area is Harvard professor Edward O. Wilson, whose books include *Sociobiology*, the most important text on the subject, and *On Human Nature*. He was also cowriter of *The Ants* (both the latter two books won Pulitzer prizes) and author of the recent *Biophilia: The Human Bond with Other Species*.

"To the degree that we come to understand other organisms, we will place greater value on them and on ourselves," says Wilson.

Through his work as a renowned entomologist, Wilson has come to believe that humans have an "inherent need" to be connected with life and lifelike processes. Wilson labels this human affinity "biophilia."

Simply put, Wilson's "inherent need" suggests that we are all genetically predisposed to be close to animals, plants, and nature. Certainly, this does not mean that biophilia will develop and manifest itself in each and every person. In some humans, early childhood exposure to nature and living beings may be necessary for it to come to fruition. In others, the affinity may be so strong that the biophilia-related urgings develop on their own.

Consider my situation: I was raised in an urban environment with little exposure to wilderness and animals, yet as far back as my parents can recall, nature was foremost on my mind. Clearly, no environmental stimulus brought this interest forth—I didn't see a cow until I was eight years old, I didn't touch a horse until I was twelve. But I did in my mind and in my heart.

Numerous veterinarians have told me similar stories, particularly those who grew up in cities where they weren't exposed to the lifestyles they eventually carved out for themselves. And many of my clients who live in the country with a menagerie of animals share comparable backgrounds.

For me, one of biophilia's most potent manifestations appears in the human desire, whether conscious or subconscious, to share our dwellings with other life-forms—flora or fauna, or most often, both. Even those of us who choose to remain in an urban environment create space for plants, or place a high premium on views of nature from our apartment windows, or ensure that we have an animal companion waiting for us when we come home from the office.

Although people have always believed that this kind of desire to be with nature is positive, Wilson has taken it one step further, proposing that the predisposition is actually hardwired into our genetic makeup.

Biophilia may, in fact, help explain co-species healing. As noted earlier, the classic definition of healing is to make whole. And if we acknowledge that we are part of nature, being whole means taking advantage of all the opportunities nature provides to calm our soul and spirit. Although science has no definite answers, why not assume that sharing a home with a dog, a cat, or a bird—or sharing our lives with a horse or any other large animal—has therapeutic benefits that are deeper than simple stimulation of the opiate receptors in the skin through touch? Perhaps, through our connection with animals, we are stimulating some deeply buried aspect of nature within us, rekindling a lost connection that allows us to be more than solitary creatures, but a part of something greater—and therefore more healthy, more whole.

Biophilia has served the human race well. It has given us the advantage of creating a social connection with other living beings, and from that we have been able to further our own understanding of love and intimacy. It has also helped us learn and develop the abstract concepts of protection (by allowing animals to protect us and vice versa); strength in numbers (a lesson learned from watching smaller animals defeat larger ones); altruism (by giving up a part of our lives for the sake of animals); the ability to cooperate with others (by learning how to become a part of a group or pack).

Furthermore, through understanding other animals' behaviors and lifestyles, humans gained the ability to become more successful hunters, gatherers, foragers. We were able to form bonds and create communities that would not have existed without animals. For example, Great Pyrenees dogs were able to protect sheep, allowing a shepherd to increase the size of his flock; hunting dogs helped hunters find and capture more prey.

If we try to ignore the nurturing aspects of biophilia, a part of our evolutionary past, as well as our ability to heal ourselves, may be lost forever. Because of this, I feel it is imperative that we nourish our hereditary predisposition early on in life to help ensure that our children waken their biophilian genes, which will have a positive impact on their lives and how they treat all living beings.

•

Looking into the matter from a very different perspective is Larry Dossey, a physician who is board certified in internal medicine and former chief of staff of Medical City Dallas Hospital. Once a battalion surgeon in Vietnam, Dossey has written five books, including *Healing Words: The Power of Prayer and the Practice of Medicine.*

Dossey believes that between all living beings exists a connection, unrestricted by locality, which he calls the "nonlocal mind." Consciousness, he maintains, is not limited to specific points in space, such as the brain or the body, nor is it limited to specific points in time, such as the present moment. As well-documented premonitions illustrate, consciousness may include both future and past events.

Because it is not place-specific, nonlocal mind could explain how people and animals may have a mutual impact on one another while being physically distant. Dossey calls this area of study "distant intentionality" (also known as "long-distance prayer"). In other words, Dossey feels humans have the potential ability to focus their attention on another living being over great distances and have a positive or negative impact on that being's health.

Dossey bases his theory on the research of a number of world-renowned physicists, including John Stewart Bell, Nick Herbert, and Amit Goswami. For instance, in 1964 Irish physicist Bell published a mathematical proof, now called Bell's theorem, which demonstrates at a subatomic level the concept of nonlocal connections and influences. These nonlocal effects act instantaneously and are not affected by, nor are diminished with, distance. Bell states that "an essential connectedness and unity underlie all the levels of reality."

From Bell's work comes an experiment showing that, when particles are emitted from a common source—for example, two photons of light out of the same atom—they retain some kind of common connection so that what happens to one of them is instantly reflected in the other.

Dossey has applied the research of Bell and others to some remarkable projects and has come away with equally remarkable conclusions; he mentions many of them in a recent article entitled "Prayer as Distant Intentionality." For example, in an experiment designed to test the existence of a nonlocal effect and its impact on the health of living organisms, ten subjects tried to inhibit the growth of fungal cultures in a laboratory through conscious intent. They concentrated on the cultures for fifteen minutes from a distance of approximately 1.5 yards. After several hours, 151 of 194 cultures showed retarded growth.

Other results showed that nonlocal conscious intentionality can have an influence on biochemical processes in humans as well. And in still another study recently reported on *Salon.com*, researchers at the Mid-America Heart Institute of St. Luke's Hospital in Kansas City randomly divided 990 patients admitted to the institute's coronary care unit into two groups. None of the patients knew that they were involved in a study. In one group, community volunteers were given the patients' first names and were asked to pray daily for a speedy recovery with no complications. No one prayed for the second group.

The researchers, led by Dr. William Harris, found that the prayed-for patients suffered 10 percent fewer complications, ranging from chest pain to full-blown cardiac arrest. "This result suggests that prayer may be an effective adjunct to standard medical care," says Harris.

Dossey labels this effect "distant healing." Some of the more famous studies which he mentions in his book *Reinventing Medicine* include seminal work by Elizabeth Targ, M.D., and her team at San Francisco's California Pacific Medical Center. Targ, a psychiatrist, is the director of Psychosocial Oncology Research and is on the clinical staff of the University of California, San Francisco. There Targ and her colleagues tested whether distant healing could have a therapeutic effect on AIDS patients.

Forty patients with advanced AIDS were recruited and given standard medical care; half also received distant healing prayers. It was a double-blind study, i.e., neither patients nor doctors knew who was part of which group.

Says Dossey, "Each healer was given a patient's first name and photograph to help that healer develop a personal connection with the subject. Healers were asked to focus their mental energies on the patient's health and well-being for an hour a day, six days a week, for ten weeks." These healers, who had an average of seventeen years' experience each, were recruited from many different healing traditions and included Christians, Buddhists, Jews, and Native Americans.

The results: "The patients who had received distant healing intentions had undergone significantly fewer new AIDS-related illnesses, had less severe illnesses, required fewer doctor visits, fewer hospitalizations, and fewer days of hospitalizations. Moreover, those receiving distant healing showed significantly improved mood compared with controls."

Dossey also discusses the effects of nonlocal mind in animals, recounting the countless familiar stories of animals, separated from their owners, who have nonetheless managed to find their way back home, sometimes clear across continents. Perhaps one of the most extraordinary is the story of the dog Prince, who lived with an Irish soldier and his wife in Hammersmith, London, during World War I. When the soldier left for the front, the dog soon disappeared. The wife couldn't find him and finally was forced to write to her husband to tell him his beloved Prince was gone. She was astonished to receive a return letter saying that Prince had found the soldier in the heavily bombarded trenches at Armentières in northern France, making his way through London's crowded streets, across the Channel, and over sixty miles of war-torn French countryside reeking of bursting shells and tear gas.

Another case Dossey related to me in a recent phone conversation involved a diabetic woman whose dog used to sleep in her lap. Whenever this woman would drift toward diabetic coma, the dog would bark to alert her, so she could take action. "It was as if this dog was a diabetes monitoring device," says Dossey. "He seemed to be so in tune with her that he could pick up on her depth of respiration, which changes as one is drifting toward a diabetic coma—or perhaps the odor of her breath changed." Regardless, the dog was able to save this woman's life repeatedly.

Consciousness, says Dossey, "is not restricted to humans. Neither is it restricted to the brain of individuals. You cannot put it in a box and wall it off as we have claimed to be able to do. We have so many dramatic examples where one cannot come up with any other explanation except that there is some quality of the mind that extends beyond individuals; one that envelops not just people, but people and animals.

"And there does seem to be some kind of uncanny communication that links up the owner and the pet; something that cannot be explained by pheromones, or acute hearing, or sensitivities of any sort when such great distances are involved. It seems the human-animal bond is not just a metaphor, not just poetry, but something real."

To me, nonlocal connections is a highly valuable concept and one that may eventually help explain many of the unusual phenomena that occur between humans and animals that others feel are inexplicable, based on our current knowledge base.

◆

Rupert Sheldrake, the world-renowned biologist, has completed some extraordinary studies documenting these nonlocal connections between humans and their animals. Sheldrake, who studied philosophy at Harvard and received a Ph.D. in biochemistry at Cambridge University, was a Fellow of Clare College, Cambridge, and Director of Studies in biochemistry and cell biology. Subsequently, as a Research Fellow of the Royal Society, he carried out research at Cambridge on the development of plants and the aging of cells. He has also written several influential books, including *Seven Experiments That Could Change the World* and, most recently, *Dogs That Know When Their Owners Are Coming Home.*

Sheldrake proposes a form of mental telepathy between sentient beings, all of whom may be connected through what he calls "morphic fields."

Since the 1920s, biologists have posited the existence of morphogenetic fields, which are akin to "invisible blueprints" that underlie the form of each organism as it grows. These fields help explain what is essentially a mystery: Considering that all the cells in the body contain the same genes, why is it that each individual part—the heart, the skin, the nose—knows how to develop so differently?

True, says Sheldrake, some genes code for the sequence of amino acids in protein and others are involved in the control of protein synthesis, allowing organisms to manufacture certain chemicals. But these different functions alone cannot account for form. "Your arms and your legs are chemically identical. If they were ground up and analyzed biochemically, they would be indistinguishable. But they have different shapes. Something over and above the genes and proteins they code for is needed to explain their form."

Sheldrake feels that above these morphogenetic fields are morphic fields. Morphic fields guide and shape all chemical, physical, and biological systems—atoms, molecules, crystals, organisms, ecosystems, solar systems, and so on at all levels of complexity—"like an invisible hand, acting across space and through time."

As a result of the process of what he calls "morphic resonance," morphic fields also have an inherent, collective memory. "For example, crystals of a given kind are influenced by all past crystals of that kind, date palms by past date palms, giraffes by past giraffes, etc." As to possible examples of morphic resonance, he points to flocks of birds or schools of fish which can change direction very rapidly without separate individuals bumping into each other.

Morphic fields could link group members together and may continue to connect them even when they are far apart. These invisible bonds therefore could act as channels for telepathic communication between animals and animals, animals and people, and people and people. Sheldrake also proposes that these morphic fields "extend beyond the brain into the environment, linking us to the objects of our perception and making us capable of affecting them through our intention and attention."

I realize that to many this may sound far-fetched. But I always remind people of other ideas once ridiculed by the scientific establishment, such as X-rays, radio waves, communication by telephone, and electromagnetic fields. We have been forced to change even our mode of scientific experimentation, as the wildness of quantum theory has subverted the cut-and-dried gridlike truths of the Cartesian model that preceded it. After all, as Sheldrake points out, according to Heisenberg's uncertainty principle, certain experiments cannot be performed with absolute accuracy, because the measuring process itself interferes with the variable to be measured. The old Cartesian view would never have allowed for such a notion, as it held that knowledge was objective and that humankind would eventually possess a complete and total understanding of the universe.

Sheldrake has collected a huge database of animals—from dogs and cats to parrots and horses to reptiles and fish—that have exhibited co-species connections that defy explanation. In his *Dogs That Know When Their Owners Are Coming Home*, he relates almost 200 stories of dogs that seemed to understand the whereabouts of their companions. Among the most impressive is Jaytee, a mutt in England whose ability to tell when his companion, Pamela Smart, was on her way home was fully documented in studies over several years. Timers were placed on both Pamela and Jaytee so that the exact timing of their activity and response respectively could be monitored. Jaytee would become excited almost immediately after Pamela left the office, jumping and pacing in front of the door, wagging his tail. Eventually, over 120 videotaped records of Jaytee's behavior were recorded. A well-known debunker of psychic phenomena was brought in to discredit the dog's gift; he was unable to do so.

To be fair, not only dogs show such gifts. Many species of animals that have bonded with their human companion have done the same. My cowriter, Gene Stone, has been living with his tortoiseshell cat, Minnie, for over fourteen years. For a long time they did not bond, particularly while Gene's Maine coon cat, Jay, was around. But when Minnie became the household's sole feline, she and Gene bonded more than he had with any other animal.

For years, veterinarians have told Gene that cats have no sense of time. But Minnie seems to. Gene works out of his home, so Minnie spends most of the day sharing the space with him. The more he's home, the farther away she tends to stay. But after he's been gone for a day, she'll sit in a chair near him when he returns home. If he's been gone longer, she'll sit by his feet. And if he's been gone for a week or more, she sits, if she can, on his face; barring that, on his feet, or in his lap, or wherever she can be as physically close to him as possible.

What's more noteworthy, however, is that she not only seems to know how long he's been gone, she can tell when he's about to come home. When Gene returns after an absence of a few hours, Minnie is disinterested, unless it's dinnertime. When he comes home after having been gone for a longer period of time, she is usually waiting on the living room couch, where she can see the door. But if he comes home after an absence of more than a day, she is sitting right by the door when he walks in. Because the door of his apartment is metal and the stairs are heavily carpeted, she can hear nothing until the key is in the lock. Yet when he opens the door, she is always sitting there.

Maybe she's always waiting there, I thought. She doesn't. If Gene's gone over an extended period of time and a friend stops by to take care of her, Minnie comes to the door from wherever she had been sitting to say hello. Only when she knows that Gene is coming home after a long absence is she sitting right by the door to greet him. Somehow, before he comes in, she knows it's him and not just some friend with a key.

According to Sheldrake, this kind of telepathic communication can work both ways. For instance, he tells the story of a man in Surrey, England, who knew whenever his cat Suzie wanted to come in the house without her scratching or crying out. He and his wife would be in bed, and the man would suddenly say, "Suzie wants to come in." He would then open his curtains to find the cat sitting on the gatepost, staring as only cats can stare at the bedroom window. He knew exactly when to open the door.

Other researchers have reported stories about lost cats and dogs who were able to signal their location to their owners. And then there are stories of animals who made their presence known even before they bonded with their owner. Dr. Marc Bekoff, a professor at the University of Colorado with a Ph.D. in animal behavior, tells how he first met Jethro, his part-rottweiler, part-German shepherd: "I simply walked into the Humane Society and felt this instantaneous connection. It was as though my whole body was magnetized toward the very back corner of the room, where I found this dog staring up at me. I can't explain it, but it was a warm, wonderful feeling that completely overcame me, something I felt seventy-five feet across all those cages. I knew I'd found a companion even before I saw him.

"I'm a trained scientist," he says. "I'm not supposed to have these kind of universal connections—they put me in hot water with my associates. But I do."

Since that time, Marc has experienced other moments of connection. "Once I came home after a disastrous day at work. Normally, Jethro greets me right away and wants to be fed immediately. But this time he was completely subdued. He seemed to know I needed looking after. He was very compassionate, very empathic, leaning into me, looking at me as though he was thinking, 'Marc needs help.' I'd never seen him act that way before—and never again. He just knew it was time to think about me, rather than him."

You could call this phenomena: dogs who know when their owners are coming home feeling despondent.

It is hardly news to say that Western science tends to scoff at this kind of thinking, and Marc runs into trouble at work for believing it. Yet biologists are able to accept that other kinds of nonverbal communication exist within species. For instance, E. O. Wilson talks about how a society of ants can act as one organism, able to move strategically as a single army in vast aggregations without any form of currently identifiable verbalization. Fish too work in formations, able to coordinate moves in ways that defy simple sensory explanations, as do flocks of birds.

Says Sheldrake, the British horse trainer Harry Blake has carried out experiments showing that horses who were raised together as an unrelated pair or were brothers and sisters, when separated, were able to know when the other was being fed or exercised and showed a similar desire to eat or play. There are no scientific answers yet for any of these occurrences, only a great deal of anecdotal evidence waiting for clarification.

·

The researchers described above aren't the only scientists who are investigating the far reaches of co-species connections, but they are among the few willing to challenge the conventional take on the relationship between human and animal, as well as that of Western science in general.

Other scientists are approaching the area from their own particular perspective, such as Michael Fox, who, besides being a close friend, is vice president of the Humane Society of the United States and the author of over forty books, including *Understanding Your Cat* and *Understanding Your Dog*.

Michael's studies have led him to coin the term "empathosphere," by which he means "a realm of feeling, which is not limited by time or space." Like Dossey's nonlocal mind, Michael uses it to explain what he calls "the so-called psychic phenomena in animals and in humans."

According to Michael, certain aboriginals extant today have the ability to feel and see "in a kind of clairvoyant, empathic way." Michael doubts this ability was limited to only these ethnic groups: "But today

I believe that we are rapidly losing this ability. We are becoming more rational, more intellectual, and less and less in touch with the wisdom. We must relearn how to trust our intuition."

Deepak Chopra, a pioneer in mind-body medicine, has integrated neurobiology, quantum physics, spirituality, and nonlocal connections into a cohesive theory that he describes in his most recent book *How to Know God*. The essence of this integration is that all of our connections are a form of energy that we are only now becoming able to measure and quantify. This energy is most powerful when the connections are based on love.

It often seems that the more we move forward, the more we step backward. As modern scientists begin to analyze new possibilities in human-animal connections, they are stumbling upon truths known to humans centuries ago. We have already seen how Western science turned its back on the animal as compeer, starting with Aristotle and progressing through Descartes, the mechanists, and the behaviorists. What we often forget is that many indigenous tribes or cultures, some dating back to the dawn of history, some still existing, didn't think that animals were different from people or unworthy of respect. They felt an intimate, respectful connection to all the beings with whom they shared their days, their lives, their Earth.

I do not believe that earlier eras were necessarily utopias for either humans or animals. The past was as replete with disease, ignorance, and aggression as the present—and, I sometimes fear, the future, too. Humans grow and change, sometimes for the better, sometimes for the worse. It is always our choice, I suspect, whether conscious or not.

Still, all evidence points to a human-animal relationship that was more harmonious, more understanding than the twenty-first century's. There was a time when humans lived more as equals than masters of other species, cohabiting the planet in predator-prey relationships that didn't encourage us to dominate other species. The world was more holistic, a totality greater than the sum of its parts, a living, breathing organism of which man was a component rather than its proprietor.

In sum, we were dependent on animals for our food and our daily survival. Clearly, humans have always hunted animals for food. But within the Native American tradition, for instance, killing an animal didn't connote contempt for the prey. Instead, the hunter respected the animal he chose to kill. After all, he had to fully understand the behavior patterns of his prey—where they lived, when they traveled, how they gathered their own food—in order to be a successful hunter.

By learning who animals were and how they interacted with others of their own species, we developed an awareness for their strengths as well as their weaknesses. Above all, this created in us a respectful admiration for animals as fellow creatures rather than as objects as separate from us and our lives as furniture and appliances are today.

Everything belonged on Earth for a reason. Said Shooter, a Teton Sioux, "All birds, even those of the same species, are not alike, and it is the same with animals and with human beings. The reason Wakantanka [the Indian word for the Great Being or Great Spirit] does not make two birds, or two animals, or human beings exactly alike is because each is placed here by Wakantanka to be an independent individuality and to rely upon itself."

Humankind did not regard itself to be better—or worse—than the animals. "In the beginning of all things, wisdom and knowledge were with the animals, for Tirawa, the One Above, did not speak directly to man. He sent certain animals to tell that he showed himself through the beasts and that from them—and from the stars and the sun and the moon—should man learn. . . . All things tell of Tirawa," said Eagle Chief, Pawnee.

Because indigenous cultures shared such a respect for the natural world, they tended to create societies that nurtured the relationship between species. Humans could not shoot all the buffalo, for example, or deplete all the fish from the local river. They needed to live in balance with other beings.

One of the most endearing of stories, told by David Suzuki and Peter Knudsen in *Wisdom of the Elders*, concerns the Chewong people of Malaysia. Once a populous society, as of 1979 its numbers had dwindled down to 131 because of centuries-old encroachment on their land.

The Chewong feel so strongly that humans and animals share the world that they have a sacred law against laughing at animals. This doesn't signify a lack of humor in the culture, but a deep respect for animals that precludes teasing them cruelly, just as no one would taunt another human worthy of regard. The Chewong do not deem humans superior to animals. They are one of many varieties of animals, part of a living family in which each member sees the world differently, but each with an equally valid perspective.

When teaching a workshop on acupuncture for animals in the Himalayas of Bhutan, the last independent Buddhist kingdom in the world, I continually came across *tangkas*, murals painted on monastery walls and homes. Depicting what is commonly known as the story of the four partners, this is an ancient parable about one of the basic tenets of Buddhism—the interdependence of all beings. Here a monkey, a hare, and a bird are riding on top of an elephant, the bird on top of the hare on top of the monkey, which is sitting on the elephant's back. The tower of animals is standing under a blossoming tree bursting with fruit. The bird is picking the fruit, the rabbit is dropping its dung, the monkey is spreading the dung, the elephant is watering the tree with its trunk, allowing it to stay fertilized so it can provide shade, blossom, and feed all.

This lesson is not only depicted everywhere throughout Bhutan, but is taught to all schoolchildren as a key fable by which to live.

◆

Co-species connections can be mystical. They can be illuminating. They can be magical. They put us in touch with bonds that modern civilization has forgotten; they allow us to believe that there is more to life than what Western science tells us.

But there's more. I believe that the true beauty of co-species connections is that they allow humans and animals alike the chance to develop into something greater than each could be alone. Once you open yourself to the possibility that there is more to a human-animal companion relationship than the simple offer of food or shelter, you open yourself to any number of wonderful prospects.

A friend of a friend, Mark, is a twenty-seven-year-old New Hampshire native who has led a painful life, in part due to an unhappy childhood spent in a cold, unnurturing family. His father was distant, seldom speaking to him for months at a time; his mother was highly narcissistic, uninterested in anyone other than herself; his older brother physically abused him. Along the way, Mark developed a severe antipathy toward many animals, especially cats. He never knew why.

By the time he went off to college, Mark was a dangerous mix of anger and vulnerability, and he barely obtained his degree, transferring several times to different schools, always unhappy, always searching for a happier place, and making one halfhearted attempt at suicide.

For several years after school, Mark lived alone, struggling to deal with his psychological issues with the help of a therapist. But progress was slow. He did, however, find a house he loved and tried to make a home for himself, however lonely he felt.

Near the end of a cold winter three years ago, Mark noticed that whenever he drove into his garage, a pair of glistening cat's eyes was staring at him from behind the backyard shrubbery. When Mark was younger, he had tortured a neighbor's Siamese, for which he felt continual guilt, and he had always assumed that he could never handle sharing his life with an animal—partly because he doubted he was responsible enough but also because something about cats continued to make him nervous and angry.

But Mark was also very lonely, and when the gray tabby tentatively approached him, he petted her. She then jumped up on his lap as he sat on the front steps, and Mark decided to make an effort to take care of her. So he took the cat inside, fed her a little tuna, gave her some water, and let her sleep by his side. He quickly fell in love with her little whiskered face, which he thought radiated a fine intelligence, as though behind those feline eyes was a mind capable of discernment. He even felt flattered that of all the households in the neighborhood, she'd chosen his.

When he first took her in, the cat was not in good shape. Clearly, she'd been on her own too long. Mark took her to a veterinarian. (This simple act was something that Mark once said he could never imagine doing: Taking an animal to see a medical professional, paying good money for it, caring about the results—it all seemed to Mark to be too responsible, too tied in to a world to which he felt completely unconnected.) The veterinarian said the cat was malnourished and worm-infested, but with time and care she would recover.

It didn't take long for the cat, whom he named Sophie, to make a home for herself. It also didn't take long for Mark's anger to erupt. It seemed to come from nowhere—without prompting or incident. It usually ended with his hurling a skidding and meowing Sophie across the wooden floors into the wall. Mark was immediately remorseful and would lie on the floor crying, expecting the cat to disappear back into the bushes. Instead, he was amazed to see that she usually crawled over to his side and brushed her head against him. He would pet her, and she would close her eyes, purring.

This pattern played itself out several times over the next month. Each time rage would enter his heart, Mark would hurt Sophie, sometimes hurling her across a room, sometimes slapping her on the head, and occasionally spanking her as though she had been a bad child. Each time she'd disappear. But she always returned to soothe him, sidling against him when he was lying in bed, purring into his ear. He interpreted her actions as forgiveness—she loved him enough to want to reconcile with him. He didn't know such love was possible.

Once Mark came home from his office in a terrible mood; as he changed out of his work clothes, he felt his rage edging dangerously close to the surface. He kicked a shoe toward Sophie, who was watching him from across the room, cautiously eyeing his demeanor. He then nailed her with the other shoe. She took off like a shot, and again Mark figured that was the last of Sophie.

It wasn't. A few minutes later, she jumped up on Mark's lap and looked him directly in the eye. Mark could have sworn that Sophie was completely aware of what she was doing—she was telling him that try as he might, he wasn't going to lose her, and she wasn't letting go of him, either. For better or for worse, they were a couple, and they would work it out together.

Mark burst into tears, wondering how a strange little animal could cause such great emotional disturbances. He also wondered who he was crying for: Sophie, himself, or the child who had been hurt so badly two decades earlier.

In talking about Sophie with his psychiatrist, Mark began to realize how part of him hated Sophie—and all cats—for being as vulnerable as he once was and how enraged he felt that she wasn't being punished as he had been. Gradually, he also began to accept, through the cat, that he was capable of being loved and that the abuse he had undergone wasn't his fault. He was a good person who had been the victim of his family's excesses, just as Sophie was currently the innocent victim of his own.

Using the lessons Sophie taught him, Mark was able to work through much of the mental and physical pain of his childhood. He credits Sophie for understanding that his soul was good despite his problems. True, Mark says, maybe the real story was that the cat had been so abused herself that she was willing to settle for whatever crumbs of kindness came her way. But he doubts it. Sophie's stubborn attachment struck him as stronger than a stray's desire for food; he knew enough about cats to know they are not masochistic.

They grew even closer. Mark says that Sophie was able to let him know what she wanted. Mark would be watching television and then suddenly, without knowing why, would go to the kitchen. When he did, Sophie was there, and usually either her bowl of dry food or her water dish was empty. And like the man in Surrey, England, Mark could often tell when Sophie wanted to come inside.

When he was lying down, feeling depressed, Sophie would come over to him and lick his forehead. She would do it as patiently, as diligently as a mother calming a child. Although Sophie's ministrations didn't necessarily relieve Mark's unhappiness, they made him realize that, if nothing else, he had a loving cat.

Sophie also seemed to know whenever he was having a bad dream—those dark nights when he would wake up in a sweat, she would be sitting right next to his face, staring at him. Usually she stayed at the far end of the bed—Mark was a restless sleeper, and she had learned if she got too close she might get inadvertently whacked, but if the dream was truly frightening, she would be nearer to his face.

Mark tells me that the two of them have learned to communicate so intimately that he fears it borders on the surreal, and he was heartened to hear from me that there are plenty of others who share the same kind of telepathy.

Mark hasn't yet been able to establish this kind of a close relationship with another human. But he is not worried—he feels his bond with Sophie had to come first. In fact, without in any way diminishing his appreciation for all she has done for him, he sometimes wonders if it isn't a dress rehearsal for a human-human relationship. The rest of the time he considers it one of the greatest blessings of his life.

At its best, a co-species connection makes it possible for humans and animals alike to grow as Mark and Sophie have—and, I suspect, to evolve to new places that would not be otherwise possible.

The work of professor Marian Diamond at the University of California, Berkeley, has taken the notion of co-species connections into what I call "co-species evolvement," meaning that through these connections, both human and animal have a chance to develop into more fully evolved beings. For instance, based on the latest research in brain development and neurophysiology, it appears that many animals have the ability to achieve more advanced levels of cognition than previously acknowledged—a progress that can now be traced in single life spans rather than over eons.

In 1963, Diamond and her colleagues discovered that, given the appropriate mental, physical, and/or sensory stimulation, the brain's interconnected neurons can sprout and branch. At the same time, in a prolonged condition of understimulation, the neurons stop growing. Previously, the traditional scientific attitude toward the brain adhered to a no-growth policy—as a person reached maturity, the brain's plasticity terminated. Diamond's ideas are potentially life-transforming: Enrich your own experiences and you enlarge your cerebral cortex; deprive yourself of stimulation and your brain will shrink from disuse.

Most of Diamond's work has been done on rats. But, as she points out in her book *Magic Trees of the Mind*, although the rat's brain is smoother, simpler, and smaller than a person's, the rat's nerve cells—or the living units that comprise most of the brain—are virtually identical to a human's brain. And the physiological processes are basically the same, which is true, Diamond says, "of the cat, dog, guinea pig, and monkey as well."

Oddly, prior to Diamond's work, neurologists had noted a decrease rather than an increase of brain cells in rats and humans over the typical life span. The shrinkage was apparent at the microscopic level: Scientists could literally count the disappearance of nerve cells in a given region over time. Macroscopically, it also seemed to diminish— the brain weighed less at increasingly older ages.

In one study, researchers found a 20 percent decrease in the number of cells in the brains of two octogenarians, as compared to twenty-year-olds. Another neurologist extrapolated this data to estimate that between young adulthood and old age 100,000 cells are lost each day.

But consider this: The researchers obtained the brains from coroners, who had turned over the bodies of indigents, alcoholics, and the like. Likewise, animal researchers invariably studied mice, rats, and other lab animals housed in small sterile cages—a picture of mental impoverishment.

Diamond's team collected their brain tissue from research animals maintained in enriched environments and from people who had lived healthy, mentally active lives. This seems to explain why they found no thinning of the cortex or relentless depletion of neurons with age.

Studies demonstrate that the brains of various species develop in different areas, based on the relative importance and uses of their various senses. For example, rats' brains have smooth cerebral hemispheres and their olfactory bulbs are huge, meaning that the rat depends heavily on its nose to monitor its environment. In cats and sheep, the olfactory bulbs are smaller and the cerebral hemispheres are extremely fissured—because these animals rely less on smell and more on other sensory cognition. In more intelligent mammals, such as humans, dolphins, or chimpanzees, the cerebral hemispheres—the brain's thought center—are much larger and the convolutions considerably deeper.

On every mammal's brain, a narrow top layer—or cerebral cortex—contains the acme of the organism's thinking powers. The part of the cortex that is the newest evolutionary addition is called the neocortex. "From rat to cat to person, the neocortex differs mainly in area, not in basic interior design," says Diamond.

Since the initial publication of her book, Diamond's research team has produced more unexpected results. For example:

1. A stimulating or nonstimulating environment affects the regions of the brain involved in learning and remembering. Neurons in other parts of the brain besides the cerebral cortex can also respond—by growing new dendritic branches and spines or by shrinking.

2. Enriching the environment of a pregnant female rat can result in newborn pups with a thicker cerebral cortex than pups born to impoverished females.

3. The brain of a nursing rat pup is able to grow as much as 16 percent thicker in an enriched environment.

4. In "teenage" rats, the impact of an enriched environment on cortical thickness was greater than in young weaned rats. Also: A more monotonous environment had a more powerful thinning effect on the cortex than an exciting environment had on cortex thickening.

5. Brain changes were found in young adult rats, middle-aged rats, and old rats.

The implications here are considerable. Challenging the ancient dogma that you can't teach an old dog new tricks, this research suggests that our companion animals have the ability to become smarter, more aware, more conscious in a positive, stimulating environment. That means our relationships with them have greater potential for mutual satisfaction when we treat them with respect and offer appropriate stimulation than when we ignore or undervalue them.

As Kelly Bollen of the Syracuse Zoo pointed out earlier, zoo animals who develop stereotypic behavior patterns can benefit from enrichment programs. These kinds of enrichment programs are critical for other animals as well, whether they are in humane society shelters or homes. Touch, eye contact, love—they all aid the animals' growth and development.

There has been much inauspicious news in the world recently regarding our animal friends—so many species are becoming extinct, so many animals are in trouble, so many frightening stories of human cruelty abound. But let's also take the time to give ourselves an occasional pat on the back (just as we give our animals a pat). Every year more and more animals become companions to humans; every year more and more people learn how to take better care of their new friends. The beauty is that the company of a loving human truly seems to give animals the potential to evolve into smarter, higher-functioning creatures than they would without us.

•

It's not just animals who evolve—as we've seen, humans can, too, because of all the gifts that co-species connections provide.

For example, by showering us with their attention, their rubs, licks, and purrs, animals teach us how to love ourselves.

They allow us to smile. We laugh at their comical behavior, and we laugh at ourselves when we act like fools in front of them.

They allow us to talk without criticism, without judgment, to a loving, open ear. I have met several therapists who consider pet therapy an adjunct of their work, offering their animal companions to patients as another therapeutic sensibility, one that is nonjudgmental and comfortable. As mentioned, one of my clients regularly brings her Bijon Frise to her office, and another client always keeps her calico cat, Cassie, around because she claims her clients are comforted by Cassie's presence and, during moments of verbal inhibition, seem more able to talk to Cassie than to her.

Animals teach us about living in the moment. No one can live constantly in the present, because part of being human is feeling responsible for our past and our future. But so many of us spend too much of our time worrying about what has happened—or what will happen. Animals bring us back to the moment; their comfort and love help us appreciate what we are feeling now.

Animals allow us to comprehend the idea of refuge. They are always available whenever we need them, at hand with just a beckoning call, always willing to take our problems and help us by being present for us. (Well, okay, maybe not when they're eating—but at any other time.)

Just as animals are able to evolve in our presence, I believe that we evolve in theirs. Something happens when a person comes into loving contact with an animal, something wonderful, something inexplicable, something worth aspiring to.

Let's say you come home after a hard day at work. You've been stuck inside your mind all day, thinking about all you have to do, all the demands on your time, all the bruises to your ego, all the hurts and stresses and pains.

Then you see your dog wagging her tail, or you hear your cat meowing, or your bird chirping—or you sense any other form of affection from your animal friend. You begin to change. You move from being inside your head to your heart. You move from being stuck in the past, worrying about what you've done, or the future, anxious about what you will do, to the present. Your whole being responds positively.

And that is one of the principal reasons why animals can support our health—they relieve our stress. Like many outside influences on the human body, stress can be good or bad. It's good when it stimulates creativity and efficiency. When we are under the gun, needing to meet a

deadline, stress helps us focus, keeping us on target as we feel a mild release of epinephrine or adrenaline, the biochemicals that increase our
heart rate, that give us zest and energy. The fight-or-flight mechanism,
one of our instinctual responses, allowing us to dash out of the way of
a speeding car or escape quickly from some other dangerous situation,
is based on this immediate, short-term chemical release.

However, if stress becomes a constant in our lives, not only is
there a continuous release of adrenaline but also of cortisone from the
adrenal glands. This ongoing release eventually exhausts our supply of
both adrenaline and cortisone, overwhelming the adrenal glands and
preventing them from functioning well. Cortisone suppresses the immune system, decreases our resistance to infections, and has long-term
detrimental effects on the liver and kidneys.

If you are not immediately familiar with the feelings these biochemical releases create, try two exercises, similar to those I share with
veterinarians at seminars: Imagine you have received a phone call at your
office saying that your home has just burned to the ground. Sense what
this feels like, first in your mind, then in your muscles. Feel the temperature of your hands. Feel your heart race.

If you are truly experiencing the sensations, you are experiencing
a release of adrenaline, also called epinephrine. Your heart rate is increasing, the blood vessels in your extremities are constricting, the
muscles in your shoulders, neck, and face are tightening. Soon parts of
the brain, including the sensory cortex, the thalamus, the amygdala, and
the hippocampus, begin to release biochemicals that stimulate the pi-
tuitary gland to release ACTH (adrenocorticotropic hormone). This
goes into the bloodstream and acts on the adrenal cortex, the outer part
of the adrenal gland, causing it to release steroid hormones into the cir-
culatory system.

These adrenal steroids help the body activate its energy resources.
Also activated is one of the body's numerous feedback systems, where
the steroid hormones go back up to the hippocampus and prevent further release of hormones.

If stress persists for too long a time, the hippocampus and other parts of the brain begin losing control of their release of stress hormones. At this point, stressed rats are unable to learn and can't remember how to perform certain tasks that depend on the hippocampus. Both monkeys and mice living under social stress have been found to develop not only stomach ulcers but also significant degeneration of the hippocampus. There is a similar effect in humans as well. Long-term stress also appears to impair conscious memory.

Now try a second exercise. Imagine that phone call was from someone you love deeply, someone who tells you how much he or she looks forward to seeing you tonight. If you are imaging this well, you will soon feel the release of 5-hydroxytryptamin, seratonin, enkephalins, and endorphins, neurotransmitters: all chemicals that make us happy, the same ones we feel after a good physical workout.

I believe that, at some level, these prolonged periods of stress are what keep us from being centered, from evolving to a better place.

What do I mean by evolvement?

When humans are highly evolved, we are not reacting to any particular situation based on our past patterns or on our psychological weaknesses. Instead, our response comes from a centered, tranquil place, one that represents our inner peace and our inner clarity. We react with compassion toward all living beings. We tolerate what is different from us, and we learn to love those differences rather than scorn them. We understand that we are not the center of the world.

Yes, we are all our own centers, but none of us is *the* center. We see that other beings—whether a physically challenged child, a stray kitten, a powerful executive, or a famous celebrity—all have the same nobility of life within them. All deserve respect and understanding. We are all different, and we are all the same.

I have always felt that one of the central questions of life is: When we interact with other living beings, do we choose to respond from a place of stressful fear or from a place of tranquil love?

If our thoughts center on a place of fear, we respond with a defensive posture, more likely to hurt rather than to help other living beings. This condition tends to be contagious; it spreads fearfulness to all others we encounter. If, on the other hand, our thoughts are loving and compassionate, animals (as well as humans) respond to our love with love in kind.

Acting from love, I believe, provides the best trajectory to a healthy and fruitful life. And few outside influences motivate us to act from love more than a caring relationship with an animal.

We must be careful here. There is often a tendency in books about animals to romanticize, to fantasize, to make claims that verge on senseless. I am not saying that the human-animal bond is the most important one on Earth or the most powerful. But I do feel when this bond is strong, it can help create a solid foundation for a healthy, evolved life.

At this point in time, I feel that human evolution is more related to the development of consciousness than to an actual genetic physical change. Evolving consciously means cultivating a quiet, peaceful, reflective mind to focus one's mental, physical, and spiritual energy, to allow us to deepen our personal reservoir of compassion and wisdom. Conscious evolution means that humans commit our life energy to making this planet a better place to live for all sentient beings.

The story of Bessie the horse and her companion Eliza clearly illustrates the conscious evolution that takes place when two beings open up their hearts and souls through love. Bessie was raised to be a racehorse, which meant that she was given only a year or so to live with her mother and behave like any other happy, healthy foal before she was packed off to start her intense training at a horse-breeding farm. Jerked away from a juvenile's life of playing and gamboling, she was suddenly surrounded by stable boys, grooms, caretakers, and trainers.

To Bessie's new owners, she was no more or less than a money-making commodity, something to be molded, yanked, pulled, pushed, dominated, and manipulated, all in the name of getting her fiery temper under control. Her trainers used her natural exuberance the way an unscrupulous football coach uses a young quarterback, blowing out knees and shoulders until someone younger and fresher comes along.

As she was molded into a successful machine, Bessie's emotional system froze and she withdrew from the humans around her. She had no place in her life for kindness, because no one exhibited it to her. At best, her mother and her childhood were only memories.

In my experience, most racehorses are treated equally—and that means equally poorly. If these horses aren't running fast enough, their owners are happy to inject their joints and ligaments with potentially dangerous medications. And because a racing career usually begins too early for a horse's joints to develop properly, grave lifelong problems are created.

As long as Bessie won, it didn't matter that her training caused her constant suffering. The trainers' only pain maintenance was to take care of immediate problems, not caring that this pain was a warning sign of something much more grave.

For a while, Bessie won a fair number of races. Then, like most horses, she couldn't handle the pain anymore and she started losing. It was time to unload her, so her owners sold her off to a horse trader who in turn found Eliza, an ambitious, hard-driving lawyer who'd wanted to own a horse since she was a girl. Eliza was an expert when it came to tough litigation, but she didn't know enough about horses to see up front that Bessie wasn't a loving animal but one who had been bullied into subservience and who'd survived only by controlling her emotions, which were, up to this point, mostly fear and pain.

But Eliza bought her dream, and now she had her own horse, a respite from her exhausting twelve-hour workdays in midtown Manhattan. But whenever she came to her barn to caress Bessie, the horse stood motionless, ears back, the whites of her eyes showing. Eliza's presence seemed to terrify Bessie, whose every experience with people evoked pain or a sense of being controlled. But she also knew there was no option, for if she misbehaved or tried to run, she'd be beaten. So she stayed still, quiet, afraid.

Eliza's veterinarian had conducted a prepurchase examination, checking Bessie for any lameness problems, infectious diseases, or other conditions, but he found little—just some arthritic changes in her knees and hocks; nothing, he said, that wasn't uncommon for a race-horse. He couldn't find any physical reason for her to be so difficult.

So when Bessie continued to act tense and distant, Eliza called a friend who in turn recommended that she talk to me. Because I've seen so many of these horses, I recognized the problem immediately from Bessie's withdrawn, stoic demeanor; from the way she was anxiously glancing left and right, lifting her head up as high as possible so no one could reach her, as though she knew that at any minute someone would put a twitch over her nose to restrain her and, if she didn't cooperate, smack her hard.

I went over to Bessie, gently stroked her lower neck, mane, and withers, and let her smell my hands, my armpits, and anywhere else she wanted to place her nose. I also tried some mental visualization—in my thoughts, I always try to express: I'm here to help you. I'm not here to hurt you.

Bessie then looked me right in the eyes, as though she'd heard my unspoken words and was asking, "Hey! Are you talking to me?"

I started my examination. Feeling and palpating her body, I touched the atlas. The right side was a half-inch farther forward than the left. When I carefully pressed on Bessie's neck, she couldn't control herself and she reared.

Clearly, Bessie felt that if a human came near her head, she was going to be hurt, and her natural defense mechanism was to retreat. Many other horses will strike back. Luckily, Bessie chose flight.

Still, I was able to calm Bessie down and we continued.

Bessie was a walking muscle spasm, from her neck, shoulders, and withers down to her back and hind limbs; her muscles were as tight as a taut rubber band.

And when Eliza attempted to put a saddle on Bessie, she spasmed even more, because she associated any contact with people as pain. Basically, this poor horse hurt all over.

I asked Eliza if Bessie had a hard time turning to the right.

"Yes!" she said. "How did you know?"

The answer was that the horse's body had told me, based on the extreme sensitivity I felt at different acupressure points. Some of this tenderness came from genuine pain and some of it from pure fear—but we couldn't know which part was mental and later became physical or which was physical and then became mental (the classic enigma of what comes first, mental anguish or physical pain).

I explained my techniques to Eliza as I adjusted Bessie's atlas. The horse reared up, came back down, shook her head, and then dropped it in my arms, letting out an enormous sigh as her stress and anxiety were released.

Then she began to lick my hands. The sight of Bessie licking me calmly and lovingly made Eliza cry. "Oh, my God," she said, "I had no idea she hurt so much."

I resumed the treatment with some acupuncture therapy along Bessie's back. As the deep, painful muscle spasms stopped, the softened muscles relaxed, and the endorphins flowed through her body, her head dropped lower and lower, her eyes became bleary. Her whole being eased into bliss.

Then we completed the therapeutic sessions with additional physical manipulation to correct the rest of her misalignments. For the first time in her adult life, Bessie was a pain-free horse.

I told Eliza that we had resolved Bessie's physical problems, but we still needed to work on the emotional ones. And I reassured her that with compassionate training and kindness, Bessie's fear and panic issues should gradually lessen. I also taught Eliza some exercises to help Bessie stretch.

When I returned in two weeks, Eliza was joyful. "This is just what I'd hoped for," she said. "A horse who's a friend. She used to turn her head to avoid me. Now when she sees me, she whinnies and comes galloping from the paddock. I love her, and I swear that she loves me, too."

Eliza took me out to the barn to show how true it was—the moment Bessie spotted her friend she ran over to say hello, nudging Eliza's shoulder with her face, looking deeply into her eyes. Some part of me thought I could spot in Bessie's face a sense of gratitude to this loving human who had saved her from such an unhappy life.

In Eliza's face, I could see something equally special. Her time with Bessie had worked magic. When I had first met her, she was abrupt and distant, with the demeanor of a stressed-out high-powered corporate lawyer. Now she was visibly softer, more open to the wonders of her relationship with her new animal companion.

Over time, Eliza's interaction with Bessie proved even more remarkable, teaching her how harmful abuse and fear can be to any living being, how love can work miracles. This made Eliza think more about her own friends who had been emotionally scarred and about the different episodes of abuse which she now told me had taken place in her own life—incidents that she had studiously avoided for decades, but now was taking the time to discuss with a therapist.

Wonderfully, Eliza took the issue further. Over the next few months, she looked into groups that helped neglected or abused children around the world and eventually became an energetic member of such an organization. Thanks to her connection with Bessie, Eliza was able to transform herself from what I call a "human doing" to a "human being"—instead of going through life checking off her never-ending self-created to-do list, she became a woman able to live in the moment.

Through Bessie, Eliza learned to help others. Through Eliza, Bessie learned to love.

The next thirty pages or so get preachy/New Age-y. You have been warned...

"The difference in mind between man and the higher animals, great as it is, certainly is one of degree and not of kind," wrote Charles Darwin in *Descent of Man*.

Humankind has long suffered from a tendency to search for what separates us from animals—what makes us better, what makes us unique, both as a species and as individuals. I find this investigation invariably leads to the same conclusion: The more we study what makes us different from other life-forms, the more we discover how similar we are.

As the world gets more crowded, more polluted, and more unhealthy, doesn't it seem wiser to focus more on what we share, on what can transform us from an *us-versus-them* mentality to a *we-are-all-in-this-together* approach? To think that humans can survive on Earth even as we methodically wipe out other species is not only anthropocentric and narrow-minded but potentially life-threatening.

Although it may be humbling to realize we are but the newest step in an ever-continuing chain of evolution, we can also reframe this thought: What a blessing it is that humans are indeed intimately and genetically connected to everything else. After all, aren't all of us constantly searching for a feeling of connection outside of our individual selves, always looking for community, allies, people with whom to share some goal in common? If we recognize that we truly are connected to all of life, then we can celebrate this connection each and every moment of the day, as we realize that humankind is not separate from the rest of the world but very much part and parcel of all creation.

Harvard University zoology professor and writer Stephen Jay Gould calls "dichotomization" our worst and oldest mental habit. We are continually looking for what he calls the "golden barrier," which is "a firm criterion to mark an unbridgeable gap between the mentality and behavior of humans and all other creatures."

Each time we think we have found that golden barrier, it inevitably proves to be a red herring. As we saw earlier, we once thought it was the use of tools that distinguishes us from other animals, then we found that chimps used twigs to extract termites out of nests. We thought altruistic behavior was unique to humans, then we found clear examples of altruism elsewhere. Domestication of other species seemed to be the answer until we found that ants had gotten there eons earlier.

No one will deny that structures in the human brain—notably the prefrontal cortex—have been responsible for our ability to develop the extraordinary civilizations that dot the entire world. But for the most

part, 96 percent of us is the same protoplasm as our fellow animals, another reason why co-species connections seem to take place everywhere
we go—if we can only just keep our eyes open.

A few summers back I was kayaking in Desolation Sound by
the Northern Gulf Islands on the western coast of Canada. Behind me
were majestic snowcapped peaks surrounding the mist-covered islands,
around me were the vivid gray-blue waves, gently tossing anything and
everything on their surface.

Kayaking—sitting at water level with eyes flush with the sea lions
and waterbirds—is among the most exhilarating means of communicating with marine life. The birds and sea lions appear to accept you as
one of them rather than as some foreigner looking down at their world.

I'd become accustomed to playing with sea lions when I spent time
in the Galápagos Islands, where humans have left them alone, and they
share the oceans with other beings as equals. We would frolic in the
ocean as they pulled on my snorkeling fins and tossed me pieces of coral
to catch, all the while swirling around my body as if I were another sea
creature, swimming up to my mask, inches away from my face, staring
right into my face with their big blue-brown eyes.

But up in Desolation Sound, the local fishermen have blamed a recent decrease in the population of salmon (and other fish) on the sea
lions. Actually, sea lions and salmon have thrived together in these waters for millennia, and the population decrease occurred only in tandem
with a tremendous increase in commercial fishing by fleets from
Canada, the United States, and other foreign nations.

Regardless, the fishermen's response was to shoot the sea lions.
So, over the past few months, these lovely marine mammals were being
systematically killed. Naturally, the surviving sea lions had become wary
around humans.

As I kayaked these waters that summer, I became acutely aware of
this unfortunate scenario. The sea lions watched me cautiously from a
distance, keeping themselves as unobtrusive as large animals can. Still,
I could sense that they wished to come closer—and perhaps even play
with me and my kayak. They would pop their heads up behind my boat

curiously, but when I turned my head around to look, they would quickly dive under.

After a half hour of hide-and-seek, all the while developing a modicum of trust, they stopped diving under when I turned my head around. But they still didn't come close enough to endanger their lives—in case I had happened to be one of the avenging fishermen.

Enjoying the moment, appreciating the sea lions' presence, I also felt sadness. I sat in my kayak quietly, putting down the paddle, allowing the boat to rock back and forth with the waves while the strong current began to drag me back to Cortes Island. Now the curious lions approached, checking out the scene. I closed my eyes and, trying to maintain peaceful, receptive thoughts, I allowed myself to envision the animals without fear while experiencing the sounds and smells of the saltwater inland passage.

Eventually, they came closer, bobbing their heads up higher out of the water for longer periods of time, not diving out of sight so quickly—but never as innocently as my Galápagos playmates.

When I returned to my cabin, a local friend told me that my experience was unusual. Since the recent shootings, few people had even seen a sea lion.

That evening at sunset I looked out over the calm waters and wondered how many species of animals would relate to us in special ways if they had not had prior harmful experiences. What would our lives be like if all animals had an opportunity to share their love with us, if they could approach us without the fear of death?

When I was in the Galápagos Islands, I remember, a pigeon landed on my head, and for a moment, I couldn't imagine what he would want up there. It turned out that he thought my bushy hairdo might make a wonderful place to nest, so he started digging around with his feet, cooing, nuzzling into my head, trying to make a little home; he had no fear of me whatsoever. He looked upon me as a friend rather than a predator.

This is one of the Galápagos's wonders. In his book *The Beak of the Finch*, author Jonathan Weiner tells of animals so unaccustomed to humans that many are less afraid of us than of other animals. When people walk near a group of finches, the birds often act unperturbed, yet when an owl approaches, they become alarmed. Flying up off the ground and looking for a safe haven, they may land on a nearby person. Sometimes an islander will be carrying a bamboo pole and it will suddenly seem heavy—until a glance backward reveals that a hawk has seen the opportunity for a free ride and settled on one end.

Perhaps the greatest wonder of the Galápagos is that, even today, humans still treat the animals with respect and consideration. I only wish it were like this in more places, that there were more Gardens of Eden where we could live together with love and respect.

Certainly, environmental health is a macroscopic metaphor of our own health. And as optimistic as I would like to be, I have to accept that there is more bad news than good. The quality of the environment is declining, as is our potential for good health and the good health of our animal friends. What follows are just a few examples.

The well-documented hole in the ozone layer over Antarctica is increasing faster than any scientists predicted and is causing an increase in the rate of skin cancer worldwide. Furthermore, the U.S. National Science Foundation and the Scripps Institute of Oceanography have also discovered a 3.8-million-square-mile cloud of haze (the size of the United States) hovering over the Indian Ocean during winter months. Apparently, this haze, blown over the ocean from the Indian subcontinent, China, and Southeast Asia, consists of mostly minute particles from the burning of fossil fuels. The haze causes acid rain when it returns to land and reflects solar radiation, cooling the part of the Earth beneath it, leading to less evaporation, decreased rainfall, and droughts.

Water pollution is making large areas of our seas hostile to life. There is an ever-expanding dead zone in the Gulf of Mexico where fishermen are now finding only empty nets in areas where marine life used to thrive. The zone has been blamed on the chemical runoff from the Midwest through the Mississippi River, leaving deadly pesticides and fertilizers on the Gulf's floor.

Meanwhile, whales on both America's East and West coasts have been dying in record numbers, apparently due to decreased food resources, toxins, noise and water pollution, as well as collisions with boats and fishing nets. Beluga whales in the St. Lawrence River are so filled with toxic chemicals that, when they die, they are required to be buried as toxic waste.

As for ocean noise pollution: A National Resource Defense Council report, entitled *Sounding the Depths: Supertankers, Sonar, and the Rise of Undersea Noise*, stresses that there likely exists an "acoustic threshold of viability" for many marine species and that "we are in effect carrying out a giant, uncontrolled experiment on marine life, possibly with disastrous consequences." The offshore oil industry has proposed an experiment that would allow a dozen transoceanic loudspeakers to blast 195-decibel low-frequency tones across the oceans for decades in order to conduct seismic surveys for the more than 500 new wells it drills each year on the U.S. continental shelf.

Some marine species experience hearing loss at levels below 140 decibels. Dr. Sylvia Earl, former chief scientist at the National Oceanic and Atmospheric Administration, states that: "Undersea noise is like the death of a thousand cuts. . . . The noise from shipping, seismic surveys, and military activity is creating a totally different environment than existed even fifty years ago." Try, if you can, to imagine what our marine friends are living with: a constant bombardment of ear-damaging noise levels, with nowhere to escape.

In short, the warning signs are all around us. This is not a fire drill. This is not a test. Twenty percent or more of the Earth's species will disappear—or be consigned to early extinction—during the next thirty years. The five paragraphs above could easily be extended to five huge tomes.

I am not sharing this with you to shock you into hopelessness or despair. I only want to help spread the word about this sad reality. If we are to acknowledge and benefit from biophilia, or nonlocal mind, or morphic fields, or any yet undiscovered deeper interspecies connections, we need to act now to preserve our environment.

As far as I am concerned, there is a worthy triad of goals to be addressed: the healing of people, the healing of animals, and the healing of the environment. We are all intimately and inseparably interconnected. We cannot heal our bodies of disease without healing our environment and our animals, too. We cannot find inner peace without outer peace. Likewise, we cannot create outer peace without inner peace.

My greatest hope is that whatever connections you discover between you and your animal, you can extrapolate them to all the animals in the environment. Anytime we make a loving connection with another living being, we are given a wonderful opportunity: Build on that love to help all the other beings that aren't so lucky.

I don't believe that everyone has to become an activist. I don't believe everyone should push his or her beliefs upon others. But I do feel that we should extend the discussion about the importance of the co-species connections into a few arenas where it can make a wonderful difference:

Family: By presenting our children with the gift of an animal companion, we help them establish firm foundations for developing character based on respect, love, forgiveness, and altruism. Children raised on small farms where animals are considered part of a larger family develop a different attitude toward animals than inner-city kids; they are often blessed with an awareness that all living beings are part of a larger extended family, not limited only to two-legged beings.

Medicine: If animals indeed have feelings, we need to rethink how we treat them in animal hospitals and laboratories. In many animal hospitals, their psychological well-being is often ignored. In laboratories, we should consider creating a space of gratitude for the sacrifices they make for our benefit. Better housing for lab animals should be required. Conscious enrichment development programs should be made to keep them stimulated. And of utmost priority should be an awareness of their pain and suffering, with the goal of doing everything possible to keep it as minimal as possible.

We can also create much warmer hospital environments for ailing animals. Cats, for example, love to hide; simply placing a paper bag in a cage can give them a feeling of security around barking dogs and other unfamiliar noises. I always recommend that clients who are leaving their animal friend at a hospital or a boarding kennel bring something that is imbued with their own as well as their animal's smell, such as a stuffed toy or a favorite blanket. Some care facilities go further: Colorado State University's Veterinary School has instituted both indoor and outdoor visiting areas, as well as a meditation area where people can spend peaceful time with their companion.

Food: The way we raise and slaughter animals for food production must be reevaluated. I don't necessarily advocate unqualified vegetarianism, but why not become aware of the sacrifices animals make to become our daily meals? Wouldn't an agro industry that is mindful of humane methods of slaughter be a welcome alternative from today's harsh, frightening reality? The truth is, I know few people who have witnessed animals being led to their deaths who ever want to eat meat again.

Care Facilities: Why not add co-species love to the lives of individuals who are missing it by locating animal shelters in close proximity to orphanages and senior citizen homes? The children can train and take care of stray animals, and lonely senior citizens can share the joy of connectedness.

Not far from my practice is an inspiring institution called Green Chimneys, which takes in neglected, abused, and otherwise troubled children and gives them stray animals to care for. The animals, many of whom were abused or nearly killed themselves, are given a chance to thrive. Remarkably often, the children learn lessons valuable enough to put them back on their feet and give them a sense of love, respect, and compassion for all beings.

Recent programs in corrections facilities have incorporated animal companions for repeat offenders. Many of these prisoners have never learned about love and responsibility, and through caring for the animals they begin to understand both. So far these programs have been enormously successful.

The Environment: One of the many gifts our animal friends can give us is a renewed relationship to the natural world—a walk in the woods accompanied by an animal is a powerful healing modality. But this will be an increasingly rare experience if there are no woods to walk in.

In an attempt to protect our greenspaces from the ever-increasing onslaught of development, numerous organizations are not only trying to purchase land and gain conservation easements but are connecting many of these greenspaces into vaster areas known as greenways or greenbelts. One such organization is the Conservation Fund, which cosponsors with the Kodak Corporation and the National Geographic Society an annual National Greenways Award, supporting local efforts to create greenbelts throughout the country.

One trail currently in formation will connect all the major cities on the East coast. Other greenbelts are being developed along rivers, such as the Housatonic Valley Association in northwestern Connecticut and Massachusetts, from the beginning of the once polluted and dying Housatonic to the end. Another group in this region, the Roxbury Horse Association, is creating a long path of horse trails through different farms so that people and animals can travel through a continuous, contiguous space.

On a larger scale, the Tucson-based Wildlands Project is attempting to ensure the vitality of ecosystems by establishing a group of vast wildlife corridors—large parcels of land free from subdivisions, mining, timber, roads, and other invasive activities—where animals can roam safely.

I call this vision the connection from *our heartspace to our greenspace.* The opening of our hearts to our animal companions needs to be expanded to the environment we all inhabit—after all, if we do not preserve the environment, we will have no animal companions to connect with.

I am not being a dreamy romantic, not by any means. This is a true call for self-preservation, because our species is dependent on all other species for existence. We are not isolated pieces of DNA, distinct from all other life. We are all part of the same environment, kindred spirits capable of deriving great gifts from the remarkable connections we can make with the living, breathing, loving creatures all around us. It is inappropriate for us to act as omniscient gods, deciding which species on our planet are expendable and which are worth preserving. Consciousness resides in all beings, and all consciousness deserves a chance to prosper.

This is why, at this precious moment at the beginning of the new millennium, amid the disappearance of species and ecological devastation, we must take advantage of this window of opportunity to do everything possible to support all manner of life. If humans are able to understand the potential impact of our relationships with our fellow creatures, we can learn how to open up our hearts, how to stimulate buried compassion, how to care for other beings.

Today many people believe that technology has all the answers for our future. But a technological world where faster is never fast enough and where newer is never new enough leaves us little room for our heartspace, that quiet, peaceful place within each of us that connects us with all living beings. Technology can do many extraordinary things, but it can't teach us to have a more compassionate heart.

So go forth and make a conscious, active effort to rejoice in the interconnectedness of all of life, every day. Love yourself by extending love to all other living beings. And whenever possible, do something special to support the beauty of life on our one and only planet, Mother Earth.

PART IV

Becoming Kindred

Spirits

One

Creating a

Spiritual Bond:

Seven Ways to Foster

Kindred Connections

Will humanity love life enough to save it?
—E. O. Wilson

I believe that it is time for every one of us to acknowledge

a deep, spiritual connection with all of life, that it is time

to act moment by moment, day by day, in a loving, com-

passionate manner with all beings with whom we share this planet.

As we enter the new millenium, I believe that it is time to reeval-

uate our relationships with every living being and look for ways to

deepen and strengthen those connections. Above all, we must remember that animals and humans share similar feelings of pain, fear, joy, and love. We must realize that care for all animals, humans, and their environment must be based on compassion for all beings and a respect for their body, mind, and spirit. This care must also be based on the awareness of the power of the human-animal bond. We must create a new paradigm for animal health care, Integrative Veterinary Medicine, and appreciate the interrelatedness of human health, animal health, and environmental health. Finally, we must always remember that kindred connections are grounded in an awareness and acknowledgment of deeper levels of communication and healing that we all share.

Throughout my life, I have always extrapolated the experiences I've accrued along my spiritual journey to my connections with animals. Indeed, the more I grow in spirit, the deeper my connection with nature. And as I dared to step beyond the limits of conventional veterinary medical thinking to share these thoughts with friends and colleagues, I realized that many other people were having similar experiences—but were as reluctant to express them as I was for fear of being ridiculed by the Western medicine establishment.

In this chapter, I would like to share some methods that I have found helpful in deepening our relationships with our kindred spirits. The goal is to connect with our animal companions at a much deeper level than any of us ever realized was possible—a connection that goes past taking a dog out for a walk, or giving your horse food, or changing the litter box. Instead, I mean the connections that prove we are all living beings capable of more than just a moment in time together, but a commingling of the mind, body, and soul.

Deepak Chopra states that if we consider the body as a vessel or a cup, any injury or wound, whether physical, emotional, or spiritual, is a crack in that cup, and no matter how much love you pour into it, it will always leak out until the crack is fully healed.

As you have seen throughout this book, animals help us heal that crack, because the kindred love we share with animals can regenerate that healing potential in all of us. This fills our cup with love and then we can share that love with others as it overflows out of our own cup, becoming like a salve on a wound, like the soothing lick of a dog's tongue.

The stories of these loving connections, which I keep hearing about every day, continue to surprise me with their diversity, their warmth, and sometimes their humor. For instance, not long ago, a neighbor introduced me to Makito, a Japanese cowboy who had come to America to follow his passion, which was to raise bison. The man bought some land in Colorado and some animals, and soon he was living his dream.

One day, not many winters later, Makito found a tiny baby bison who had been abandoned by her mother in a snowdrift. Amelia, as Makito soon named her, was half-dead, starving, lying on her back, waving her spindly legs in the air. Stricken with love, Makito picked her up and took her home. He fed her from a bottle, caring for the infant as though she were his own.

Amelia, knowing no one else, soon imprinted on the cowboy, assuming he was her mother. She began following him throughout the house, observing him shave, sharing food with him in the kitchen, watching television with him at night. But also, because she was a bison, Amelia grew far too big to stay in the house, so reluctantly Makito introduced her to the herd. There she seemed to make friends, and he walked sadly back to his cabin.

But imprinting is one of nature's strongest forces, and Amelia loved humans. So whenever she saw one, she would rush over to be petted, to be touched, to be loved. Normally, the instinct to love isn't a problem, but in this case the other bison, highly sensitive to movement in the herd, joined in the rush, which meant that anytime Amelia saw a human, she caused a stampede of bison across the plains.

This wouldn't do at all, so Makito had to take Amelia back home (perhaps this was what she really wanted) and prepare a pen for her adjacent to the house. Now Amelia and Makito could be together again—forever.

There was one more problem. As a baby, Amelia had grown to enjoy watching television with her friend, so whenever Makito turned on the set, Amelia would try to push her head through a window, breaking anything her enormous body came near. An alteration had to be made to Makito's home: a window large enough so that whenever Amelia felt like watching television, she could do so. When I met them, they were sharing a quiet moment together at sunset, watching an old Hollywood Western.

·

Every one of us can incorporate co-species connections with our kindred spirits into our lives in a multitude of ways, even if all we can give is a little time each week. The following are seven ways that may help you create a kindred connection, one perhaps a bit more intimate than the one you already share.

Co-Species Meditation

We now know that a good relationship with your companion animal is good for your health. We also know that meditation helps to lower stress and enhance our overall well-being.

Why not combine the two?

During our normal daily life, we rarely create moments of quiet, when our mind is silent and our thoughts are not running through our brains at the speed of light. When we meditate, there is a moment of silence between our thoughts, what Deepak Chopra calls "the gap." This is a time when our minds are quiet, yet awake. This gap between our thoughts is where magic can occur, where we lapse into clarity, where creativity can begin. If you experience this new level of peace within yourself and with your animal friend, it will enhance not only your kindred connection but, ultimately, the way you live each day.

According to Dr. Herb Benson at the Harvard University Medical School, who has conducted excellent research on the physiologic benefits of meditation, all religions and all meditation techniques appear to share certain traits. The most obvious is the continuous repetition of one particular vowel, sound, word, or thought that helps to focus the mind. This focus has varied around the world, from Hail Marys to the Hindu chants of Om Nama Shivaya, the Buddhist chants of Om Mani Padme Hung, the Jewish prayer Shema Yisrael, and so on.

One simple technique that I have found to be universal, nonsectarian, and very effective, is to visualize the breath moving in and out of our bodies. Breathing often reflects our moods. And from a scientific perspective, it affects our entire physiology. Breathing too fast or too slow can actually change the chemical balance in our body, making it more or less alkaline or acidic.

Occasionally, when clients enter my office extremely upset over their companion's condition, before we do anything else, I suggest they sit down and take some deep, slow breaths. If they tell me that they can't, I offer to help. I help them visualize their breathing, as if the air flowing in and out of their body was a shining stream of brilliant energy.

After a few minutes, I watch as the anxiety disappears from their faces, their eyes soften, their faces unwrinkle. They exhale a sigh of relief.

Just like my clients, you can change your feelings and state of mind—and those of your animal—just by changing your breathing. Try this exercise in your home:

1. Find a quiet, peaceful place.

2. Sit in a comfortable position in an easy chair or on a cushion. You do not have to sit cross-legged in the lotus position—anything you find comfortable will do, including sitting upright. But if you can keep your back straight—horizontally or vertically—you will find it easier to breathe.

3. Close your eyes. Breathe very slowly and deeply through your nose. Visualize your breath as a clear or white light gradually

moving from your nose down into your throat, into your lungs, broadening into your chest, and then continuing down into your abdomen.

Finally, let it go deep into your pelvis and hold it there for as long as you feel comfortable. As you practice, you will be able to hold your breath longer and control it more easily.

Then slowly exhale and visualize the breath of light traveling up your back, through your spine, up into the abdomen, the chest, your neck, head, and then out through your mouth.

Personally, I find it helpful to count from one to five to center my mind; others use a repetitive sound or chant. Whichever you prefer is fine. Begin with just a few minutes and, as you gain comfort, increase it to five, ten, fifteen, and finally twenty minutes once or even twice a day. Many people find the best time is early in the morning and late at night, when your pace tends to slow.

If you find it hard to focus and want some object to help you concentrate, try looking at a candle, or summoning up pleasurable images, or using audio stimulation, such as tapes of specific sounds such as rainy days or soft ocean waves, to help tune your brain waves away from everyday cares and into a state of focused calm and clarity.

By stimulating and directing positive feelings, we can actually change the essence of our inner patterns, because when these attitudes circulate through our system, our physical and chemical energies are transformed. Our neurotransmitters and other biochemical information substances will increase and will improve our overall health of mind, body, and spirit, thereby allowing us to connect with—and benefit—all other beings.

Anguttara Nkaya in the *Gradual Sayings* describes the benefits of meditation eloquently: "Suppose a pool of water, turbid, stirred up, and muddied, exists. Just so a turbid mind is. Suppose a pool of water, pure, tranquil, and unstirred, where a man sees oysters and shells, pebbles and gravels, and schools of fish. Just so is an untroubled mind."

4. Once you feel comfortable with this exercise, try visualizing yourself together with your favorite animal as you do your breathing exercise. I find my animal friends inevitably surround me when I am meditating, most often lying by my side or near my feet, and it sounds as though they too begin meditating— or perhaps they just fall asleep.

My cat Chi always lies by my side. Quietude seems to come easily to a cat. However, these still moments sometimes make my ever-persistent golden retriever Shanti think this would be a great time to play, and he drops his slimy tennis ball into my meditative lap and waits for me to throw it across the room. Still, most of the time he realizes that this is a serene time and he will sit down quietly.

Such meditation, surrounded by our animals and at peace with ourselves, allows us all an opportunity to return to a pace of life that was normal to humankind until this last century. When our pace slows down, we perceive and experience life differently. We feel calmer, we are more receptive to feelings of joy and inner peace, we live in the present. We experience the finer details of life that often go unnoticed: the sun shining through the window glass, throwing off prisms of refracted light; the trees in the backyard glistening in the rain; or the unconditional love our animal companions feel for us and the love we feel for them.

Kindred Relaxation

*J*f meditating isn't easy for you, try this exercise instead.

Have you ever seen a cat perfectly relaxed, his eyes gently closed, his body limp as an overcooked noodle, curled on a chair with his paws hanging out into thin air? Or a dog, sleeping quietly, almost melting into a plush carpet? Or a horse, on her side, lying out in a field of grass, snoring gently and rhythmically?

Have you ever wished you could be so relaxed? You can—by using your animal friends as the focus of your visualization.

Once when I was camping at 12,000 feet in the Himalayas on a frosty cold spring night, I was accompanied by some yak herders and their yaks, as well as stout horses, goats, and Bhutanese mountain dogs. When dusk came, I set up my tent in a spot that looked quiet and peaceful. But shortly after I fell asleep, my tent began to move. Looking up, I saw snouts poking in, making me realize that my tent was a novel curiosity to all these animals.

Recognizing that there was no danger, I used the animals' heavy breathing as a focus of my concentration, breathing in and out as deeply as they did until I fell into blissful sleep. This worked for a while. But later that night, one of the horses lay down just outside the tent and began to snore. If any of you have a snoring partner—animal or human—you can imagine the challenge I now faced.

But again, I took advantage of the deep, rhythmic inhalation and exhalation as a meditative device and eventually dozed off again.

When I woke up at sunrise and looked outside, I discovered it wasn't just one horse lying near me—it was a veritable zoo of sleeping beauties, all still fast asleep, their slow breathing creating clouds of vapor as they inhaled and exhaled with serene depth into the cold air.

Here is an exercise that can help you relax at home—or wherever you find yourself with your animal friend.

1. Again, find a quiet, peaceful place.

2. Sit upright comfortably on a pillow or in a chair or lay down on your back in what in yoga is called the "corpse pose."

3. Close your eyes.

4. Visualize your animal friend or a favorite animal in his absolutely most relaxed bodily position, flat out on the ground, his eyes gently closed, his breath deep, his sleep relaxed and

pure. (You may find your dog or cat will lie down close by you at this time—somehow both my dog and cat inevitably end up alongside me whenever I envision them sleeping.)

5. Begin breathing as recommended in the meditation exercise above: deeply, through your nose, into your throat, chest, and then your abdomen. Allow the breath to sit there for a moment. Visualize your breath doing this, either as a ball or mist of white light.

6. Slowly breathe as described previously. Visualize the breath slowly and gently being released from your abdomen up through your back, neck, head, and out through your nose in a slow, calm, rhythmic pattern.

7. Feel your body and mind relax, again thinking about your favorite animal friend, equally relaxed.

8. After five to twenty minutes have gone by, feel how relaxed you are. There you are, mind, body, and spirit all at peace. Ahhhh. . . .

9. Try to incorporate this exercise into your life. By visualizing your animal friends in pure repose, you will find it easier to reach that state of relaxation many of us yearn for but seldom find. If other thoughts come to your mind, don't be upset. Acknowledge those thoughts and let them leave without resistance. My first acupuncture teacher told me that he envisioned his thoughts as waves in the ocean; as a thought enters one side of his brain, he sees another leave like a wave washing out the other side of his brain. Eventually, the waves settle down into ripples and finally into a peaceful, still pond. You will begin to yearn for those moments more and more.

Sharing Mindful Moments

A MINDFUL WALK WITH A DOG

Heeding your dogs as they encounter their world offers you special insight into their lives, their interests, their presence. You become more aware of their environment: the smells, the sounds, the beauty. Through them, you extend your own sense of touch, your feelings, your sight—allowing your world to become wondrous and more engaging. You are more inclined to stay in the moment rather than worry about tomorrow or yesterday. How concerned can you be over your taxes when you and your dog are luxuriating in a beautiful spring day? You can always return to your work. You can't always share a golden moment with a true friend.

As you walk, recede into a moment of quiet within yourself. Breathe in, breathe out, breathe in again, breathe out, and as you do, visualize yourself alongside your dog, walking at your dog's level.

Then visualize being inside your dog's head, inside his mind, inside his body. Imagine what the world would be like from his perspective. Watch what he watches—the butterfly dancing up ahead, the fluttering leaves in nearby trees. Look at his ears. What makes them perk up, what sounds do they hear? Watch his interaction with the environment, watch what happens when he comes into contact with another dog. Is he being dominant or passive? Is he scrunching down on the ground, wagging his tail submissively, or does his tail go up, his ears forward, and signs of aggression are clear?

Understand—if you can—what he's smelling. Feel how your dog appreciates the miracle of the moment. Use this as a reminder to stop and smell the roses along the way.

Just today I took my dog Shanti for a walk on a perfect, crisp fall day by a beautiful brook. Although it was a marvelous afternoon, I found myself slipping into worries about my patients. Just then Shanti caught my attention with a bark, and he looked up, sniffing the fresh air by a large boulder decorated with lush ferns, shadowed by bright yellow-, red-, and orange-leafed maple trees, alongside a small waterfall lending trickling sounds to this magical moment. He and I stood still, soaking in the full magnificence of our unmitigated sensual pleasure. How could I divert my energy fretting about work when Shanti was offering me such a lovely alternative?

Just as your dog does, try experiencing sensations before you have words for them. Say you're walking in the park in the springtime and the flowers are coming up. Close your eyes, rid yourself of all other thoughts, and immerse yourself in their smell. You're connecting to them purely through sensuous experience.

Besides giving you a chance to feel closer to your dog, this is also a wonderful way to bring joy into your life. Maybe your life isn't as happy or fulfilling as you'd like it to be. Chances are your dog's life is. Take him for a walk and let him introduce you to the simple pleasure a wonderful smell can provide and let him guide you into finding the little moments of peace and happiness that are buried in the world around us.

And, of course, your dog benefits, too. He experiences the joy of your presence rather than being rushed back inside.

By the way, although it's unusual, there are cats too who enjoy a walk. Philippa Kaye is a Manhattan-based choreographer and dancer whose companion is a one-year-old ruddy Abyssinian named Spreewell (loosely named after the infamous New York Knick, as Spreewell can jump high and has a tendency to claw on Philippa's neck). When Spreewell was only three months old, Philippa bought him a small dog's harness and began taking him for walks in the city. "I grew up with cats in the country," she says, "and it made me sad to think he wouldn't be able to go outside." She walks her cat daily, and he loves it, pawing at the door and meowing whenever he thinks it's time for an outing. They do run into dogs, but for the most part, "if the dog is medium or small," Kaye says, "Spree wants to check them out and sometimes chases them. If they're big, he puffs up and snarls. He doesn't ever run."

A MINDFUL MOMENT WITH A CAT

True, most cats don't like being walked. Some don't even like to move when you're as much as looking at them. But there are many other ways to connect with felines. Spend some real time in their presence, get down to their level, take a walk into their mind, if you can.

Let's say you come home from a stressful day at work and your cat is lying on a sofa or chair, waiting for you. You may be exhausted, but your cat is overjoyed to see you.

Connect with him. Put down all your physical and mental baggage and sit. Talk to him. Say hello, just as though he were a person. Pet him. You're releasing his endorphins. He starts purring. You feel like purring inside. It's a loving connection.

But, you say, your cat always wants his food first. Do you blame him? Maybe he's been waiting all day to eat. In this case, feed him right away and wait until he's done with his meal. Then he'll come rubbing against your feet or jump in your lap.

Just as you have a personality, your cat has a "felinality." Get to know it, honor it, enjoy it. If he is a lap cat, take him in your lap. If he wants to rub against you, let him do that. If he doesn't relish being picked up, don't. He'll like you all the more for respecting his wishes.

Scratch his neck, pat his back, discover where he wants to be touched. Some cats love being scratched at the far end of their back, by their tail—but some don't and may swat you. A small minority will roll over on their back and let you caress their tummy. Some cats love having their ears massaged, while others enjoy having the very top of their head gently stroked. Learn what he likes and delight in your shared connection.

Don't always stand up above your cat. Move to his level. Lie on the floor, the couch, the bed, and acquaint yourself with the view of his world. Get to know his pace, his speed, his metabolism. One of the worst things you can do is assume that your pace is also your cat's. You come home frenetic and you fuss about at your stepped-up rhythm.

Your cat doesn't like that. He hasn't had a rough day. Start breathing at his rate and slow down to his rhythm. You may be surprised how much more he will communicate with you once he feels that you're both on the same wavelength.

Many of you may be thinking that you already do this with your cat or dog. But do you always consciously recognize the benefits that you both are giving and receiving in those moments? This conscious acknowledgment is the key.

As with dogs, the point is to be in the moment. Your animal companion is giving you a marvelous opportunity to experience life from a new perspective. Take him up on the offer. Leave your world and enter his and consider it a minivacation.

A MINDFUL MOMENT WITH A HORSE

To me, there are few sweeter, more meditative sounds than the munching of horses at dinnertime, when the barn is closed down and you are alone with your animals. A mindful moment with a horse in a quintessential country barn can be absolutely magical. However, it can also be challenging amid some of the more modern touches, including vacuum cleaners, lawnmowers, and all the noisy business of show barns. If this is your situation, try to find a quieter spot or a quiet time in the barn for this exercise.

Horses communicate with one another through a full range of sensory signals. You can connect with your animal at a deeper level by being aware of all these forms of expression and then mimicking them.

Begin by rubbing your hands on your horse, getting her smell on you and vice versa; this is both a sensory and a chemical signal, allowing her to recognize you via your odor.

Put your nose near her nostril and breathe in, breathe out as she does. (Be very, very careful, however, or you may be nipped—you must know your horse well prior to doing this.)

As you breathe, slow down to her breathing rate, and you may find she actually takes a deep breath at that moment, sighs, and relaxes.

Touch her in some manner—lean against her, let her head hang over your shoulders, or gently pet or groom her. Stay quiet, soak in the hushed sounds of the barn, and just be. Sense how it feels to just be with her.

Horses are highly sensitive creatures and can attune themselves to our emotions if we just give them the chance. They want to communicate with us and often appear perplexed when we don't make the effort.

As I've mentioned, grooming is one of the most important means of communication between animals. Intraspecific (horse to horse) grooming of preferred sites such as the neck and withers will actually decrease the animal's heart rate, as compared to grooming of less favored spots such as the belly. It is also interesting to note that when a stallion nips at the inside of a mare's lower leg to stimulate sexual interest, this coincides with a very important acupuncture point, Spleen 6, which has important hormone regulating effects. I imagine animals instinctively know that touching certain points on the body can produce physiologic effects.

When you're alone with your horse, talk to her as you imagine she would talk to you. Speak in a soothing voice or attempt a nicker. Don't shout or become irritated if you don't get a response. Sometimes, out of frustration, we may yell at a horse or dog or cat, assuming in the moment that our animal friends actually understand us. I often think of a scene in the movie *Bananas*, where Woody Allen is being introduced to a South American general. Instead of interpreting Allen's words into Spanish, his translator merely repeats them, louder and slower, still in English.

Since we are the species that possesses the more flexible problem-solving brain, it's our responsibility to understand the communications gap and figure out how to overcome it. It is not the horse's job to learn to read our minds.

A MINDFUL MOMENT WITH BIRDS

People who don't own birds seldom understand how intelligent and communicative they can be. I have experienced many remarkable moments connecting with winged creatures—parakeets, cockatiels, parrots, even wild birds at the bird feeder—and found them remarkably uplifting.

My cowriter, Gene, never quite believed me until recently, when a wren flew into an open window in his city apartment. His cat Minnie decided that the bird would make a nice lunch, so she chased her around the apartment until Gene heard the terrified wren bang into a skylight. She fell to the floor slightly dazed, which gave Gene the chance to throw a light blanket over her. He then gently bundled her up and brought her to his roof garden. The bird was still in shock when Gene unfolded the blanket, so he sat with her as she recovered her senses. When she finally came to, she simply stared at him curiously, as if to say, "Why am I sitting on this human's lap?" The answer seemed to be: "This is not a good idea," for she suddenly flew off.

Gene assumed that was the end of it. But the next morning when he went up to his garden, the bird was sitting on his table (she was easily identifiable by two white tufts by her wing). He said hello, and she watched him as he read his paper. More remarkably, she appeared every morning for a month, not looking to Gene for food, but just sitting by him as he read the paper. It seemed to be a form of gratitude, perhaps even of bonding.

Something similar happened to me not long ago. As I was working on this book, a strangely marked chickadee accidentally flew into our bedroom window and fell on the deck unconscious, despite the normally effective multitude of hawk decals that we have applied to the glass. By administering CPR, the Bach flower rescue remedy, and acupressure, I was able to revive my dazed friend. After a few moments of calmly sitting in my hands looking at me, she took off.

The next morning as I was staring out the bathroom window, I saw this same chickadee looking eye-to-eye at me through the glass. At first I thought she had been mesmerized by a reflection, so I walked out on the deck to confirm my hunch and found the light wasn't appropriate for any reflection. For the next few days, she came by the bathroom window each morning to watch me, and whenever I sat out on the deck, she'd fly within a few feet of me and chirp. Like Gene, I couldn't help but think that she was showing her appreciation for saving her life.

As with other animals, the more you think about what you would do, think, or say if you were a bird, and how birds would express themselves to you in human talk, the better your connection will be. Here are some exercises and thoughts to help you communicate better with your winged companions:

1. Create a peaceful environment. Birds like stationary objects; fast movement is often an alarm signal in their language and translates into quick exit, stage left. So whether you are connecting with a wild bird or your domestic companion, sit quietly. Avoid body language that might be interpreted as aggressive, such as standing right by a bird feeder.

   If your bird is in a cage, sit next to her. Or, if you allow her to sit on your shoulder, try that. Close your eyes and visualize peacefulness. Breathe deeply and slowly. Whenever I do this outside near my bird feeder, the message seems to get out quickly. I see the boughs of the spruce, ash, and hickory trees that surround my back deck quickly fill with chickadees, tufted tit mouse, nuthatches, woodpeckers, and more. If there is no feed in the feeder, they let me know instantly by landing on the railing and chirping incessantly.

   As soon as I put out seeds, the sound of their chirps changes and they become more patient. One particular chickadee comes over, sits within arm's reach, and just looks at me right in the eye. Another isn't quite that brave, and he lands, grabs some seeds, and takes off. The sound of their fluttering wings brings a level of peace that no words can describe. Perhaps it resonates with some primitive genetic link, a biophilian connection to an ancient time when primates and birds lived together in the forests.

Birds enjoy consistency; a new object or a new animal in the household or anything out of the ordinary can perturb them. A routine provides them with security, so try to connect with them at the same time each day, so they know to look forward to it.

Fill their lives with gracious sounds. My bookkeepers' birds love to sing along with music on the radio. They particularly seem to relish Mozart.

2. Communicate with touch. Your bird may begin to nuzzle you or groom you as you fall into a quiet, peaceful moment. You may choose to scratch him gently on his head, the back of his neck, his breast, or even his ears, which often makes them quiet and peaceful. He is constantly acquiring new feathers; when you pet him against the base of his feathers, they open up more, as they do when he preens and grooms himself.

Most birds are as sensitive as other animals to nervous, frenetic energy. So when you touch them, breathe deeply and find that calm place within you.

3. Talk. Birds love to be sung to. Or talk to them in a quiet tone, as if you were sharing thoughts with a human friend. Try mimicking their sounds and see if you get a response. It always amazes me that whenever I do this, they respond quickly, looking at me with their heads cocked sideways as if they know exactly what I am saying. On the other hand, perhaps they are merely wondering why my imitation was so poor, as though I were speaking a foreign language with a terrible accent.

Birds tend to be flock animals, so it is better to have more than one. They also like to eat with you, too. By sharing meals, just as by talking to them, you become part of their flock. So go forth and fly together!

Think Like an Animal

*O*ne way to become closer to your animal companions is to try to think the way your animal friend may be thinking.

Temple Grandin, a professor of animal science at Colorado State University and the author of *Thinking in Pictures*, grew up an autistic child. As difficult as that was, Temple nonetheless gained many remarkable insights into the way creatures—human and nonhuman—behave.

Temple believes that animals think in sensory images—visual pictures combined with smell, light, and sound patterns—just as she does. Most people think using words, and their response to an image or experience derives from their intellect rather than their senses. When Temple remembers something, she does not see or hear a word in her mind, but experiences the memory emotionally, *feeling* the image rather than intellectualizing it. This causes other visual clues to be released, as well as other emotions.

I find Temple's personal story inspiring because she has been able to take a painful childhood affliction and turn it into something positive. By combining her visual abilities with her love of animals, she began to observe cattle and sheep by trying to see the world from their point of view. In doing so, she helped develop revolutionary new guidelines and more humane approaches to the care and slaughter of food animals.

For instance, through exploring these places at eye level along with the animals, she was able to extrapolate from her own emotional reactions how they responded to various stimuli and determined what made them unhappy, what frightened them, and so on. She then developed pathways with proper lighting and curves, as well as minimal distractions, that allowed the animals to follow their normal behavioral patterns and neither hear nor see other animals slaughtered in front of them.

On the basis of her research, Temple feels that people who are picture-based may connect better with animals than those who are word-based. What that suggests to me is that all of us can communicate and understand our animal friends' responses more clearly if we attempt to perceive life more visually.

Here is an exercise I have developed to help you connect with your animal friends via their picture-based thinking patterns:

Get down to eye level with your animal friend—dog, cat, horse, goat, sheep, cow, whomever—and notice what you both can see. What objects, forms, shapes, colors are in your line of sight? Do you see faces? Scenery? Moving objects? Other living beings? How do these objects make you feel?

For instance, I find my dog Shanti likes to stick his neck through the posts on my deck. When I got down to his level, I realized why— he was observing the view across the valley, unobstructed by the posts. If I were him, I would like that view as well. This made me realize that Shanti has just as many preferred ways of seeing the world as I do— which made me begin to understand more fully his other behavior patterns.

Try to visualize what your animal companions are seeing at different times and think about how you might experience the world with those images in your mind. Looking at the world through your friends' picture-based thinking can give you a new appreciation of the way they respond to you, other animals, and their environment. After all, isn't switching positions with others the best way to understand them better and be more sensitive to their needs?

Remember, when you truly connect with animals, you can learn wonderful lessons. For instance, I recently went to Eastern Washington University to interview Washoe, the chimp who learned sign language over thirty years ago and has been communicating with humans ever since. On my way to see her, I pondered what I would ask a chimp who can actually share some of her thoughts. What is the meaning of life? What are your greatest desires? Do you think much about the past? The future? Are you happy? All these questions crossed my mind.

When I arrived, the caretakers said that I could communicate through sign language through the glass windows. I quietly entered the room, wondering how the conversation might proceed. What deep inner secrets might she share?

Washoe immediately signed for me to untie my shoelace and take my shoe off. Next she signaled that I should tickle the bottom of my feet and that she wanted hers tickled, too. And then she laughed and laughed.

Washoe taught me one of my life's greatest lessons: Lighten up! Don't take things so seriously. When you are troubled, truly listen to your animal friends—see what they do to play or have fun or what they do that makes you laugh—and savor the joy of the moment.

A Blessing Exercise

*W*hy a blessing exercise? Because such an observance helps us develop what I call an "attitude of gratitude" for all of life. It shows our appreciation for our animal friends, it helps us remember to thank them for all their gifts.

The next time you are sitting on a chair and your cat is in your lap, or your dog is by your feet, or your bird is chirping in her cage, or your snake or your iguana or your turtle is nearby, or when you are standing next to your horse or cow at the barn, think of all the ways that your friend brings you joy.

Start by thanking them verbally for bringing you that joy. From there, bless them. Yes, actually say, "Bless you" or "Thank you."

Just by saying those words aloud, you stimulate a particular thought process in your mind. Your animals will pick up on your mood—your joy—and they will begin to appreciate you more. The more they appreciate you, the more you appreciate them, and you've started a gratitude-attitude cycle.

By creating these new, loving patterns in your mind, you will form deeper relationships not only with your animal companions but with all beings: two-legged, four-legged, or winged.

If you wish, take this a step further and redirect your positive connection with your animal companions outward to the humans you come into contact with that day. Maybe these thoughts can help remind you to come from a place of gratitude and appreciation for those around you. Try doing this even when confronted with people who might otherwise anger or upset you, such as that rude cashier at the supermarket. The right attitude can help you move from being angry to understanding that, maybe, the cashier was just having a bad day. Imagine how amazed he will be if, after he's rude to you, you gently thank him for packing your bags. The advantages of this kind of behavior come back to reward you: Instead of leaving the store enraged, you leave cheerful and smiling.

How does this blessing exercise improve your life? By respecting all living beings as sacred, you'll be able to treat your animal friends with a new level of respect, compassion, and love. No one is a saint, and I'm not saying that in the space of a week you'll walk through life without grudges, grumbles, or groans. But just a step in this direction will help. You will start to feel how blessed you are to share this time, and this Earth, with your friends. And I believe they will want to be closer to you, because they will perceive your love, and they will respond with more love.

Talking and Listening

J am endlessly impressed with Charles Darwin. For instance, in his book *The Expression of the Emotions in Man and Animals*, Darwin was noting similarities between humans and nonhumans at a time when few other scientists ventured near the subject. The idea was too frightening for readers for decades to come.

Certainly, we now realize that all species share certain genetic traits. If a scared cat is hissing, we know this reflects a reflex fear reaction, not dissimilar to our own crying or yelling. Today it is not so odd to say that if you listen to your animals' vocalizations, you may discover a great deal about them.

So listen to their whinnies, meows, barks, chirps, or hisses. Take an anthropomorphic stretch and think: If I were making those intonations, with that voice, with that expression, what would I be saying? What would I be wanting? What would I be thinking?

For example, I've learned that my cat Chi talks like clockwork. At 5 P.M., he wants his dinner and he starts meowing until he gets it. Then there's another kind of meow that happens in the morning, and after he eats, which says, "I want to go outside." There are still more meows for attention, for love, for a bird on the window, for a jump off a chair. Some of my clients swear their cats have vocabularies of twenty-five or more sounds.

We are all trying to live in this world together. But not everyone speaks English (and that includes humans, too). Animals cohabit your environment, and if you really think about it, when they talk to you, they probably assume you know what they are saying. Why not? You give them food, you give them shelter—doesn't it follow they figure you're smart enough to understand even their most simple utterances?

As the self-designated caretakers of the world, we have the responsibility to strive to comprehend our fellow living beings. When you stop to listen, you are being mindful, attentive, and conscious. You are fostering a co-species connection. Animals don't ask for just a little attention. When they want your attention, they want it all. Unfortunately, most of us are frantically running around, leading our complicated human existences, rarely being fully present, always thinking about past or future. Listening to your animals and working to create those deep connections can be a wonderful source of grounding.

When you're listening to animals, your best move is to be receptive. Don't thrust your will onto them. Come from an open, loving, nonaggressive place. When your mind visualizes that place, you can become the embodiment of it to your animal; your body language will reflect this, and your friend will be more receptive, more willing to talk to you.

And remember to talk back. I talk to my cat and my dog all the time. I listen to their vocalizations, mimic them, and watch their responses. When I talk to my cat, it seems as though he looks back at me and says, "Now you're talking my language." I believe he then launches into a much more profound discussion, giving me a different meow whenever I meow back at him. I'm not always sure what we're saying when we talk back and forth, but he seems to enjoy it, even if he may think my words aren't well chosen.

I always feel that dogs infuse their talk with a great deal of body language. When they're submissive, they bow to you, conceding your place as the leader of the pack, rolling over on their belly. (You always want to be dominant with a dog—this may not sound appropriately sensitive, but if you're not on top, he will be, which means he won't obey you, and that can mean real trouble. So be a leader of the pack, but lead with gentleness.)

Watch your dog for anxiety, frustration, joy, and concern. Some dogs wrinkle their eyes, some move their ears back. When my dog wants me to play with him and I'm not in the mood, his ears swivel forward, he wrinkles his brow, and he stomps his feet. Then he goes for his ball and tries to guide me to do what he wants. That's frustration. It's pretty evident, and he's telling me with his body.

With horses, you need to talk differently. Some people say that horses are not very smart. On the contrary, I think they are much more perceptive than we give them credit for. As I said earlier, they try to communicate with us through all means possible, including body language, touch, and verbalizations. And they listen very intently to our intonations, trying to interpret what we want them to do.

Listen to them, too—and watch. Like all species, horses have distinctive vocalizations, each expressing a particular emotion or desire. Any horse lover knows the heartwarming whinny of welcome when your horse is happy to see you. Horses also let you know, through other kinds of whinnies, when they are hungry, or frightened, or when they want to acknowledge an equine friend in the area. They make that distinctive *Bhhhhhh!* sound when frustrated or concerned. When they're very scared, the ears turn back; when they're feeling good, the ears move forward. If they start to rear, that means they're really scared, so back off. If you're patient, perhaps you can sense what they fear, and see if you can allay their anxieties.

A horse's nickers seem to be a signal used to encourage approach. Mares use these sounds toward their foals and toward stallions when they wish to mate. Horses of both sexes use them toward people they like. Try nickering back to your horse and see what happens.

So talk to the animals. You may not understand everything they say to you, but both of you will thoroughly enjoy the process.

Practices for a Busy Day

Each of us has days when we don't have the time to do everything we'd like, but if we can remember to take time for our animals on a regular basis, we profit, as do our friends. And even though some of these exercises might sound simplistic, you may be amazed how these brief moments can create magic and peace, imbuing us with subtle yet profound long-lasting effects on our inner and outer lives.

- When standing and waiting with your animal friend—whether on a walk, at a barn, in an elevator, or in the park—stand still, take in a deep, slow abdominal breath, and for a minute or less, let go and just be, enjoying the present and forgetting about all else. Some call this a standing—or a perching—meditation.

- Whenever you and your companion enter a house, barn, obedience class, park, or wildlife reserve, take a moment of silence and envision that you are entering a sacred place and appreciate that special feeling.

- As you walk through nature with your animal friend, stop and be aware of each sensory experience: the smells of fresh air after a summer shower, the sounds of the chirping birds, the sight of green trees glistening with newly fallen snow. Whether you are feeling the winds of change or the colors of life, the crisp snow of winter or the bursting blossoms of spring, take a moment to share the beauty of being alive together.

- When feeding your animal friends, be grateful for the bounty of nature. Say grace and appreciate the animals and plants that have given their *chi*—or their life force—to provide food for all of you.

- Before talking to your animal friends or other beings, ask yourself: If I were speaking from a place of love, what words would I use? See if that changes your language.

- Recognize the light of love and compassion within each living being that you encounter, whether two-legged, four-legged, winged, or other. Thank each creature, and treat him or her accordingly.

- Whenever you feel troubled, close your eyes and envision something funny that your animal friend—or any other animal you know—has done. Feel the laughter within. Then express it aloud and enjoy the lovely lightness of the moment.

- Wherever you are, think about the beauty of nature and all living beings. If you are in an urban environment (say, a subway station or a crowded city street), picture the spot filled with playful animals and feel the joy of being surrounded by them.

Two

The Journey Toward

Kindred Healing

*Of course, it is worth searching for the best
treatment, since treatment comes from outside.
But healing comes from within, its source in
our very nature as living organisms.*

—Dr. Andrew Weil

y clients and friends often ask me what they can
do to prevent illness or to assist in the healing of
their animal companions outside of bringing them to
my office. I tell them that there are actually many beneficial approaches
and therapies that anyone—veterinarian or not—can do in their home.

In this section, I would like to share a few with you. Many of them
are natural therapies, such as massage, homeopathy, and herbs. These

recommendations will not only give you the chance to help your friend, they allow you to become an integral part of the healing process. This too deepens your connection, and that is why these exercises represent more than just disease treatment, but are a true form of kindred healing.

A Natural Pet Scan

One of the most basic steps you can take when learning to interact closely with your animal friends is to become a home physician—certainly not to replace your regular veterinarian but to serve as your friend's early warning system.

Both in Eastern and Western medicine, the physical exam is an essential part of understanding animals and their problems. While you will not be able to give your furry companions a comprehensive physical, you can pick up an immense amount of information by observing, listening, examining, and even smelling them. With this brief list of possible spots to check, not only might you observe early danger signs, you will be learning a great deal about their bodies as well as their minds. Imagine how good you will feel if you find something now that could save their lives later.

1. Observe your animals when they are lying down, or sitting, or sleeping. Do they appear comfortable? Are they favoring a particular leg, wing, or paw? Are they huddled up? Do they show any sign of pain in their abdomen? Are they breathing normally from their chest?

   If you spot any problems as a recurring pattern, you might want to seek further medical attention from a veterinarian. Some of these signs can signal potentially serious disorders: for example, difficulty finding a comfortable position or growling just as they lie down may indicate the discomfort associated with arthritis or an affliction in an internal organ.

If you notice that your companion is favoring a particular leg or other part of her body, gently see if she will let you palpate (or examine by touching) that area. If she snarls, growls, or gives you any other message that she wants you to stay away, respect her wishes. Even the best-tempered animal may snip or bite if you touch an extremely painful spot.

If you are able to touch her, however, and you do sense a swelling or you run into an obvious place of pain, alert your veterinarian. You may have found an abscess, an infection, a tumor, or merely a fatty cyst.

2. Listen to her as she sits in repose: Do you hear any unusual sounds? Do you see any breathing problems? Do you hear wheezing, excessive gastrointestinal gurgling, or burping?

   It's quite valuable to learn to listen well so that you are cognizant of what is normal—or abnormal—in your friend. Unusual sounds, such as strange coughing or snorting, may be early warning signs of respiratory problems, from a collapsed trachea to what is commonly (and aptly, in canines) called "old dog lung."

3. Smell your friend. Use your nose to sniff just as animals do. Do you detect any foul odors from the mouth, the ears, the paws, or the skin? Odors can indicate potential afflictions. For example, unusually unpleasant breath can indicate gum disease, a bad tooth, or intestinal problems. Breath that smells like ammonia or urine can mean a troubled kidney; a sweet, sugary smell can signal diabetes.

   If the odor is emanating from the ears, check them out carefully. Some animals will be extremely sensitive here if they have an infection. A common underlying cause of ear infections is a food allergy, which can inflame the ears, causing the animal to scratch at them, which in turn abrades, or wears down, the ear canal and allows bacterial or fungal infectious agents to invade.

4. Now begin the actual physical part of the examination. Put yourself in a warm, caring place, as if you were about to start a loving massage and/or grooming session—you don't want the poor thing to feel like your seventh-grade science project. Pet her, talk to her in a gentle voice, tell her that you're just going to look her over to make sure she's okay. The best time to do this is at the end of the day, when she's relaxed, slightly tired, and happy to see you.

Begin with the head. Look in the eyes. Are they bright and alert, as they should be? Gently lower the lower lids and look to see if they are pink, which is normal. If they seem pale, examine the gums to see if they are pale, too; this may indicate anemia, from either blood loss or insufficient production of red blood cells. Purplish or blue gums may mean your companion isn't getting enough oxygen; your veterinarian should check her immediately.

A bright red line at the gum line could indicate periodontal or gum disease; tartar around the teeth could also hint at deeper dental problems.

Being extremely careful, feel for any pain around the teeth, which could indicate a problem in the tooth at the root level. Remember: Your animals aren't used to human hands poking around in their mouths. Even if they love you dearly, the discomfort or surprise of your intrusive fingers may result in a nasty bite. Use common sense.

The Chinese consider the tongue a visual gateway to the entire body. In *Four Paws, Five Directions,* her book on Chinese medicine for dogs and cats, Dr. Cheryl Schwartz describes the extrapolation of Chinese human tongue diagnosis to our animal companions. After examining hundreds of dogs' and cats' tongues, looking at coating, texture, shape, and color, Schwartz found the same abnormalities in animals that Chinese doctors have observed in humans for thousands of years. For instance, a thin white tongue coating is considered normal in healthy dogs, while a dark coating may indicate illness; a thick yellow coating may mean digestive problems.

The tongue's color is also important. A normal tongue is pink; if it's too pale, it may mean anemia, while purple could mean a circulation problem.

Look at the ears. Does the ear canal (the part you can easily see) look clean? If there's a thick brown discharge, that can mean a yeast infection; a yellow discharge is indicative of a bacterial infection. Little white specks may hint at a mite infestation.

Next inspect the coat. A normal healthy coat should be shiny without excess flakiness or oil. Look at the quality of the hair coat (or, in the case of birds, feathers). Is it fine and glossy, or does it lack luster? A dry and flaky coat can be an indication of nutritional deficiencies, such as a lack of quality nonrancid essential fatty acids, or quality protein, or an indication of poor absorption of nutrients in the gastrointestinal tract. In this case, an additional supplement such as flax seed, cod liver, sesame seed, or evening primrose oils may be beneficial.

An excessively oily coat may mean eczema; scales and odor can indicate mange; redness and bloody areas could be signs of food or seasonal allergies or fleas.

A normal healthy coat should not have an excessive body odor. Of course, dogs may smell wet if they just went for a swim or had a bath, but a continuing odor can indicate a problem such as an inadequate diet or food allergies.

The skin can serve as a reflection of general body health and is an easy way to gather information about your animal friend. How does the skin look at the base of the hairs? Is it normal skin color, or is it extremely red? From the perspective of Western medicine, red skin can be due to allergies, inflammation, or a skin infection. From a traditional Chinese medical perspective, it may be an indication of excessive internal heat in the body. This heat can be due to either an infection or an inflammation or from eating too many foods that are considered "hot" foods, such as red meat.

Now, gently run your hands over your friend from the head, down the neck, down the front legs, then over the back and the hind legs, along the chest and belly, feeling for any abnormal swellings, lumps, or bumps. Besides being on the alert for abscesses or tumors, you may find a cut beneath the skin and be able to disinfect it before it festers.

Gently flex the front legs and back legs and see if they move comfortably—here you are looking for arthritis, which you can manage quite well with supplements that can prevent or at least slow down the progression of future lameness.

If you do this exam once a week, not only will you be giving your friend a pleasant experience that she will look forward to, you will learn what is normal and abnormal on her body.

Touching and grooming are universal means of communication between animals of all species, an intimate form of co-species connection, and perhaps of co-species healing, too, because your hands help stimulate opiate receptors in the skin. By committing yourself to this once-a-week, half-an-hour exercise, you will become aware of your animal at a new, more intimate level.

How to Help Heal Your Ailing Animal

When your animal companion is ill, you seek the best possible medical care. That's a given.

But there are more ways to help than simply making sure your friend has a good veterinarian. You'll want to do whatever you can to help at home, too.

Say, for instance, that your cat has cancer. If you become distraught and anxious, telling him that you can't let go now, moaning about how unhappy you are that he's leaving you, he may pick up on that negative energy. Sensing your emotions might propel him into his own form of sadness. This in turn can cause the release of various neurotransmitters that act to suppress his immune system. As we've seen, emotions have an impact on health, whether you are a seventy-year-old woman or a seven-year-old Siamese.

I am not recommending that you repress your thoughts or emotions—that too can be detrimental to health. But in your animals' presence, consider being as loving and cheerful as possible. This will help them feel positive, allowing them to release biochemicals that will help boost their immune systems. In other words, it's not out of the realm of possibility that your positive outlook can help your animal heal. King Solomon, in Proverbs 17:22, shares a similar perspective: "A cheerful heart is good medicine, but a downcast spirit dries up the bones."

At the same time, it's certainly possible that no matter how much love you give your animals, they may still pass away. You can only do your best, and hope, and pray.

Something else I tell my clients: Learn to love without being attached. By that I mean, do your 100 percent best for your animals without regard to the outcome. I know too many people who tell their animals, "You better get well because I need you too much to let you go. Don't leave me alone." Death is not failure—it's just another stage on our journey.

Instead, try loving for its own sake. Love your animals, whether in sickness or health, for who they are, without attaching any clauses or conditions to your feelings. "If you need to go," you can tell them, "then you need to go. But I love you and I will do whatever I can to help you in the meantime."

If you can approach a sick animal from a place of love rather than one of neediness, you can establish a healthier connection.

Remain unattached and love in the moment. If you play appropriately with your ailing animals, you'll cheer them up, you'll make them more active, you'll stimulate their chemical messengers, you'll help them take in oxygen by increasing their circulation. But don't overdo it, either. You don't throw a Frisbee to a dog with bone cancer.

Equally important is to provide a good diet, which establishes the essential foundation for health. I can't emphasize enough how important it is to change your animals' food habits when they are ill (or just when you want to improve their well-being). Over and over again, I have seen animals' health transformed by switching from processed food to a balanced, homemade diet of organic vegetables and meat. If nothing else, just ridding the diet of pesticides and preservatives while adding *chi* and fresh vitamins is a positive step.

Two final elements to home care: visualization and touch. More and more evidence shows that visualization—or being able to picture in your mind the outcome you desire in reality—has a positive impact on health. Thoughts are indeed energy. Visualization can help make thoughts real. I'm not saying that you can think your animal to health. But if Larry Dossey's research is borne out, creating a mental picture of your animals as happy, joyous, playful beings may well have some kind of impact on their well-being—along with prayer, as evidenced by Dossey's work on long-distance intentional healing.

So pray for your friend. Say, "Dear God (or Jesus, or Muhammad, or Buddha, or Goddess—whatever you prefer), may my animal be blessed with good health, vitality, joy, and life." Then visualize him or her playing, romping, smiling, living happily. Be as specific as you can— in other words, try to imagine your friend as healthy as possible, with glowing eyes, a shining coat, bounding happily through the woods.

As we saw earlier, touch is an eons-old, genetically programmed means of connecting and bonding between all animals: mother and child, mates, grooming partners, friends. Touch and massage have been identified as factors capable of boosting the immune system by increasing certain types of white blood cells. Touch also causes the release of many other biochemicals that act on the brain and the central nervous system.

Touch your animal friends. But remember, be relaxed. If your thoughts are filled with tension and frenetic energy, the blood vessels to your extremities will be constricted, giving you cold hands. Your friend may not respond to you as well as if your hands are warm. You can change your hand temperature by returning to that calm, peaceful part of yourself. Your friend will pick up on it and feel better.

Finding Kindred Veterinary Support

*F*inding the right veterinarian is a personal affair. So often I hear someone tell me that it's like trying to find the right pediatrician. "I want someone I like," people say, "and someone I trust." These are the two most critical issues. But you might also look for kindred veterinary support—a veterinarian who not only practices quality medicine but who is sympathetic to the mental, physical, and spiritual connections that we share with our animal friends.

A veterinarian may have a wonderful cage- or barn-side manner and may have received excellent advanced training—but not always both. Veterinary medicine is changing as rapidly as human medicine, making it challenging for any one individual to have a depth of knowledge, as well as the proper training and experience, in all the different fields.

To find the right veterinarian:

1. Make a list of the traits and skills important to you. You might include: ease of access to your home, emergency access or emergency support, compassion, technical expertise, knowledge, open-mindedness to new therapies, and appreciation for the human-animal bond.

   It may be a challenge to find one veterinarian who possesses all the abilities, wisdom, and vision that you seek, so prioritize your wish list and decide which qualities you believe you cannot do without.

2. Talk to other animal lovers in your town or neighborhood. Word of mouth is often the best referral.

3. Decide whether you prefer a solo practitioner or a group practice. If you select a group practice, do you have access to the veterinarian of your choice whenever she or he is available?

4. Meet the veterinary support team. They are an integral part of the operations of an animal hospital and will be taking care of

your animal friend as well. Talk to some of the technicians and watch how they handle animals. Chat with the receptionists and ask about the philosophy of the animal hospital. (Bear in mind, however, that even the most compassionate and capable veterinarians are not necessarily the best business managers—that kind of training has not been a routine part of veterinary school.)

5. Don't choose a veterinary hospital based on prices and massive advertising campaigns. The animal hospitals that advertise the most or the ones with the lowest prices are not always the best when it comes to a commitment to the co-species connection.

6. The World Wide Web has a multitude of sites recommending veterinarians with different expertises. But be wary: Some of the veterinarians may have paid for this kind of sanction.

7. Make your first appointment with a prospective veterinarian a job interview. Bring a list of questions based on your own feelings about the human-animal bond. Ask if he or she agrees with your philosophy. See if you feel a rapport, if you trust his or her knowledge and wisdom.

8. Don't stay with a veterinarian you're ambivalent about. Many people feel that once they start seeing an animal doctor, they have to stay. Not so. Look around for someone new if you're not happy. It's like any relationship—you have to have faith in the person you're dealing with.

The Natural Approach to Diet and Food Allergies

J once treated a cat who had been taking all sorts of medications for chronic itching—cortisone, hormones, antibiotics. She was still itching and the irritation was getting worse. When I first saw the cat, I suggested stopping all medications and replacing them with a simple balanced diet. Within two weeks, the itching and skin problems were gone.

Another time I saw a German shepherd with a history of all sorts of skin and gastrointestinal problems, including itching, loss of hair, ear and skin infections, diarrhea, and constipation. He too had been treated with a variety of medications. Three weeks after I put the dog on a natural diet, all the symptoms resolved and we had another happy canine camper!

Over the past few decades, dogs and cats have begun to develop food allergies to many ingredients in pet foods. Dr. Donald Strombeck, in his book *Home-Prepared Dog and Cat Diets*, states that dogs rarely have food allergies in geographical areas where commercial pet foods are not routinely sold. This may be due to the fact that grains, which dogs and cats are not designed to consume as a major part of their diet, are the largest single ingredient in store-bought pet foods.

Allergies to meat products such as beef may be due to the overuse of vaccines in our dogs and cats. Many of these vaccines are based on beef broth, and therefore the animal develops an immune response to beef as well as the disease they are vaccinated against.

Food allergies have become so prevalent among domestic animals that I feel it is imperative to discuss them as an integral part of preventing disease.

While not all cases will be resolved as easily as those above, it is often surprising what a switch to a healthier diet can do.

A food allergy is defined simply as an allergic reaction caused by the ingestion of particular food substances. The most common food allergens for animals include beef, chicken, wheat, corn, soybeans, eggs, and dairy products. Such allergies can be a significant cause of a wide range of symptoms in both people and animals: At least 60 percent of the U.S. population may suffer from negative reactions to foods or chemical additives such as preservatives or artificial colors and flavors. As for animals, experts estimate that 5 percent of all skin disease and 10–15 percent of all allergic skin reactions in dogs and cats are due to hypersensitivity to certain foods as well as to medications such as antibiotics or drugs for heartworm or flea prevention.

Food allergies may appear at any time and can mimic other hypersensitivity reactions—such as allergies to fleas, dust, or poison ivy—or even parasitic infections. They are easy to differentiate from seasonal allergies because food allergies occur all year round—as long as your animal friend is consuming the offending food. Food allergies affect male and female animals equally, and they appear to be no more common in one breed than another, although in my practice German shepherds and Labrador retrievers seem to have a higher than usual incidence.

Food allergies can affect not only the animals' skin but also the gastrointestinal tract and (rarely) the nervous system. Typical skin symptoms may include severe pruritis (itching), hair loss, or erythema (redness), along with vomiting, diarrhea (sometimes bloody), constipation, and increased frequency of bowel movements. Although rare, seizures have been associated with food hypersensitivity, too. In humans, food allergies can cause irritable bowel syndrome, hyperactivity, depression, headaches, irritability, arthritis and joint pain, asthma, chronic bronchitis, hypoglycemia, and sinusitis. Occasionally, I see some of these symptoms in dogs or cats, as well as horses, and suspect food allergies may play a role. However, this is difficult to prove.

How can you tell if your animal companion has food allergies? If he or she has any of the above symptoms, check with your veterinarian. Blood tests are available, but these are not always reliable (although new ones are getting more so every year). However, sometimes you can figure it out on your own by doing some simple detective work. First, ask yourself: When did the itching or other symptoms begin to appear? Was it soon after you started using a new prepared food? If so, try switching back to the previous diet and see if the symptoms subside.

Once you know your friend is allergic to a particular pet food, then the question is: Which ingredient or ingredients are causing the allergies? Is it the carbohydrate source, perhaps wheat or corn, or the protein source, such as beef or chicken? Could it be something else entirely, such as artificial colors, flavors, or preservatives?

To find out, I usually recommend a food elimination diet. Ideally, limit your animal companion to one protein source to which she has had limited to no previous exposure. For instance, if your friend was on a basic generic dog or cat food diet with wheat, corn, and beef as its main ingredients, you might want to choose either a homemade or prepared diet consisting of fish and potatoes.

Then you add back one food source at a time. (This method is commonly known as a food provocation trial.) For instance, if you add wheat to your friend's diet and the symptoms reoccur, you've likely found the offending ingredient. The challenge with food trials is patience. Although I often see improvement within a few weeks, it may take as long as three to six months.

During the avoidance trial, you should not give your animal antibiotics, steroids, heartworm medications, or any other potential allergens. Certain toys and snacks, such as bones or other chewables, may also contain the problem substance and need to be removed during food elimination trials.

After you've confirmed the diagnosis of food allergy, you need to decide how to handle it.

Sometimes simple nutritional supplements may help. I recommend a good essential fatty acid supplement, such as organic refrigerated flax seed oil, black currant oil, fish oils, or evening primrose oil at a dose of about one teaspoon daily for a fifty-pound dog. In addition, I sometimes suggest using a combination of digestive enzymes and supplements such as quercetin (a bioflavonoid) and bromelain (derived from pineapple). Quercetin actually helps prevent the release of histamines in the gastrointestinal tract. For more challenging cases, I may prescribe other natural supplements.

Of course, the best—and easiest—solution to food allergies is to keep the offending allergen away from your friend. Usually you can find a brand of dog or cat food that your friend does not react to. However, with all the different foods and chemicals potentially found in these products, this is easier said than done.

One sure alternative: Try a homemade diet. I am a firm believer that animals do best on a homemade diet that is natural, organic, and balanced. Recipes for healthy homemade pet foods can be found in books, including my *Love, Miracles, and Animal Healing* and *Dr. Pitcairn's Complete Guide to Natural Health for Dogs and Cats*, as well as a number of diet guides published by dog breeders and owners.

Travel Tips for Dogs and Cats

*C*ome summer, many of us travel on vacation and wish to take our animal companions along for some kindred adventures—something which can be enjoyable, stressful, or both. Whatever the situation, proper preparation is key. While it's difficult to anticipate every little thing that can go wrong, there are plenty of ways to minimize problems.

First on your trip-planning agenda should be a standard checklist of pet items to bring along: water and a water bowl; a quality commercial pet food (health food variety); a leash or harness; identification tags; copies of health certificates; medications; a carrying case; an animal first-aid kit (see below); a brush for grooming and dislodging anything unexpected from a shaggy coat; and your friend's favorite toy or blanket, something they can play with in an unfamiliar place or lie down on for comfort.

Don't forget to bring a pooper scooper and plastic bags to clean up after your dog. For cats, a portable litter pan is essential, along with a scoop and towels to clean it out. Bring extra catbox filler and nontoxic air-freshener sprays if you can't clean the box out immediately.

It's crucial that when you are traveling far from home, your buddy wear proper identification in case he gets loose and runs away. Though we often hear miraculous tales of lost dogs or cats who found their way home over hundreds of miles, don't count on it. Many types of identification tags are available. Information on the tag (or in a waterproof container on the collar) should include your friend's name, your name, and a phone number. It's also a good idea to list any severe medical conditions, such as epilepsy or diabetes. (For example: "My name is Rover and I am diabetic. If I am lost, please call John or Mary Smith collect: 212–555–1234.")

There is even a new system available whereby a veterinarian can implant a computer chip with all pertinent information under your friend's skin, usually in the neck and shoulder region. With this technology, animals can be identified by other veterinarians and humane societies. Ask your veterinarian whether your friend is a candidate for this system. (Some holistic practitioners are concerned about potential health problems resulting from such an implant, but none have been identified so far.)

If your friend does have a serious medical problem, consider whether it is better for him to be with you or to stay home with someone who can provide proper supervision. Check with your vet if you have any doubts.

Let's say your animal companions are healthy and ready to travel. If you're going by car, make sure they don't get under your feet or try to jump out a window while you're driving. Many cats prefer the security of their carrying case, and that is certainly safest for both of you. However, if you've got a kitty who meows like crazy in a carrier, she may do better perched where she can watch what is going on. For dogs (and cats), various screens are available to assure that they stay in a safe part of the vehicle. Safety harnesses are also worth investigating.

Never leave animals in a sealed car on a hot day—they can overheat and collapse very quickly. If the weather is too hot and/or humid, don't travel with your animal friends. But if you have no choice, leave enough windows open to allow a current of fresh cooler air to pass through, and make sure that a water source is within easy reach—untippable water bowls are now available. Window shades and even solar fans can be used to keep cars cooler.

Make sure your friend is having normal bowel movements. Like people, animals can be predisposed to constipation from the irregularities of travel.

Some animals love to travel; others feel anxious or succumb to motion sickness. What if your buddy gets carsick? Your veterinarian may want to prescribe a mild tranquilizer or some medication for gastrointestinal motility. There are also some excellent herbal and homeopathic remedies to prevent or treat this type of distress.

As I mentioned earlier, ginger is a good home cure for motion sickness. According to a 1982 article in the English medical journal *Lancet*, ginger "appears to work in the gastrointestinal tract by slowing down the feedback interaction between the stomach and the nausea center in the brain." A number of other studies have documented the benefits of ginger over conventional motion-sickness drugs such as antihistamines. And while it is easy for an animal to overdose on antihistamines, ginger appears to be quite safe. The typical human dose is 940–1,000 mg. of ginger half an hour before travel, then as needed every one to two hours. For an animal, this translates to about 50–75 mg. per ten pounds of body weight every few hours as needed. For instance, for a twenty-pound dog, 100 to 150 mg. would be reasonable.

Other useful holistic options include the Bach flower rescue remedy, which many of my clients swear helps alleviate the stress and anxiety of travel. Try one drop for a cat and between two and five for a dog, depending on weight. Other useful homeopathic remedies include cocculus, tabascum, or homeopathic petroleum. A few granules of a 30C potency of any of these one hour prior to travel often works.

If your animal companion is traveling by plane, discuss arrangements with the airline and your veterinarian beforehand. Don't take a sick animal on an airplane unless it's absolutely unavoidable. And if you're staying in a hotel or motel, make sure in advance that it is animal-friendly. I have heard sad tales from owners of giant breeds such as Great Danes and Newfoundlands who arrived at their lodgings only to be told management did not allow dogs over a certain size. What kind of a vacation is it when you find yourself having to board your best friend in a strange kennel at the last minute?

Preventing and Treating Cancer the Natural Way

*T*here are few words more dreaded by both veterinarian and client than "I am sorry to tell you that your pet has cancer." Because cancer is a leading cause of death in our animal companions, I feel it's essential to look at nontraditional forms of treatment in addition to—or instead of—more aggressive conventional ones. Fortunately, holistic medicine offers many nontoxic therapeutic options to help cancer patients.

If your friend is unfortunate enough to be diagnosed with cancer, you have a number of natural, nontoxic, innovative approaches in addition to surgery, chemotherapy, and radiation therapy. In my practice, we work with herbal medicine, nutrition, acupuncture, and homeopathy and use nutritional supplements to maintain an alkaline pH of the body and to support the immune system while maintaining optimal health.

We also recommend dietary changes, which my friend Dr. Greg Ogilvie at the Colorado State University Veterinary School believes is the first step in treating cancer. This helps counteract the effects of cachexia, a complex process in which cancer cells seem to metabolize nutrients such as carbohydrates, fats, and proteins differently from normal cells. Dr. Ogilvie has found that carbohydrates actually feed the cancer at the expense of the host. Therefore, your friend's diet should limit carbohydrates.

Dr. Ogilvie also found that, because cancer cells and normal cells compete for amino acids, if the diet does not provide them, the tumor process actually leaches them from the host. He suggests a diet of high-quality protein in moderate amounts as well as the amino acids arginine and glutamine, which enhance the immune system and decrease toxicity in the gastrointestinal tract.

Another interesting fact is that many cancer cells cannot metabolize certain fats known as n-3 fatty acids. These fats appear to have anticancer effects. Good sources of n-3 fatty acids include fish oils, evening primrose oil, flax seed oil, borage oil, and black currant oil. The oils must be fresh and kept refrigerated. (Rancid oils can be worse for your friend than no oil at all.)

So what are the best foods for a dog or cat with cancer? Certainly not most processed pet foods, which are composed primarily of carbohydrates and poor-quality protein and fats. Instead, feed your friend a balanced homemade diet of fresh, organic, quality proteins such as fish, white meat turkey, or tofu.

You may supplement this with additional arginine and glutamine from a health food store or a holistic veterinarian and the fatty acids mentioned above. Before making dietary changes, discuss your plans with a holistically oriented veterinarian.

Certain vitamins, such as retinoids, beta-carotene, and vitamins C, D, and E may help prevent and actually be therapeutic in the treatment of various types of cancers. Similarly, extensive research has shown that selenium has a positive effect in warding off certain cancers, and it should be part of every cancer prevention and treatment regimen. Garlic too has been shown to be effective in the prevention and treatment of cancer.

Many other herbs have been noted as beneficial. In fact, vincristine, a major agent used in chemotherapy, is derived from the periwinkle plant. Traditional native American folk remedies for cancer include combinations of Turkish rhubarb root, red clover, sheep sorrel, blessed thistle, burdock root, and slippery elm bark. I have used this blend with some success in slowing down the growth of tumors.

The Chinese and Japanese alike use medicinal mushrooms, including the shiitake and reishi varieties, as anticancer agents, believing they strengthen the immune system. (Recent research studying extracts of these medicinal mushrooms appear promising and I too have found a significant clinical response to them.) The Chinese employ hundreds of different herbs and herbal formulas to treat cancer and the side effects of chemotherapy and radiation therapy. Some of the more common include ginseng and astragalus. Consult a veterinarian trained in herbal medicine before you use them. (You can find one by contacting the American Holistic Veterinary Medical Association in Bel Air, Maryland [410–569–0795].

Acupuncture has also been used with cancer patients for pain relief, as well as to support the immune system. Classical homeopathic veterinarians claim that homeopathy may also be useful in slowing down the growth of certain cancers, as well as helping to stimulate the body's defense mechanisms. Numerous other more controversial therapies are being tried as well, with varying degrees of success. In my practice, my associates and I use an individualized integrative approach, incorporating a natural diet, nutritional supplements, herbal supplements, and acupuncture, as well as conventional approaches when they are appropriate.

A Holistic First-Aid Kit

You never know when it may happen: You are playing with your four-legged friend at home or traveling together out of town. Then suddenly, he or she spies something interesting and takes off without you, only to return injured or poisoned. Panic immediately sets in: What should you do?

First, regain your composure, take a deep breath, and assess the situation from a rational place. First-aid support is much more than a first-aid kit. Then decide which condition is the most critical to get under control, whether that means a major hemorrhage, shock, or stabilizing a severe fracture.

Normally, your first move would be to obtain immediate professional help from your veterinarian or veterinary clinic. But what if you are far from home or help isn't available? That's why it's always important to have access to an animal first-aid kit.

This is where a holistic first-aid kit can make the difference between life and death in most common types of medical emergencies: if your pet is suffering from shock and/or broken bones after being struck by a car; poisoning; cuts and wounds from fights with other animals; burns; convulsions; heatstroke; insect bites; and puncture wounds.

Here are the necessary items to include in an emergency kit, all of which are available at most pharmacies. Keep them handy in a plastic waterproof container. Include a laminated list of the kit's contents along with a small instruction book—bookstores, catalogs, and pet stores usually sell such brief first-aid guides.

Bandage material is essential for cuts, wounds, fractures, and so on. This should include one package of gauze pads, three to four gauze rolls, two three-inch-wide elastic bandages, and a small pair of scissors. It's a good idea to include an extra gauze roll to wrap around your pet's mouth like a muzzle. Sometimes a hurt or frightened animal will bite anyone who touches a fracture or painful area—even you, who only want to help.

A blanket is handy as a makeshift stretcher if you have to carry your friend. It will also insulate her if she is in shock or suffering from hypothermia.

Antibacterial disinfectant. For cuts and abrasions. I especially recommend hydrogen peroxide, which can be used both topically (for wounds) and orally (to induce vomiting if your friend has ingested poison). My other favorites include Betadine, an iodine solution, and Nolvasan. (If you choose Betadine, make sure it's in an unbreakable bottle with a secure top—it can stain and make quite a mess.)

Activated charcoal capsules are administered orally to absorb poisons. (These are neater than powdered charcoal and go down fairly easily.) One capsule is usually sufficient for a cat or small dog; give two for larger dogs. There is also a Chinese herbal formula aptly named "Pill-Curing," which is wonderful for food poisoning. You can taper the suggested human dose down to the weight of your animal friend.

Certain homeopathic and natural remedies are also good to keep on hand. They come in a variety of potencies or strengths, but I usually like to use 30C (centesimal) potencies, which are normally quite safe with no side effects. You can purchase homeopathic remedies at health food stores, through natural pet catalogs, or from a holistic veterinarian.

Arnica montana 30C is my first choice to treat shock, trauma, swelling, or bruises such as those caused by an automobile accident. Administer one to five pellets orally (under the tongue), so they are quickly absorbed. Do not give with food. If water is available, you can dilute the pellets and administer them that way. I've always felt this remedy alone could prove the validity of homeopathy.

Aconitum napellus (aconite) 30C is the first-choice treatment for anxiety and fear, as well as for an acute fever. If your buddy is panicky from shock or due to an accident or if he's afraid of thunderstorms or loud noises, this is an excellent remedy to try. If aconite doesn't work, other remedies are also effective.

Apis mellifica 30C is a wonderful remedy for allergic reactions due to insect stings. Typically, a dog will chase a bee and bite it. If he is allergic, the mouth and gums will swell immediately, followed by severe breathing difficulties and even an anaphylactic reaction, which can cause shock and occasionally death. Apis is easy to administer orally and can work almost as well if not better than conventional medicine.

Once, when hiking, I ran across a fellow hiker with his bulldog. The dog had gotten into a wasp's nest and received multiple stings around his face, which was so swollen we could barely see his eyes, and the animal was breathing heavily. Fortunately, I had apis in my first-aid kit. We treated the dog, and within five minutes, he felt more comfortable and his breathing improved. Within fifteen minutes, the swelling had decreased significantly. What a relief for this hiker!

Another handy item for bug bites that sting or itch are the little penlike tubes known as "sting ease," a combination of vinegar and mink oil. You can also use white vinegar topically on the bite—this helps neutralize the venom.

Nux vomica 30C induces vomiting and is a handy remedy for poisoning. It may also be used to treat vomiting.

Phosphorous 30C orally assists in clotting for cases of bleeding, hemorrhage, and so on.

Ledum 30C is an excellent remedy for puncture wounds.

Finally, I also recommend carrying a formula called Dr. Bach's Rescue Remedy to help animals relieve the anxiety associated with shock. And since good first-aid support also includes mind-body medicine for you so that you can maintain your calm in the midst of the storm, consider taking a few drops of Rescue Remedy for yourself, too.

Three

Bittersweet Farewells

I have sometimes thought of the final cause of
dogs having such short lives and I am quite
satisfied it is in compassion to the human race; for
if we suffer so much in losing a dog after an
acquaintance of ten or twelve years,
what would it be if they were to
double that time?

—Sir Walter Scott

oving spiritual bonds with your animals can do wonders for both you and them. And learning how to develop your own healing skills can also be of great benefit. But there are times when nothing can save your animal from the realities of life and death. Just like people, animals can't live forever.

I often feel that the most difficult part of sharing your life with animals is dealing with their departure from it. How do we act, how do we think, how do we cope with such a challenging time?

I believe that the acceptance of death's inevitability and the willingness to discuss it openly, as well as the ability to comfort the bereaved, can prevent long-term emotional and physical turmoil. Meaningful rituals and the opportunity to talk about loved ones can help mourners immensely.

Throughout history, humankind has honored the departed and helped those who mourn. Thirty-five thousand years ago, Neanderthals buried their dead with cornflowers, grape hyacinths, and hollyhocks; the Cro-Magnons adorned their deceased with elaborate ivory necklaces; the bodies of ancient Egyptians were mummified and interred with favorite objects, including mummified animals who may well have been their favorite friends.

According to Carol Wogrin, director of the Bereavement Studies Program at Mount Ida College in Massachusetts, all cultures have some set of beliefs concerning the human soul or spirit existing beyond the physical form. Ideas about the afterlife of animals, however, vary greatly, from those who feel animals have no soul to those, such as Buddhists, who believe animals may reincarnate into human beings, as well as vice versa. (Some Buddhists also feel that monks may sometimes choose to take a lifetime off from being human to return as a dog, or another animal, in order to benefit other beings.) In fact, recent research at the University of Arizona by Drs. Gary Schwartz and Linda Russek suggests that there is a continuity of energy that continues after death.

For the most part, though, Americans have tended to side with those who downplay the death of an animal. Too often I have heard someone tell a friend grieving over a death: "It's just a cat [or a bird, a dog, or a turtle, or a horse . . .]. Get over it."

But that's not how animal lovers feel. We are often overwhelmed with difficult questions in the face of death. The most common query I hear is: "How will I know when to put my friend to sleep if he doesn't die on his own?" Given medicine's capacity to keep animals alive longer than ever—but with questionable quality of life—as well as the popularity of euthanasia, it has become more challenging than ever to answer this question, because it leads to so many others. Is it fair to put him to sleep? Is it fair to let him suffer? How bad does he feel? Will he let me know? How will he let me know?

There is no one correct answer to any of these questions. But I tell my clients that your animal companion will indeed let you know when it is time. If death is imminent through a chronic disease or aging, you will see your friend begin to lose interest in eating and drinking. He will sleep more, he will breathe more deeply; the essence of his being will slowly dissipate. If you are close to your friend, you will begin to feel as if he is no longer truly with you. If you are both lucky, he will die peacefully, while sleeping, or take a few sudden deep breaths and let go.

I suggest to clients that they talk to their animal friend and ask him to let them know when it is time. This may sound odd, but my experience over the years has shown that it often works. Many of my clients have shared intimate stories about touching last moments together.

I remember one client, Jennifer, who came to me with her nineteen-year-old orange male tabby, Tulku, on a cold December day. It is not uncommon that with the onset of winter, many geriatric animals who have been hanging on to life appear to fall into an acute crisis, let go, and pass on—and this seemed to be the case with Tulku.

When Jennifer first brought Tulku to me a year earlier, he had severe kidney problems. Due to his age and condition, dialysis or kidney transplants weren't feasible; his previous veterinarian had recommended euthanasia. But Tulku rebounded and became energetic and playful, appearing happy and content while undergoing monthly acupuncture treatments. In addition, Jennifer administered nutritional and herbal supplements, as well as subcutaneous fluids, at home.

Now Tulku had taken a turn for the worse. Jennifer had decided to let Tulku die peacefully at home and she asked how she would know if the time had come.

"Each animal companion is different," I said. "Some tell you with a special look, others by changes in their eating or sleeping habits." I knew Jennifer didn't wish Tulku to suffer needlessly, nor did she want to end his life prematurely. I suggested that she talk to him as she would to her best friend and ask him to let her know in some demonstrative way when it was his time.

The first few times Jennifer tried this Tulku stood up, jumped out of her lap, ran for his food bowl. This seemed to be a pretty clear answer that it wasn't his time. However, one night as she was again bringing up the subject, Tulku looked up at her with soulful eyes, licked her fingers, and gently laid his head on her hand.

Later that night, he let out a loud meow and walked onto her chest. Jennifer woke up and held him in her arms while he looked into her eyes, took in one last breath, and let go. Jennifer hugged him, cried, and thanked him for saying goodbye.

Once your friend has died, pioneers in the field of bereavement counseling say that you can ease this difficult journey with proactive steps. Although universal, grief is also highly individual, and you will want to do whatever makes you feel best. Grief counselors Laurel Lagoni and Carolyn Butler at Colorado State University Veterinary School say that grief can manifest itself in many ways—crying, shock, numbness, exhaustion, sleep disturbances. You may feel sadness, anxiety, grief, resentment, embarrassment, self-doubt, helplessness, or hopelessness. You may also find yourself challenging your belief systems— something I have seen in many of my clients who, although devoutly religious, wonder about the existence of God or life-after-death issues at such a solemn time.

There's no reason to think you are odd if you feel in need of support after a beloved animal's passing. Discussing the death, sharing your emotions with friends, consulting with a compassionate veterinarian: These are all essential parts of the grieving process. Most veterinary schools now have bereavement groups and hot lines. Your veterinarian can help find one that is right just for you.

It can also be extremely healing to create a memorial service or a peaceful, spiritual environment in which to grieve, surrounded by soft music, your friend's favorite people, toys, and smells. Make a gesture that honors your friend's life, such as planting a tree over a burial site or sprinkling their ashes over favorite haunts.

Ask friends to share happy moments about your lives together. Think and talk about favorite qualities. Reflect on how you can incorporate these qualities into your life right now. For example, if your cat forgave you when you lost your patience, forgive another who may have lost patience with you. If your dog loved you when you came home from a long, exhausting day at work, do that for somebody else. Integrate their strengths and beautiful qualities into yourself so that each time you share one of those qualities with another, fond thoughts of your animal friends come to mind, helping you realize that they are still in your life in wonderful ways.

Do something positive that helps other animals or the environment. Adopt another animal or make a donation to your favorite animal charity in your friend's memory. Volunteer time in an animal shelter, a humane society, or a senior citizen home. You are not replacing your friend. You are transforming his memory into a gift for others.

Or you could create a memory box into which you place strands of hair, perhaps a collar, a clay mold of a pawprint, favorite toys, or photographs. This can be exceptionally comforting for children who have lost their friend.

When I was trekking in Bhutan, I noticed small statues in beautiful spots with magnificent views or near monasteries. A monk later told me that these were clay molds that contained ashes of the deceased, which their loved ones would place in their favorite locations.

Grief has no timetable. It is a journey filled with peaks and valleys. Just when you think you are getting over your loss, a fresh wave of pain pulls you back. But grieving is part of the human experience; it is a journey to a new stage of life. The goal is not forgetting, but reconciling yourself to your loss and creating new meaning out of it. You will always have a relationship with your animal friend, but in a different form. You may bury your friends' bodies in the ground, but you bury their souls in your heart.

Four

The Single Best

Way to Find Your

Kindred Spirit

Lord help me be the person my dog
thinks I am.

—Anonymous

hether I'm out on the lecture circuit or treating
patients at a barn or in the office, I often hear the
question: "Dr. Schoen, what is the best way I can
personally help a kindred spirit?"

Here's my answer: Find an abandoned or a homeless or an abused
animal friend and bring him or her into your life. Share your home with

your new companion and provide as much love and nurturance as you can. Receive the same love and affection back and allow the two of you to grow together. Your life—and the life of your friend—will never be the same. Your joy will be great and your souls will flourish. Their cup and yours will truly runneth over with love!

A Final Word (or Two)

We Are Kindred Spirits
(After "Please Call Me by My True Names" by Thich Nhat Hanh)

We are the eagle looking down from the sky
We are the puppy playing with a ball
We are the cat purring meditatively
We are the horse nuzzling your hair
We are the lamb bleating for food
We are the calf nursing

We are also the fawn watching the hunter take aim
We are the dog whimpering in pain after an accident
We are the kitten peeking through steel bars at the shelter
We are the baby gorilla being grabbed by poachers
We are the steer in a slaughterhouse
We are the monkey locked in a cage

We are the naïveté of youth exploring the adventures of life
We are the wisdom of elders after years of exploration
We are the joy of all mothers
We are the pride of all fathers
We are also the pain of those who suffer
We are the fear of those who cower
We are the shared emotions of all our brethren
We are truly a kindred spirit with all of life

Resources

*We need a boundless ethic which will
include the animals also.*
—Albert Schweitzer

*A*sk yourself, ask your friends—ask anyone at all
whom you feel might have an answer—for ideas to help
you put the concepts of co-species healing and co-
species connections into action in your life each and every day. Action
turns knowledge into wisdom. Following are more suggestions on how
you can cultivate strong human-animal bonds.

Please don't forget to let me know how this book may have stim-

ulated your thoughts and actions in new ways. Tell me what you are doing to help us re-create healthier, happier connections with all of life.
Also let me know if you are interested in seminars, workshops, and information on both or if you wish to be included in future editions of
this book. Drop a note to *www.drschoen.com* with any stories you wish to
share.

Some of the following books were referenced in the text or con-
tributed to the writing of this book, and others offer more suggestions
on how you can achieve remarkable kindred connections through a multitude of resources.

BOOKS

Animals as Teachers and Healers, Susan Chernak McElroy, NewSage Press
A moving affirmation of the wonderful gifts that animals have given to
humankind, full of touching stories and insight.

The Biophilia Hypothesis, edited by Stephen R. Kellert and Edward O. Wilson, Island Press
A definitive, if academic, collection of essays on the theory of biophilia,
as developed by Harvard professor and two-time Pulitzer prize–winning author Wilson.

Dogs That Know When Their Owners Are Coming Home, Rupert Sheldrake,
Crown
Proposing new theories on the ineffable bonds between animals and humans, this is a fascinating, well-documented study by one of the most important and controversial scientists in the field.

The Dog Whisperer, Paul Owens, Adams Media Corp.
A remarkable, compassionate approach to training your dog, this book
describes dog communication and humane solutions to the most common canine behavior issues.

Dr. Pitcairn's Complete Guide to Natural Health Care for Dogs and Cats, Dr.
Richard Pitcairn and Susan Pitcairn, Rodale Press
The classic introduction to natural health care for dogs and cats—still
one of the best.

Eating with Conscience, Michael W. Fox, NewSage Press
Dr. Fox, a true pioneer in the field of the human-animal bond and ani-

mal rights, eloquently describes the bioethical facts and considerations concerning animals in factory farming (farms so large that the animals are simply fed for production with little concern for their well-being) and what we as individuals can do to change the way we treat food animals.

Encyclopedia of Animal Rights and Animal Welfare, Marc Bekoff, editor, Greenwood Press

Dr. Bekoff, a professor of animal behavior at the University of Colorado in Boulder, provides an excellent overview of many different perspectives on the issues of animal welfare and rights. The book's appendix provides a wealth of resource information.

Foods Pet Die For, Ann Martin, NewSage Press

Exactly what the title says: an exposé of the ingredients that actually go into pet foods and into the feed of most farm animals whose meat and other by-products we consume.

Four Paws, Five Directions: A Guide to Chinese Medicine for Cats and Dogs, Cheryl Schwartz, Celestial Arts Publishing

A trailblazer in traditional Chinese medicine for dogs and cats shares her practical experience, insights, and wisdom.

The Hidden Life of Dogs, Elizabeth Marshall Thomas, Houghton Mifflin

A personal account by a novelist and anthropologist of a life spent living with—and loving—dogs.

Home-Prepared Dog and Cat Diets, Donald Strombeck, Iowa State University Press

This book is a must for anyone wanting to make a scientifically balanced homemade diet for an animal, offering the latest approach to eating plans for specific diseases and conditions.

Homeopathic Care for Cats and Dogs: Small Doses for Small Animals, Don Hamilton, Homeopathic Educational Services

The latest and most detailed book focusing specifically on homeopathy for small animals by a veterinarian dedicated totally to this medical approach. (Order from: Don Hamilton, P.O. Box 67, Ocate, NM 87734.)

Improve Your Horse's Well-Being: A Step-by-Step Guide to Touch and Team Training, Linda Tellington-Jones, Trafalgar Square Publishing

Tellington-Jones's newest book on a humane approach to training your horse (see Tellington Equine Awareness Method under organizations).

In the Company of Animals, James Serpell, Cambridge University Press
One of the best summaries of the relationship between human and animal companions, covering subjects as diverse as health, history, and the unfortunate tendencies of humankind to abuse its friends.

Magic Trees of the Mind, Marian Diamond and Janet Hopson, Plume
Diamond, a leading brain researcher, reports her findings on the mind and how it matures, as well as her original studies on the role animals play in a child's mental development.

Minds of Their Own, Lesley Rogers, Westview Press
A courageous attempt to examine and consider consciousness in animals, this book makes it impossible to look at animals in the same light again.

Molecules of Emotion, Candace B. Pert, Touchstone
A leading scientist shares her wisdom on the impact of our biochemical constitution on our emotions and our identity as humans.

The Nature of Animal Healing, Martin Goldstein, Knopf
A fellow veterinarian's guide to taking care of your animal in a healthy way, with prescriptive advice and warm sentiment.

New Choices in Natural Healing for Dogs and Cats, edited by Amy D. Shojai, Rodale Press
This book offers practical home remedies and natural health care tips from a variety of holistic veterinarians.

The New Natural Cat, Anitra Frazier, Penguin
A classic in the field of natural veterinary care for our feline friends.

Next of Kin, Roger Fouts, Morrow
A heartwarming and illuminating account of the author's attempts at communication with a chimp, Washoe. Fouts, a professor of psychology, is also codirector of the Chimpanzee and Human Communications Institute.

Pack of Two, Caroline Knapp, Delta
An intimate exploration of the relationship between dogs and dog owners.

A Perfect Harmony, Roger A. Caras, Fireside
Written simply and sensibly, this is a fascinating tour through the history of humans and domesticated animals.

Reinventing Medicine, Larry Dossey, HarperCollins
Expanding the boundaries of medicine and looking presciently into the

future, Dr. Dossey's research and wisdom will change all but the most stubborn readers' perspectives on health and health care.

Thinking in Pictures, Temple Grandin, Vintage

Grandin, who is autistic, explains what it is like to think in pictures rather than words. More than anyone I know, she sees through an animal's eyes, and her insights have had an enormous impact on the design of slaughterhouses and livestock restraint systems. An outstanding book.

The Third Chimpanzee, Jared Diamond, HarperCollins

A penetrating look at the numerous traits shared by humans (the third chimp species) and animals. This should not be surprising, given the fact that our genes are more than 98 percent identical to chimps. One of the most fascinating books ever written on the subject.

When Elephants Weep, Susan McCarthy and Jeffrey Moussaieff Masson, Delacorte

A well-written account of emotions in animals, told with both scientific and anecdotal support.

Wisdom of the Elders, David Suzuki and Peter Knudsen, Bantam

This collection of the ancient wisdom of indigenous peoples around the world reminds us that so-called primitive societies are a lot smarter than we might like to think.

PUBLICATIONS

Best Friends Magazine
Best Friends Animal Sanctuary
5001 Angel Canyon Drive
Kanab, UT 84741
Committed to saving and helping animals, this is a magazine full of helpful information. Their sanctuary in a sacred canyon in Utah is a true blessing for all abused and abandoned animals.

E/The Environmental Magazine
P.O. Box 5098
Westport, CT 06881
203–854–5559/X 106
emagazine@prodigy.net
An excellent journal describing the latest advances, challenges, and efforts in working to save the environment we share with our animal friends.

Animal Life
P.O. Box 1842
Lenox, MA 01240
877–264–5433 (toll-free)
www/animalife.com

A wonderful example of a local magazine dedicated totally to the co-species connection.

Animal Issues
The Animal Protection Institute
P.O. Box 22505
Sacramento, CA 95822
800–348–7387 (toll-free)
www.api4animals.org
onlineapi@aol.com

A dynamic quarterly aimed at informing and educating the public about major animal protection issues.

The Holistic Horse
20 Prospect Avenue
Ardsley, NY 10502
914–693–2553
www.holistichorse.com

For horse lovers, an invaluable newsletter that helps us all understand holistic approaches to equine care.

National Geographic World
1145 17th Street NW
Washington, DC 20036
800–647–5463 (toll-free)
www.nationalgeographic.com/kids
nwhite@ngs.org

A superb interactive and educational publication that introduces children to the concept that human and animal health care is related to the conservation of the environment.

Orion
195 Main Street
Great Barrington, MA 01230
413–528–4422
www.orionsociety.org

Offering a collection of articles that focuses on a deep respect for—and the effective stewardship of—all forms of life.

Pets: Part of the Family
Rodale Press
400 S. 10th Street
Emmaus, PA 18098–0099
www.petspartofthefamily.com
A new magazine devoted to "celebrating, exploring, and standing in awe before the special relationship between pets and people."

Sierra
P.O. Box 52968
Boulder, CO 80328
800–765–7904 (toll-free)
www.sierraclub.org
The magazine of the Sierra Club, *Sierra* is dedicated to protecting our planet. In addition, *Sierra* offers information on animal and environmental health.

ORGANIZATIONS

The Animal Protection Institute
P.O. Box 22505
Sacramento, CA 95822
800–348–7387 (toll-free)
www.api4animals.org
onlineapi@aol.com
A proactive nonprofit organization that works behind the scenes to promote the latest approaches to animal welfare and to help animals wherever they are in need.

American Greenways
The Conservation Fund
1800 North Kent Street, Suite 1120
Arlington, VA 22209
703–525–6300
www.conservationfund.org
Provides some of the best and most authoritative information on how

to establish a greenway or greenbelt in your area, as well as how to preserve animal habitats.

The Delta Society
19615 Russell Road
Kent, WA 98032
800–869–6898 (toll-free)
www.deltasociety.org
The Delta Society is the premier international organization fostering the development of the human-animal bond. It focuses on integrating the science and the heart of the co-species connection and emphasizes the benefits of animal-facilitated therapy and human-animal interactions.

Dreampower Animal Rescue Foundation
P.O. Box 926
Castle Rock, CO 80104
719–390–7838
Run by my old friend Diane Benedict, Dreampower's mission is to provide a viable alternative to euthanasia for society's discarded companion animals. Dreampower rescues animals from the streets, offers sanctuary to strays, provides interim medical care, and educates the public on all related issues.

Friends of Animals
777 Post Road
Darien, CT 06820
203–656–1522
Founded in 1957, this not-for-profit organization helps protect animals from cruelty and abuse throughout the world.

The Fund for Animals
200 West 57th Street
New York, NY 10019
301–585–2591
www.fund.org
At the forefront of animal protection for more than thirty years, this group provides sanctuary to abused and rescued animals. It works on grassroots campaigns to prevent animal abuse and promote humane solutions to human/wildlife conflicts.

Goldman Environmental Foundation and Goldman Environmental Prize
One Lombard Street, Suite 303
San Francisco, CA 94111 (USA)
415–788–9090
www.goldmanprize.org
Offers awards (the equivalent of the Nobel Prize for Environmental
Preservation) to the most worthy individuals helping the environment and
preserving natural habitats throughout the world.

Green Chimneys
Putnam Lake Road
Brewster, NY 10509
914–279–2995
www.gchimney.org
This extraordinary organization provides abused and/or physically-chal-
lenged inner-city children with a supportive environment in which they can interact with and care for previously abused or abandoned farm animals and
injured wildlife.

The Humane Society of the United States
2100 L Street NW
Washington, DC 20037
301–258–3042
www.hsus.org
One of the consummate organizations leading the way in relieving animal suffering and educating the public on animal welfare.

In Defense of Animals
131 Camino Alto
Mill Valley, CA 94941
415–388–9641
ida@idausa.org
The name of this organization describes it all. It is a very compassionate, active organization with a wonderful magazine that works to defend animals everywhere.

The Jane Goodall Institute
P.O. Box 14890
Silver Spring, MD 20911
301–565–0086
www.janegoodall.org

Well-known naturalist Jane Goodall's organization is dedicated to helping save not only chimpanzees but all wildlife. Her in-school training program, "Roots and Shoots," teaches children throughout the world about improving the environment for all living beings.

Global Action Plan for the Earth
P.O. Box 428
Woodstock, NY 12198
914–679–4830
information@globalactionplan.org.

Founded in 1989, this environmental education not-for-profit organization promotes and supports the development of environmentally sustainable lifestyles in America and has worked with over 10,000 people and neighborhood groups throughout the country.

Global Communications for Conservation, Inc.
150 East 58th Street, 25th Floor
New York, NY 10155
212–935–5568
www.nyoffice@gcci.org

Dedicated to educating children throughout the world about the importance of preserving natural habitats for the survival of endangered species, GCC supports various wildlife refuges and environmental education programs. Its Center for Integrative Animal Health provides information on integrating animal, environmental, and human health care.

The Heifer Project International
P.O. Box 8106
Little Rock, AR 72203
800–422–0755 (toll-free)
www.heifer.org

This organization helps needy families around the world become self-reliant by giving them a cow, buffalo, llama, sheep, goat, rabbit, chicken, pig, or bees, as well as helping them learn how to care for them humanely.

HORSE of Connecticut
43 Wilbur Road
Washington, CT 06777
860–868–1960

A wonderful example of how a few dedicated individuals can have a major impact on helping abused animals in their local area.

Natural Resources Defense Council (NRDC)
40 West 20th Street
New York, NY 10011
212–727–2700
www.nrdc.org
A leading organization in the protection of the world's natural environment, the NRDC combines the power of science, legal action, and social commitment.

North American Riding for the Handicapped Association
P.O. Box 33150
Denver, CO 80233
800–369–RIDE (toll-free)
www.narha.org
A group dedicated to the principles of co-species healing: the horses are used in rehabilitation therapy, and they in turn bask in the love showered on them.

San Francisco Society for the Prevention of Cruelty to Animals
2500 16th Street
San Francisco, CA 94103
415–522–3546
www.sfspca.org
The San Francisco SPCA, one of the pioneer no-kill animal welfare agencies, has become a model organization for the world. With the community's involvement, it provides revolutionary animal adoption strategies and much more.

Tellington Equine Awareness Method
P.O. Box 3793
Santa Fe, NM 87501
800–854–8326 (toll-free)
www.lindatellingtonjones.com
Linda Tellington-Jones has developed a unique method of helping people connect not just with horses but with all animals. This organization offers training programs, books, and videos based on her approach.

HOW TO FIND A HOLISTIC VETERINARIAN

You may contact the following organizations to find a veterinarian in your area trained in acupuncture and/or other various complementary therapies. Note: Completion of an educational training program doesn't necessarily connote expertise—that depends on how long an individual has been practicing and how much of his or her practice time is dedicated to acupuncture.

Chi Institute
9791 NW 160th Street
Reddick, FL 32686
352–591–3165

International Veterinary Acupuncture Society (IVAS)
P.O. Box 271395
Fort Collins, CO 80527–1395
907–266–0666

Colorado State University (CSU), Department of Clinical Studies
Fort Collins, CO 80523–1620
970–491–1274

Veterinary Institute for Therapeutic Alternatives (VITA)
15 Sunset Terrace
Sherman, CT 06784
860–354–2287

American Veterinary and Chiropractic Association (AVCA)
Animal Chiropractic Center
623 Main Street
Hillsdale, IL 61257
309–658–2920

American Holistic Veterinary Medical Association (AHVMA)
2214 Old Emmorton Road
Bel Air, MD 21015
410–569–0795

American Veterinary Medical Association (AVMA)
1931 North Meacham Road, Suite 100
Schaumburg, IL 60173–4360
800–248–2862 (toll-free)

CATALOGS OF INTEREST

Anaflora Flower Essence Therapy for Animals
P.O. Box 1056
Mt. Shasta, CA 96067
530–926–6424
Anaflora flower essences and flower essence formulas made just for animals by Sharon Callahan, internationally recognized animal communication specialist and leading pioneer in the use of flower essences in the treatment of animals.

Chamisa Ridge Inc.
P.O. Box 23294
Santa Fe, NM 87502
800–743–3188 (toll-free)
www.chamisaridge.com
Here you can read about the absolute best educational material concerning the natural health care of you and your horse.

A Drop in the Bucket
586 Round Hill Road
Greenwich, CT 06831
888–783–0313 (toll-free)
www.bucket.simplenet.com
This catalog offers the best alternative health care nutritional supplements for horses.

Earthwise Animal Products
P.O. Box 654
Millwood, NY 10546
212–579–7170
www.earthwiseanimal.com
An on-line catalog for dogs and cats listing pure foods, natural supplements, toys, accessories, and books not readily available in stores.

NATURAL ANIMAL HEALTH-CARE SUPPLEMENTS

These are some of the quality suppliers offering natural animal supplements:

Animals Apawthecary
P.O. Box 212
Conner, MT 59827
406–821–4090

The Botanical Animal
Equilite Inc.
20 Prospect Avenue
Ardsley, NY 10502
914–693–2553

Halo Purely for Pets
3438 East Lake Road #14
Palm Harbor, FL 34685
800–426–4256 (toll-free)

MUSIC

It may sound odd, but there is some great music about animals, complete with nature sounds, that we can play for kids. I know that whenever I play this CD, children respond wonderfully. Called Animal Songs, you can get it by sending $15 (or $10 for an audiocassette without the lyric booklet) to:

Megha
P.O. Box 1857
Lenox, MA 01240
413–448–3482
e-mail: *Megha@aol.com*

Acknowledgments

One of my favorite writers, Thich Nhat Hanh, states, "as we cultivate peace and happiness in ourselves, we also nourish peace and happiness in those we love." I want to acknowledge all of you—dear friends, colleagues, and teachers (whether two-legged, four-legged, or winged)—who have nourished my own peace and happiness, helping guide me through my life's journey leading up to this book—as well as all the people who consented to an interview. Many of these people requested that I change their name, as well as their animal companions' names, which I have done—and in a few cases, for the sake of anonymity and brevity, two stories have been collapsed into one.

I must also thank a few specific individuals by name: my parents, Fred and Sophie Schoen, and my sister Beverly, who lovingly supported my desire to march to the beat of a different drummer; my first college teachers, Dr. Gene Somers and Dr. James Tucci, as well as my other professors at my college biology department who nourished my interests in veterinary medicine; Dr. Forrest Tenney, Dr. Don Fritz, and Dr. John Combs, for providing such a fertile foundation for integrating modern veterinary medicine along with practical old-time knowledge; Dr. Sheldon Altman, my first veterinary acupuncture teacher, who wisely and gently opened my eyes to a new world of animal healing and the spiritual basis of all of life; my colleague and friend Evan Kanouse, who created Brook Farm Veterinary Center with me in order to provide a warm, loving base to treat my small animal friends; Dr. Bill Kay and Dr. Martin DeAngelis, for their support of my vision of integrative animal health care throughout the years; my colleagues and friends at Colorado State University College of Veterinary Medicine, Cornell University College of Veterinary Medicine, and the other veterinary schools where I teach; my associates Dr. Bea Ehrsam and Dr. Rosemary Ganzer, who, by providing such loving care of our animal friends, have allowed me the time to write this book; and my incomparable support staff—my administrative assistant Melissa Perock, my office assistant Bridgette Banach, and my personal assistant Tatiana Firkusny, for their tremendous support of all the projects I take on.

I am also indebted to Laura Utley, Janet York, Dan Lufkin, the Geraldine R. Dodge Foundation, and others for their magnanimous support of my nonprofit work for animals through the Center for Integrative Animal Health, a division of Global Communications for Conservation, Inc.

I would also like to give thanks to all my spiritual guides for the many insights and wisdom they have imparted, as well as each and every kindred spirit that I have shared my veterinary career with—I am appreciative for all that they have taught me as I treated them.

I am so grateful to Amy, Mindy, and David for allowing me to share the joy of being an uncle. And most of all, throughout the yin and yang of life's journey, my wife Barbara has always been there for me with her loving compassion and support.

I can't find the right words to express my gratitude to Richard Pine, my literary agent, for understanding my vision of helping animals, people, and nature, and guiding me so carefully through the labyrinth of the publishing world. I am also grateful to everyone at Broadway Books, especially Steve Rubin, Gerry Howard, Bob Asahina, Ann Campbell, Brian Jones, and Mark Hurst.

And a final thank-you to Gene Stone, who has been my writing partner for the last two years. We have argued, laughed, struggled, and rejoiced until we eventually figured out how to bring out the best in each other. His canny ability to turn my inchoate thoughts into a finished book astounds me, as well as his efforts to balance my scientific mind with my spiritual heart. I know he has worked very hard, and I am truly indebted.

Gene, in turn, wishes to thank his remarkable cat, Minnie.

Index

A

AAT (Animal Assisted Therapy), 59–61,
 71–73
Acupressure, 129–31, 190
Acupuncture, 4, 15, 16, 99–108, 124,
 128–29, 132, 149
ADHD, 65–66
Aesculapius, 50
AIDS, 67–69
Allen, Karen, 56–57, 64
Allergies, 116–17, 120, 237–41
Alternative health care
 acupuncture, 4, 15, 16, 99–108
 aromatherapy, 134–36

Bach flower treatment, 133–34
 changing view of, 96–99
 Chinese herbs, 108–10
 chiropractic, 125–28
 glandular therapy, 136–37
 homeopathy, 121–25
 preventive nutrition, 115–18
 Tenney's use of, 31–32
 therapeutic nutrition, 118–21
 touch therapy, 128–32
 Western herbs, 111–15
Altman, Dr., 102–3, 104
Altruistic behavior, 42
Animal companions
 AIDS and, 67–69

benefits listed, 51–52
children and, 59–60, 64–66, 75, 197
death of, 250–54
the elderly and, 60–61, 62–64
heart health and, 53–57, 62–64
mental health and, 51, 69–73
negative side of, 73–77
treating like humans, 142–43
See also Human-animal bond
Animal harm by humans
experimentation, 19, 20–21, 25–27,
    28–29, 89–90, 197
growth beyond, 177–80
horse mistreatment, 89–90
physical violence, 137
psychological stress, 137–41
Animals
dichotomization from, 18–20, 191–92
similarities to humans, 41–45, 174,
    191–93, 223
slaughter of, 29, 198
thinking like, 220–22
Ants, The, 163
Anxiety, 111–12, 133, 137–41
Aristotle, 18, 174
Aromatherapy, 134–36
Arthritis, 15, 105–7, 120–21, 124
Artistic expression, 41
Averna, Tom, 161–62

B

Bach, Edward, 133–34
Bach flower therapy, 133–34, 243
Basko, Ihor, 109, 110
Beak of the Finch, The, 194
Bekoff, Marc, 171
Bell, John Stewart, 165–66
Benson, Herb, 206–7
Bernard, Shari, 60–61
Biophilia, 163–65
Biophilia, 163
Birds, 64, 194–95, 217–19
Bison, 205–6
Blake, Harry, 173
Blessing exercise, 222–23
Blood pressure, 55, 56, 57, 64
Bollen, Kelly, 91–92, 183
Books, 259–62
Brain, neuron growth in, 180–83

Breathing meditation, 207–9
Bulls, castration of, 38–40

C

Cancer, 8–10, 82–86, 150, 244–46
Carlson, Richard, 143
Catalogs, 270
Cats
chiropractic for, 127–28
colds in, 108–9
co-species connections with, 171–72,
    177–80
experimentation on, 27
human recovery and, 58–59
leukemia in, 110
mental health benefits of, 69–70, 71
mindful moments with, 214–15
talking with, 224–25
travel tips, 241–43
Cavalieri, Paolo, 44
Cheating Monkeys and Citizen Bees, 42
Children, 59–60, 64–66, 75, 197
Chimpanzees, 41, 43–44, 221–22
Chiropractic, 125–28
Chopra, Deepak, 174, 204
Communication skills in animals, 42, 170,
    178–79, 223–26
*Complementary and Alternative Veterinary
    Medicine,* 135
Consciousness in animals, 18–21, 155,
    168, 220–22
Corson, Sam and Elizabeth, 51
Co-species connections
Bell's theorem and, 165–66
biophilia, 163–65
with birds, 194–95
with bison, 205–6
with cats, 171–72, 177–80
defined, 156–57
with dogs, 1–10, 148–56, 160–61,
    167–68, 170–71, 172–73
with dolphins, 159–60
Dossey on, 165–68
environmental issues, 195–97, 198–200
evolvement via, 180–91
extending, 197–200
growth via, 176–84
with horses, 157–58, 173, 187–91
"inherent need" for, 163–64

maternal love, 4, 7, 148–51, 155
with orcas, 161–62
in past times, 174–76
prayer and, 165–67
with sea lions, 193–94
Sheldrake on, 168–70, 171–72
stress relief via, 184–86
as transcendent, 155–57
Wilson on, 163
See also Human-animal bond; Spiritual
  bonds, creating
Co-species healing, 144, 147–48
Co-species meditation, 206–9
Cows, 2–4, 34–37, 118–19, 155

D

Darwin, Charles, 19–20, 45, 155, 191, 223
Death of pets, 250–54
de Kooning, Willem, 41
Delahanty, Dr., 30, 102
Descartes, René, 19, 174
Descent of Man, 191
De Simplicibus, 112
Diabetes, 167–68
Diamond, Jared, 41, 42
Diamond, Marian, 180–82
Diet and nutrition, 104, 115–21, 237–41,
  271
Distant healing prayer, 165–67
Dogs
  acupressure for, 131
  AIDS helped by, 67–68
  allergies in, 116–17
  anxiety in, 111–12, 133, 137–41
  aromatherapy for, 135–36
  arthritis in, 15, 105–7, 120–21, 124
  bee stings in, 123–24
  bronchitis in, 137
  cancer in, 8–10, 82–86, 150
  chiropractic for, 126
  chronic myositis in, 128–29
  co-species connections with, 1–10,
    148–56, 160–61, 167–68, 170–71,
    172–73
  the elderly and, 60–61, 62–64
  empathy of, 3
  exercise benefits of, 52
  heart health and, 53–54, 55–57,
    62–63

hepatitis in, 113–14
hip dysplasia in, 14, 103, 149
knee injury in, 131–32
labor difficulties in, 32
Lyme disease and, 13–17
maternal love in, 4, 7, 148–51, 155
Megan, 1–10, 152–56
mindful moments with, 212–13
motion sickness in, 114–15
negative side for, 73–77
pain felt by, 28–29
pancreatitis in, 135–36
psychotherapy and, 70–71
Saint Guinefort's cult, 50
talking with, 224–25
travel tips, 241–43
*Dogs That Know When Their Owners Are Coming
  Home*, 169, 170
Dolphins, 159–60
Dossey, Larry, 165–68
Dr. Fulford's Touch of Life, 122
*Dr. Pitcairn's Complete Guide to Natural Health
  for Dogs and Cats*, 241

E

Earl, Sylvia, 196
Eastman, Andrea, 89–91
Elderly, the, 60–61, 62–64
Emotions/feelings in animals
  anxiety, 111–12, 133, 137–41
  conventional veterinary view of, 34,
    45–47
  of empathy, 2–3, 7–8
  maternal love, 4, 7, 148–51, 155
  Pert's research and, 44–45
  PET scan evidence for, 48
  scientific view of, 18–21
  See also Pain in animals
Environmental issues, 195–97, 198–200
Evolvement, co-species, 180–91
*Expression of the Emotions in Man and Animals,
  The*, 19, 223

F

Finding
  kindred spirits, 255–56
  veterinarians, 236–37, 269
First-aid kit, 246–49
Food allergies, 237–41

Four Paws, Five Directions, 231
Fouts, Roger, 43
Fox, Michael, 173–74
Fredrickson, Maureen, 71–73
Freud, Sigmund, 70
Friedman, Erica, 51, 55–56, 64
Fulford, Robert, 122

G

Galen, 112
Gandhi, Mohandas, 13
Gatkin, Lee, 42
Glandular therapy, 136–37
Goats, 152–54
Goodall, Jane, 43
Goswami, Amit, 165
Gough, Charles, 156
Gould, Stephen Jay, 192
Gradual Sayings, 208
Grandin, Temple, 220–21
Great Ape Project, The, 44
Green, Diane and Dan, 81–86, 89
Greenspaces, 199
Grief, 58, 62–63, 81–86, 250–54
Griffin, Donald, 21

H

Hall, Granville Stanley, 50
Hanh, Thich Nhat, 257
Harris, William, 166
Healers on Healing, 143
Healing, defined, 143
Healing methods at home
    for ailing animals, 233–35
    for cancer, 244–46
    first-aid kit, 246–49
    for food allergies, 237–41
    natural pet scan, 229–33
    travel tips, 241–43
Healing Words, 165
Health care
    animals and, 197–98
    changes for humans, 96–99
    See also Alternative health care
Heart health, 53–57, 62–63, 64
Herbal medicine, 108–15
Herbert, Nick, 165
Herriot, James, 31
Hippocrates, 119

Homeopathy, 121–25
Home-Prepared Dog and Cat Diets, 238
HORSE of Connecticut, 91–94
Horses
    acupressure for, 130–31, 190
    carrot stretches for, 127
    chiropractic for, 126–27
    co-species connections with, 157–58,
        173, 187–91
    evolution in, 187–91
    mindful moments with, 215–16
    mistreatment of, 89–90
    rehabilitation of, 90–91, 93–94
    talking with, 225–26
Houpt, Katherine, 46
How to Know God, 174
Human-animal bond, 49–77
    AIDS and, 67–69
    benefits listed, 51–52
    children and, 59–60, 64–66, 75
    early scientific studies of, 49–53
    the elderly benefited by, 62–64
    heart health and, 53–57, 62–63, 64
    human responsibility and, 88–95
    importance of, 88–89
    mental health and, 51, 69–73
    negative side of, 73–77
    recovery and, 58–61
    stress on animals from, 138–41
    See also Co-species connections; Spiritual
        bonds, creating
Human-animal similarities, 41–45, 174,
    191–93, 223

I

Integrative medicine, 98–99
In the Company of Animals, 75

J

Jessup, Diane, 76–77
Jock, Auld, 156
Journal for Diagnostic Imaging Asia Pacific,
    107
Judeo-Christian attitude, 18

K

Karl, Dr., 34–37
Katcher, Aaron, 64–66
Kava, 111–12

Kaye, Philippa, 213
Khalsa, Seva, 160–61
Kindred relaxation, 209–11
Knudsen, Peter, 175
Kundera, Milan, 81

L

Larson, Gary, 151
Levenson, Boris, 50
Loneliness, 64
Lorenz, Konrad, 21
Love for animals
    healing power of, 81–87
    human responsibility for, 87–95
Love, Miracles, and Animal Healing, 241

M

Magic Trees of the Mind, 181
Massage therapy, 129, 131–32
Masson, Jeffrey Moussaieff, 19
Maternal love, 4, 7, 148–51, 155
McCarthy, Susan, 19
Medicine Eagle, Brook, 143
Megan (dog healer), 1–10, 152–56
Mental health, 51, 69–73
Mindful moments, 212–19
Monroe, Ralph, 161, 162
Morphic fields, 169–70
Motion sickness, 114–15, 243
Munchausen syndrome by proxy,
    74–75
Music about animals, 271

N

Natural pet scan, 229–33
Nature, spirituality and, 24–25
Nkaya, Anguttara, 208–9
Nutrition, 104, 115–21, 237–41, 271

O

Ogilvie, Greg, 53–54, 58, 244
O'Neil, Jay and April, 148–51
On Human Nature, 163
*On the Origin of Species by Means of Natural
    Selection*, 19
Opiate receptors, 44–45
Orcas, 161–62
Organizations, 264–68

P

Pain in animals
    acupuncture for, 102–3
    conventional medication, 99–100
    cow dehorning and, 34–37
    lack of awareness of, 34–40
    responsibility for, 87–95
    scientific view of, 18–21, 26–29
    veterinary view of, 34, 35, 36, 37–38
    See also Emotions/feelings in animals
Palmer, Daniel David, 125–26
Periodicals, 262–64
Pert, Candace, 44–45
Pet-facilitated psychotherapy, 51
PET scan evidence for feelings, 48
Pigs, 28, 29
Pitcairn, Richard, 121–22
Plato, 18
Poison ivy, 122–23
Prayer, 165–67, 235
Preventive nutrition, 115–18
Primates, 41, 43–44
Psychological health, 51, 69–73

Q

Question of Animal Awareness, The, 21

R

Recovery from illness, 58–61
Reinventing Medicine, 166
Relaxation, kindred, 209–11
Rescue remedy, 134, 243
Resources, 258–71
Reston, James, 97
Russek, Linda, 251

S

Safdiah, Michael, 67–68
Salamander, 24
Scan for pets, 229–33
Schoen, Allen M.
    at Animal Medical Center, 45–46
    early experiences with animals, 21–30,
        37–38
    e-mail address of, 259
    integrative approach of, 98–99
    Megan (dog) with, 1–10, 152–56
    spirituality of, 24–25, 151–52

Tenney as mentor of, 4, 31–34
Schwartz, Cheryl, 231
Schwartz, Gary, 251
Schweitzer, Albert, 96, 258
Scientific view
    animal companion studies, 49–53,
        55–57, 59, 63–64, 65–66, 68–69,
        71, 77
    of animal consciousness, 18–21, 26–30
    changes in, 41–45
Scott, Sir Walter, 250
Sea lions, 193–94
Self-destructive behavior, 42
Serpell, James, 52–53, 75, 137
Seven Experiments That Could Change the World,
    169
Sheep, 32–34
Sheldrake, Rupert, 168–70, 171, 173
Shield, Benjamin, 143
Siegel, Judith, 63–64, 68–69
Singer, Peter, 44
Slaughter of animals, 29, 198
Smart, Pamela, 170
Sociobiology, 163
Sounding the Depths, 196
Spiritual bonds, creating, 203–27
    blessing exercise, 222–23
    busy day practices, 226–27
    co-species meditation, 206–9
    importance of, 203–5
    kindred relaxation, 209–11
    mindful moments, 212–19
    talking and listening, 223–26
    thinking like animals, 220–22
    See also Co-species connections
Spirituality and nature, 24–25
Spontaneous Healing, 143
Starr family, 1–3, 155
Stone, Gene, 171, 217
Stress relief, 184–86
Strombeck, Donald, 238
Suicide rescue, 159–60
Suzuki, David, 175
Syracuse Zoo, 91–92

T

Talking and listening, 223–26

Tangkas, 176
Targ, Elizabeth, 166–67
Tenney, Forrest, 4, 31–34
Therapet, 60–61
Therapeutic nutrition, 118–21
Thinking in Pictures, 220
Thinking like an animal, 220–22
Third Chimpanzee, The, 41
Touch therapy, 128–32
Traditional Chinese medicine
    acupuncture, 4, 15, 16, 99–108, 124,
        128–29, 132, 149
    herbs, 108–10
    philosophy of, 103–4
    Western medicine and, 97–98, 112
Travel tips, 241–43
Turkeys, 72–73

U

Understanding Your Cat, 173
Understanding Your Dog, 173
Urban stress, 139–41

V

Vegetarian animals, 117–18
Veterinarians, finding, 236–37, 269
Veterinary view (conventional), 34, 35, 36,
    37–38, 45–47, 98–99
Voltaire, 19

W

Wahlers, Patty, 91–94
"We Are Kindred Spirits," 257
Weil, Andrew, 143, 228
Weiner, Harold, 136
Weiner, Jonathan, 194–95
Western herbal medicine, 111–15
When Elephants Weep, 19
Willoughby, Sharon, 125, 126
Wilson, Edward O., 163, 203
Wisdom of the Elders, 175
Wolfson, Joe, 158–60
Wordsworth, William, 151, 156
Wynn, Susan, 134–35

Z

Zbelin, Sviatoslav, 147